Superfluous People

A Reflection on
Hannah Arendt and Evil

Cornelis van Hattem

UNIVERSITY PRESS OF AMERICA,® INC.
Lanham • Boulder • New York • Toronto • Oxford

Library of Congress Control Number: 2005929324
ISBN 0-7618-3304-8 (clothbound : alk. ppr.)
ISBN 0-7618-3305-6 (paperback : alk. ppr.)

Contents

Prologue

During the Second World War we, my parents and I, lived in an apartment in the Eastern part of Amsterdam. Our street ran parallel to the railway that led to the East and from our window we had a view of the railway station. On my way to school, I had to walk through a subway, because my school was in an area on the other side of the railway. About 100 meters from the end of the subway was the site where the Jews were assembled before transportation to Westerbork, a transit camp in the Eastern part of the Netherlands. I frequently saw how the trains were "loaded" with Jews. We had no idea what was going to happen to them, but it was clear to everybody that the operation didn't bode well. There were rumours about labour camps, but I could not understand what use small children and old people could be in labour camps.

Until the end of the war, we were ignorant of the final destination of the trains. Only in the months after the war ended we learned, bit by bit, the terrible truth: the end of the line was a dead end, somewhere in Poland.

In those trains there were people I knew, children from my class and boys from the football club. None of them ever came back and all that remains are old photographs.

For fifty years I have been thinking about those trains, not every day, but regularly. For fifty years I have asked myself what could be the mechanism and the ratio behind the rise of Nazism with its death factories. The introduction to Hannah Arendt's work induced me to try and fathom the origin and the essence of the catastrophe.

Abbreviations

WORKS BY HANNAH ARENDT

BF   Between Friends: The Correspondence of Hannah Arendt and Mary Mc Carthy

BPF   Between Past and Future

C   Hannah Arendt and Karl Jaspers, Correspondence, 1929–1969

CC   The Concentration Camps

CR   Crises of the Republic

EJ   Eichmann in Jerusalem

EU   Essays in Understanding, 1930–1945

HC   The Human Condition

JP   The Jew as Pariah

LK   Lectures on Kant's Political Philosophy

LM I   The Life of the Mind I: Thinking

LM II   The Life of the Mind II: Willing

MD   Men in Dark Times

OT I   The Origins of Totalitarianism, First Edition, 1951

OT II   The Origins of Totalitarianism, Second Edition, 1958

OT III   The Origins of Totalitarianism, Third Edition, 1975

OR   On Revolution

OV   On Violence

RJ   Responsibility and Judgment

TM   Thinking and Moral Considerations

WP   Was ist Politik? (What is Politics?)

BIOGRAPHY OF HANNAH ARENDT

YB   Elisabeth Young-Bruehl: Hannah Arendt: For Love of the World

WORKS BY KANT

ApH   Anthropologie in pragmatischer Hinsicht (Anthropology from a Pragmatic Point of View)
KPV   Kritik der praktischen Vernunft (Critique of Practical Reason)
KRV   Kritik der reinen Vernunft (Critique of Pure Reason)
KU   Kritik der Urteilskraft (Critique of Judgment)
MS   Die Metaphysik der Sitten (The Metaphysics of Morals)
Rel.   Die Religion innerhalb der bloszen Vernunft (Religion within the Limits of Pure Reason)

Introduction

On July 13, 1953, Hannah Arendt writes in a letter to her teacher Karl Jaspers: "If only I knew more about the problem of evil". (YB, 287)

The problem of evil, particularly political evil, is the thread of connection in the writings of Hannah Arendt. The reason for this may be found in the events in Nazi-Germany, in particular the ideology and terror that ended in the Shoah[1], the destruction of six million Jews. She wanted to understand and fathom the past.

> . . . the past is still "unmastered" and in the conviction held particularly by men of good will that the first to be done is to set about "mastering" of it. Perhaps that cannot be done with any past, but certainly not with the past of Hitler Germany. The best that can be achieved is to know precisely what it was, and to endure this knowledge and then to wait and see what comes of knowing and enduring. (MD, 20)

One of the reasons why she was so interested in Nazi-Germany was undoubtedly her own past and background. A short biography of Hannah Arendt may clarify this.

LIFE AND WORK OF HANNAH ARENDT

Johanna (Hannah) Arendt was born on October 14, 1906 in Linden, a small town near Hannover in Germany. Her parents, Paul Arendt and Martha Cohn were assimilated Jews from Königsberg.[2] Both parents had been active in the social democratic movement since their youth and were strongly influenced by the "Jugendbewegung" (Youth movement) and the pedagogic reform movement. The family belonged to the so-called "Reformjudentum" (Reform

Jewry), which defended the principles of the Enlightenment against the or-
thodox Jewry. Because of Paul Arendt's poor health the family returned to
Königsberg, where he died.

At that moment Hannah was seven years old. As a child she was already interested in literature and philosophy and in 1924 she went to Marburg University where she studied philosophy with Heidegger and theology with Bultmann.
Martin Heidegger fascinated her and for a while they had an intense relationship.
This relationship had no future for two reasons: Heidegger was married and had
children and his anti-Semitic attitude was problematic for Hannah Arendt. In
1925 Hannah continued her studies with Husserl at the university of Freiburg
and later, on Heidegger's recommendation, in Heidelberg with Karl Jaspers. Under Jaspers' supervision she took her degree as a doctor of philosophy in 1929
with her dissertation about Augustine's concept of love. Twenty years later, after her visit to the Jaspers family in 1949, a kind of father-daughter relationship
developed between her and Karl Jaspers that would last until Jaspers' death in
1969. She admired Jaspers, not only for his work, but also because he was one
of the few German philosophers who refused to collaborate with the Nazis. Her
relationship with Heidegger remained ambivalent for the rest of her life. She admired his work, especially his ideas about thinking, but she condemned his attitude during the Nazi period.

In 1929 she moved to Berlin and in 1931 she married Günther Stern, a disci-
ple of Hüsserl. Günther Stern was mainly known under his writer's pseudonym
Günther Anders. In Berlin she became active in politics and accommodated
communists in her apartment. She was arrested, but released after a few days.
However, this incident was a reason for her to flee to Paris via Prague and
Geneva.

Increasing anti-Semitism drove her to Zionism, because she considered it
the only possible answer to anti-Semitism. She realised she had to defend herself as a Jewess and therefore she became an active member of the Zionist
movement. She also met Walter Benjamin and they became very good
friends. Walter Benjamin was a German social philosopher and culture critic.
He was in favour of political engagement of art and artists. Against the belief
in progress and the idea that everything is makable, he presented a philosophy of history, which had its roots in both historical materialism and Jewish
Messianism. A member of Arendt's group of emigrated left-wing German
intellectuals was Heinrich Blücher. He had been a convinced communist in
his youth and a supporter of the soviet-style republic. He played an active
role in the Spartacus rebellion in 1919. In 1939 he was forced to flee to
Paris. Blücher was an autodidact and had an extensive knowledge of history,
literature and philosophy. His attitude reminds somewhat of Socrates. Like
Socrates, Blücher loved discussions and never put his political and philo-

sophical ideas on paper. In the meantime, Hannah Arendt and Günther Stern drifted apart and they decided to divorce. After the divorce Hannah and Heinrich married. Heinrich was the invisible source of inspiration in Hannah's life. They had a very strong intellectual bond during their entire marriage.

In 1940, after the beginning of the war, Arendt was interned in Gurs, a French camp not far from the Pyrenees. After a few weeks Arendt managed to escape and she and Heinrich succeeded in getting visas for the United States, but despite the visas, their emigration to the USA was a complicated affair. In her new homeland Arendt started publishing articles in a journal for Jewish immigrants called *Aufbau (Building Up)*. In her articles she argued in favour of a regular Jewish army to fight against National Socialism and for Jewish-Arab reconciliation for the sake of a future Jewish state in Palestine. She pointed in particular to possible conflicts with the Palestinian-Arab minority. Unfortunately, her critical remarks were not always appreciated by the Jewish society. Gradually she began to feel less at home in these circles and in the end she dissociated herself from the society. This was probably the start of a problem, which, many years later, would manifest itself in a number of controversies after her publication of *Eichmann in Jerusalem.*

After the publication of *The Origins of Totalitarianism* in 1951 she gained recognition and was invited for lectures at Princeton University (1953), The New School for Social Research in New York (1954) and the University of Chicago (1956). In 1952, there were frightening moments for Hannah and her husband because of senator McCarthy's communist hunts. In the early sixties she reported the Eichmann trial in Jerusalem in the magazine *The New Yorker*, which gave rise to the above-mentioned controversies. Heinrich Blücher died in 1970 and Hannah Arendt survived her husband by five years. During this period she was invited for the Gifford lectures. Arendt died on December 4, 1975 from a heart attack.

Hannah Arendt's most important writings with regard to the problem of evil were published after 1950. After the end of the Second World War her relation with Karl Jaspers was re-established and they started a regular correspondence. This correspondence shows how much Arendt was emotionally involved in the events during the Nazi period. Totalitarianism and the Shoah determined her thinking and they formed the dark background for her articles and books. Evil was ever-present, an evil that seemed to be incomprehensible and unfathomable.

It is as if Hitler inflicted a wound on her, which did not stop bleeding for the rest of her life. (Prins, 14)

This may be the reason that her language and style do not always show the distance that may be expected from scientists. There was a lot of passion and emotion in her writings, especially when Nazism was the subject. This sensitiveness often resulted in subjectivity and this was also a reason for criticism. Her involvement in the events in Nazi Germany induced her to start looking for the origins of the catastrophe. This resulted in a study of the modern history of the Jewish people, anti-Semitism, imperialism and finally in an analysis of the origins and elements of totalitarianism. Arendt saw two different forms of totalitarianism: Nazism and Stalinism. The two forms of totalitarianism are brought together and described in one book: *The Origins of Totalitarianism,* published in 1951.

After *The Origins of Totalitarianism,* the topics of her books and articles changed. Totalitarianism was pushed into the background. It is still there in *Between Past and Future,* but in other works Arendt concentrates herself on political theory and political philosophy. Her most important and most appreciated book is *The Human Condition,* published in 1958.

Her interest in totalitarianism returned completely when she went to Jerusalem as a correspondent for The New Yorker, to report the proceedings of the Eichmann trial. After the trial she published her articles in the New Yorker in one volume, *Eichmann in Jerusalem,* published in 1963. The publication of the book led to a number of controversies inside, but also outside the Jewish community. The controversies related to the text, the question of the Jewish Councils and Arendt's use of the term "banality of evil". I shall return to these controversies in chapter 6.

According to Arendt, Eichmann's evil was strongly related to his inability to think or in Arendt's words, his "thoughtlessness". This provokes the question whether certain mental faculties may prevent evil and this induced Arendt to start a trilogy on thinking, willing and judging. She completed the books on thinking and willing, but she died before starting the manuscript on judging. Only the title page was found in her typewriter shortly after her death. Nevertheless, we have a fairly good idea about the possible contents of this book, because she gave thirteen lectures on judging at the New School for Social Research. These lectures were based on Kant's *Kritik der Urteilskraft (Critique of Judgment)* and published in 1982 as *Lectures on Kant's political Philosophy,* edited by Ronald Beiner. The manuscripts on thinking and willing were edited by Hannah Arendt's friend, the writer Mary McCarthy and published as *The Life of the Mind* in 1977.

THE SHOAH AND PHILOSOPHY

In general philosophers have found it difficult to take a philosophical position with regard to the Shoah and this resulted in ignoring it. However, there are exceptions, such as Adorno, Baumann, Jaspers, Lyotard and Kofman. Ignoring the Shoah could be the result of the deep-rooted conviction of the rationality of mankind and of history. The Shoah does not fit in this image.

In his article "The Holocaust and Philosophy", Emil Fackenheim analyses the ignoring of the Shoah. I shall only go into two of the various reasons.

– Philosophers are mainly interested in universals and not or little in particulars and even less in the unique. With the exception of the above-mentioned authors, the Shoah is considered as a genocide that is not essentially different from preceding genocides. Nevertheless, says Fackenheim, some philosophers have paid attention to unique historical events. Both Hegel and Marx have written specifically about the French Revolution instead of revolutions in general. I would like to remark that, although these philosophers did indeed write about the French Revolution, they nevertheless tried to situate it in a general framework. Hegel, for instance, considered the French Revolution as an event in history that was indispensable for the development of the absolute spirit.

– Philosophers considered the French Revolution as a positive event in world history. The Shoah, on the contrary, is looked upon as an extremely negative one. For Theodor Adorno it was negative to such a degree that he considered it the end of dialectic thinking. This negative event, this meaningless death could not be incorporated in a dialectic way of thinking, in which something positive is developed through negative events. (Adorno, 354–400)

According to Fackenheim philosophers tend to flee from inhumanity during wars and also from the question of evil. They should, however, look this incomprehensible evil of the Shoah, this aporia, straight in the eye, because it is unique and a novelty in the history of mankind.

Philosophers from Socrates to Kant have considered evil as a form of ignorance of the actors, but this can hardly be said of Auschwitz, where the leaders were, among others, physicians and other academics. Since Kant, evil has been regarded as a weakness of the will. The inclination to do evil became stronger than the need to do one's duty according to the moral law and the categorical imperative. However, it was the categorical imperative Eichmann called upon and, according to Fackenheim, not without reason.[3] Psychiatrists consider evildoing a disease, but the Nazis wanted to be respected and rational. There was no question of a pathological process at all. Philosophy has even seen a glimpse of what theologians call "demonic evil" or "satanic evil", but Eichmann had nothing of a demon or a Satan. He was a rather ordinary citizen, a mister Average, a man that is a dime a dozen and he became an ordinary man again after the war. Eichmann was no exception. The people who committed the crimes were in most cases ordinary people. It was the system that transformed them into murderers, but this provokes the question: "Who created the system?"

According to Fackenheim this is a philosophical problem that we must try to fathom. How could ordinary people establish a kingdom of evil that was far from ordinary and without precedent? This question is aporetic, but nevertheless we must face the problem and not fall back on the familiar statement that the whole was more than the sum of the parts.

Philosophers have not only applied this statement to animal organisms, but also to human realities—a society, a state, a civilization, and a "world"—but only if the humanity had reached a higher standard than the parts, separately or jointly, would have made possible.[4] However, the Shoah showed the contrary: the total was more negative than the sum of the parts ever could have been.

> It is in contrast to this that the *novum* of the Holocaust-whole is revealed in all its stark horror. It did not enhance the humanity of its inhabitants. On the contrary, it was single-mindedly geared to the destruction of the humanity (as well as the lives) of the victims; and in pursuing this goal, the victimizers destroyed their own humanity, even as they yielded to its being destroyed. Pursuing his own age-old goal, the Socratic quest, "What is Man?", the philosopher, now as then, is filled with wonder. But the ancient wonder is now mingled with a new horror. (Fackenheim, 1985, 514)

Wonder about all that is, has always been the foundation of philosophy. Hannah Arendt picks up Fackenheim's questions in an exemplary way, although this is an anachronism, because Fackenheim asks his questions ten years after Arendt's death. As mentioned in her biography: wonder, or rather bewilderment about the Shoah is the thread of connection in her life and work. It is the same kind of bewilderment that made me ask myself questions and look for answers, mainly with the help of Arendt's writings.

QUESTIONS

– Which were the elements and factors that led to the development of Nazism and the Shoah?

– What is the relationship between Arendt's "radical evil", Kant's "radical evil" and Arendt's "banal evil" and is it possible to incorporate "banal evil" in Kant's theory?

– Are Nazi-totalitarianism and the Shoah new and unique events in history and if so, why?

– Is it possible to prevent a similar catastrophe, and which mental capacities could play a role in this prevention?

– Are we allowed to speak of a collective guilt?

SOURCES

To find an answer to these questions I made use of the work of Hannah Arendt, her correspondence with Karl Jaspers and Mary McCarthy, her biography written by Young-Bruehl and secondary literature such as books and articles about Hannah Arendt and her ideas, books and articles about the concept of evil and finally of the works of Kant, in particular of *Religion within the Limits of Pure Reason*. The three books that formed the basis of my investigation were *The Origins of Totalitarianism, Eichmann in Jerusalem* and *The Life of the Mind*.

The Origin of Totalitarianism, published in 1951, consists of three parts. The first part "Anti-Semitism", describes the history of the Jews in Europe in the 19th and 20th century. In this part, Arendt tries to explain the origin of anti-Semitism, including the role of the Jews in this phenomenon. The second part, "Imperialism", is the story of European imperialism and its concomitant phenomenon of race thinking. She also pays attention to Pan-Germanism. The contents of the first two parts form an introduction to the third part "Totalitarianism". Although both Stalinism and Nazism are totalitarian regimes, Arendt mainly pays attention to Nazism, because she considered it as the prototype of a totalitarian state. The elements of Nazism such as the development of masses, propaganda, structure, ideology, secret state police and terror are considered; these elements lead to total domination, the destruction of the vital conditions of man and finally to the Shoah, the destruction of six million innocent victims.

Eichmann in Jerusalem was published in 1963. The book is a report of the trial against Adolf Eichmann in Jerusalem. However, the book is more than a report. Arendt expresses her opinion about Eichmann's status and the role of the Jews, particularly the role of the Jewish Councils. Her opinion gave rise to the development of three controversies. Between *The Origins of Totalitarianism* and *Eichmann in Jerusalem* Arendt published *The Human Condition*, a reflection on the "vita activa" of man, in 1958. It is an interesting study, but not of great importance with regard to the subject of this book. Another book published in this period is *Between Past and Future,* a collection of essays. Two essays contain important material for this book: "What is Authority?" and "The Crisis in Culture".

After *Eichmann in Jerusalem,* Arendt wrote three books. In 1963 she published *On Revolution,* with interesting reflections on the French and American Revolutions; in 1968 *Men in Dark Times*, a series of essays on contemporaries such as Karl Jaspers, Walter Benjamin, Bertold Brecht and Rosa Luxemburg and in 1969 *Crises of the Republic* with four political-scientific essays.

Books published after Arendt's death in 1975 have all been important sources for this study. In the first place *The Life of the Mind*, published in 1977, describing Arendt's reflections on thinking and willing. *The Jew as Pariah*, published in 1978, contains the correspondence between Arendt and Gershom Scholem in 1963 about the role of the Jewish Councils and "the banality of evil".

Hannah Arendt: Lectures on Kant's Political Philosophy, published in 1982, contains thirteen lectures on judging, which, according to Arendt, is man's most political mental faculty. The last important source with regard to Hannah Arendt's writings is *Essays in Understanding*, published in 1994 and edited by Arendt's pupil, Jerome Kohn. The book contains forty essays written in different periods. The most important are: "Organized Guilt and Universal Responsibility" and particularly "On the Nature of Totalitarianism".

Moreover, I made use of the correspondence between Hannah Arendt and two of her best friends: Karl Jaspers and Mary McCarthy, published in 1985 and 1995 respectively.

Special reference must be made to *For Love of the World*, Hannah Arendt's biography written by Elisabeth Young-Bruehl and published in 1982. This biography contains many facts and details on Arendt's personality, which enabled me to get a better understanding of her life, work and character.

All other secondary literature are books and articles on Hannah Arendt's work as well as other studies directly related to the subject of this book. The amount of literature on Arendt and on the origin of evil is extensive. I had to restrict myself to the literature that helped me find answers to my questions. A complete list of all sources can be found at the end of the book.

SET-UP

Chapter One is an analysis of totalitarianism. Since Arendt does not provide a proper definition of totalitarianism, I have tried to find suitable definitions with the help of secondary literature. The genesis of Nazi-totalitarianism is the next subject. Although Arendt also considered Stalinism as a totalitarian system, I shall not pay attention to this in my study. The following elements that crystallized into Nazi-totalitarianism will be discussed: expansion, racism, the decline of the nation-state and anti-Semitism. Next subject is the anatomy of Nazi-totalitarianism. The various parts of the system will be discussed. Special reference will be made to the role of masses and the onion structure. Next are the most important characteristics of Nazi-totalitarianism: ideology and terror. In the end, these two elements would lead to total domination, concentration- and death camps and the destruction of more than six million Jews and Gypsies. Arendt speaks of a 'radical evil' that emerged in connection with a system in which all men have become equally superfluous.

Kant was the first to use the term "radical evil" and subsequently the second chapter is dedicated to Kant's "radical evil". With the help of texts by Kant, Jaspers and Allison one gets a picture of Kant's "radical evil" and its function.

In chapter three I have tried, with the help of Arendt's own texts, to indicate what she meant by "radical evil" and also if it is identical to or different from Kant's "radical evil".

Chapter four discusses the Eichmann trial and Arendt's conclusions. Eichmann's background, career and character are discussed. One of Arendt's most important conclusions was that she changed her mind with regard to the nature of evil. Instead of "radical evil" she now spoke of "the banality of evil", because she considered Eichmann a banal person, who was incapable of thinking and judging.

Chapter five is dedicated to the role of thinking, willing and judging in general and to their role in the prevention of evil in particular.

Chapter six is a reflection that leads to a number of conclusions. In this reflection I pay attention to totalitarianism and its uniqueness; the Shoah and its uniqueness; Eichmann in Jerusalem; the role of the Jewish Councils; the banality of evil; the death penalty; thinking, judging and acting in the Third Reich.

Chapter seven, the last chapter, is a reflection on guilt and responsibility, especially on the question of collective guilt.

NOTES

1. Hannah Arendt never used the word "Shoah". There was no proper word or expression for the destruction of the Jews until 1978. The makers of an American NBC-production introduced the term "Holocaust" in 1978. The literal sense of this word is "burnt offering" and this is a word with a religious connotation. The Hebrew word "Shoah", meaning annihilation, calamity, catastrophe or today "the" catastrophe, destruction, desolation, disaster (like in Psalms 35:8: "Let disaster (shoah) take them unawares") or great darkness, is now preferred by many scholars. "Shoah" was also the title of the famous film made by Claude Lanzmann in 1985. The term "Shoah" is specifically related to the destruction of the Jewish people and has no religious meaning. Because there is absolutely no question of an offering, but rather of pure destruction, I prefer "Shoah" to "Holocaust".

2. Königsberg was the former capital of East Prussia, the easternmost part of Germany. Since 1945 it has been a Russian enclave surrounded by Latvia, Lithuania and Poland. Königsberg is also the town where Kant spent his life. It is now called Kaliningrad.

3. The reason for Fackenheim's opinion that Eichmann's appeal to Kant was not entirely unfounded will be given in chapter four.

4. The best illustration of the dictum "the whole is more than the sum of the parts" can be found in art, especially in architecture. For instance: the whole of the cathedral of Paris, Notre Dame, is more than its separate parts: towers, doors, pillars, statues and windows. Something indefinable is added when the parts are brought together and this indefinable extra determines the beauty of the artwork or in other words: beauty is a sum not reducible to its parts.

Chapter One

Totalitarianism

DEFINITION

> One way to date the actual birth of historical phenomena as revolutions—
> or for that matter nation-states or imperialism or totalitarian rule and the
> like—is, of course, to find out when the word, which from then on
> remained attached to the phenomenon, appears for the first time. (OR, 35)

Hannah Arendt has not invented the term "totalitarianism", but it originates
in Italy. Originally it was a name of honour, invented by the Italian Fascists
in the years after the march on Rome in 1922. The philosopher Giovanni Gen-
tile used the word in the official exposition of the fascist doctrine in 1932,
while Mussolini used the term in an article for the *Enciclopedia Italiana*,
where he speaks of "lo stato totalitario". (Whitfield, 8) Hannah Arendt uses
the term specifically for the description of the regimes of Hitler and Stalin, although they probably never used the word themselves. Finally the word has
been used to indicate totalitarian one-party regimes in general.

In her book *The Origins of Totalitarianism* Hannah Arendt does not provide a definition of the word "totalitarianism", but at a later stage she gave a
short definition of the essence of totalitarianism: "Totalitarianism is the most
radical denial of freedom." (EU, 328) Another short, but well phrased definition comes from Bruno Bettelheim:

> . . . totalitarianism exists wherever the state abrogates the rights of the individ-
> ual and makes reason of state the highest principle, overruling all others. (Bet-
> telheim, 265)

Margaret Canovan's definition concurs with Bettelheim's:

> ... an attempt to exercise total domination and demonstrate that "everything is possible" by destroying human plurality and spontaneity at all levels, and ironing out all that is human and contingent to make it fit a determinist ideology. (Canovan, 1992, 27)

A more comprehensive description of totalitarianism can be found in *The New Illustrated Columbia Encyclopedia:*

> Totalitarianism, modern form of autocratic government in which the state involves itself in all facets of society. A totalitarian government seeks to control the daily life of its citizens by actively controlling not only all economic and political matters but all other features of society, including the attitudes, values and beliefs of its population. Totalitarian regimes erase the distinction between state and society and deny the distinction of a private sphere of living. All social roles become indistinguishable from political life, and the citizen's duty to the state becomes the primary concern of the community. An entity distinct from and superior to its components, the totalitarian state has as its purpose the replacement of existing society with a perfect society. The two most important characteristics are: the existence of an ideology that covers all aspects of life and explains the means by which to attain the final goal, and a single party through which this ideology is implemented. The party is led primarily by a single dictator and, typically, participation in politics, especially voting, is compulsory. The party has full control of the governmental system, and dissent is systematically suppressed. For this reason the use of terror and the employment of secret police force are common features of totalitarian systems. Finally, the party, through the government, has a monopoly of control over the economy, communications and the military establishment. (Bosley Woolf, 6834)

This definition corresponds with Arendt's description of totalitarianism, except for the fact that she calls the Nazi version of totalitarianism a movement instead of a party. Below I shall explain why Arendt prefers movement to party. Moreover, Arendt states that, besides the ideology, not the single party but terror is the most important symptom of totalitarianism. I agree with Arendt, since terror is not only an absolutely essential component of totalitarian regimes, but also the most frightening.

Although Arendt speaks of totalitarianism in general, her analysis is principally based on Hitler's regime. (Kateb, 74) In this dissertation I shall only discuss Nazi-totalitarianism, because certain observations in my book only relate to Nazism (such as the observations on the Jewish Councils in Chapter 6)

GENESIS

The use of the word "origins" in the title of Arendt's book *The Origins of Totalitarianism* suggests that she describes the causes of totalitarianism, as if events that preceded Nazism automatically would have resulted in its development. The original title of the book, *The Burden of our Time* does not give that impression. Arendt makes the following observation:

> The book, therefore, does not really deal with the origins of totalitarianism — as its title unfortunately claims — but gives a historical account of the elements, which crystallized into totalitarianism; this account is followed by an analysis of the elemental structure of totalitarian movements and domination itself. The elementary structure of totalitarianism is the hidden structure of the book while its more apparent unity is provided by certain fundamental concepts, which run like red threads through the whole (EU, 403)

Arendt assumes that history cannot be predicted and explained on the basis of certain events. Causal relationships, often very important for historians, are contrary to the novelty of the event and to human freedom. Human freedom enables human beings to act, that means: to start something new, take an initiative, start off a process at any moment. In an unpublished lecture at the New School for Social Research in 1954 about "The Nature of Totalitarianism", Arendt made the following statement:

> The elements of totalitarianism form its origins if by origins we do not understand "causes". Causality, i.e. the factor of determination of a process of events in which always one event causes and can be explained by another is probably an altogether alien and falsifying category in the realm of the historical and political sciences. Elements by themselves probably never cause anything. They become origins of events if and when they crystallize into fixed and definite forms. Then and only then, can we trace their history backwards. The event illuminates its own past, but it can never be deduced from it. (YB, 203)

The rejection of causality fits in with the interpretation of history by one of Arendt's best friends, Walter Benjamin, who says that the succession of historical events cannot be regarded as the movement of a rosary through the fingers. (Benjamin, 153)

Arendt also dissociates herself from the deterministic historical views of Marx and Hegel with their Messianic-teleological character. These philosophies, based on the existence of man instead of men, are in contradiction with human plurality, human freedom and human labour. The effects of labour are unlimited, because every reaction to an action may provoke a chain reaction and every process may start off new processes, which are unpredictable.

> The smallest act in the most limited circumstances bears the seed of the same boundlessness, because one deed, and sometimes one word, suffices to change every constellation. (HC, 190)

Arendt says that history becomes the storybook of mankind with many acting and speaking figures, but without specific authors who determine the ending. In conversations with her friends she called world history "that old trickster" (YB, 115) and in her correspondence with Karl Jaspers she speaks of "the insane course of history" and "world history shows little regard for our desires", while Karl Jaspers remarks:

> Ultimately no one has control over the course of history, not even in a theoretical view of it or in a prognosis. (C, 168, 250, 677)

Arendt refers to Plato, who says that the actions of men remind one of the gestures of marionettes in a puppet show, so that man seems to be a kind of plaything of a god. (HC, 185) There seems to be a figure behind the scenes, invisible for the actors in the play, who pulls the strings and is the writer of the story of mankind.

Coincidence clearly plays an important role and Arendt arrives at the conclusion that history is contingent, which means that everything that has happened might not have happened or might have happened otherwise. (EU, 326)

Going back to Nazism, we may conclude that this phenomenon, like all other historical phenomena, cannot be explained exclusively by considering it a product or result of preceding events. As we shall see later, there is another reason why Nazism is a phenomenon that is hard to explain. It cannot be denied that there was a kind of rationality behind the movement. When I speak of rationality I mean a behaviour that satisfies two conditions: consistency and the fulfilment of certain aims. However, the problem is that some of these aims (especially the systematic annihilation of Jews, Gypsies and other groups) are beyond our comprehension.

Summarizing we may say that, speaking about the origins of Nazi-totalitarianism, we must, according to Arendt, limit ourselves to the analysis of the elements that crystallized into Nazism. From the above, it will be clear that this analysis lacks any form of determinism, because the same elements could have crystallized into a completely different political structure.

In the following chapters I will take a close look at the elements that played a major role in the genesis of Nazism. The elements that will be discussed are successively: expansion and imperialism, racism, the decline of the nation-state, the alliance between the "mob" and the elite and finally anti-Semitism.

ELEMENTS IN THE GENESIS OF NAZISM

Expansion and Imperialism

According to Margareth Canovan it is obvious that for Hannah Arendt "expansion for expansion's sake" is the most important element in the genesis of Nazism. (Canovan, 1992, 29) According to Arendt, the origin of expansion can be found in Western imperialism. Originally imperialism had an exclusively economic purpose. The market for the capitalistic overproduction became too small in the home-countries and therefore new markets had to be developed for the sale of the excessive production goods and for excessive capital. Imperialism rose when the capitalists opposed governmental limitations of their economic expansion, because economic expansion is an inherent law of the capitalistic system.

In reality, expansion meant colonization, in other words annexation of areas, mainly in Africa and Asia. Superfluous capital and production resulted in another phenomenon, which was to become an extremely important factor in the development of Nazism: redundant workers. Imperialism provided a solution for this serious problem and thus the two superfluous elements, capital and workers, united and left their homeland.

As long as this was mainly an economic problem it was not a dangerous development. However, the danger is to be found in the fact that expansion, power and violence became political goals in themselves. The result of the export of political power was that the army and the police were separated from the national institutions and were promoted to national representation in the annexed areas and this resulted in exercise of power with expansion as the only and ultimate goal. This was the case when moderate imperialism was followed by totalitarian imperialism. Totalitarian imperialism destroyed all stable political structures, not only in other countries, but also in the homeland. It became a power that destroyed nations and human beings. Power became the central idea of political thinking and acting at the moment that it was separated from the political community that it was supposed to serve. The bourgeoisie, which had been excluded from political matters by the government of the nation-state for a long time, also because of their own lack of interest in public matters, became politically emancipated as a result of imperialism. Imperialism can therefore be considered the initial step of the bourgeoisie to participation in political matters.

Race Thinking and Racism

Race thinking developed at the same time in all Western countries in the 19th century and racism was to be the ideological weapon of imperialism. The first signs of racism can be seen in France. French nobility felt genealogically more connected with an international class than with France. All French racial theories adhered to Germanism i.e. the idea of superiority of the Northern European races. Paradoxical as it may sound, the fact is that the French and not the Germans were the first to bring up the idea of German superiority. (OT III, 164–165) In Germany race thinking developed after the defeat of the Prussian army by Napoleon and served mainly to unify the nation and to form a defence against foreign influences. This resulted in the development of terminology like "blood relationship" and "unmixed origin". Another source for race thinking in Germany was political romanticism with its emphasis on "innate personality" and "true nobility".

These two variations in race thinking came together in the theories of the French count Arthur de Gobineau in his book *Essai sur l'Inégalité des Races Humaines'* (1853), a kind of standard work for racial theories. Gobineau wanted to create and define an "elite" to replace the aristocracy. He invented the super race of the Aryans that was in danger of being submerged by the lower non-Aryan races.

> Human history is like an immense tapestry. The earth is the frame over which it is stretched. The successive centuries are the tireless weavers. As soon as they are born they immediately seize the shuttle and operate it in the frame, working at it until they die. The broad fabric thus goes on growing beneath their busy fingers. The two most inferior varieties of the human species, the black and yellow races, are the crude foundation, the cotton and the wool, which the secondary families of the white race make supple by adding their silk, while the Aryan group, circling its finer threads through the noble generations, designs on its surface a dazzling masterpiece of arabesques in silver and gold. (de Gobineau in Dwork & van Pelt, 20)

All this had to do with race thinking and not with racism. Racism is not only race thinking but also actual discrimination of one particular race with regard to another. Racism developed later from experiences and political constellations which were originally unknown and which would have appeared strange even to de Gobineau. Moreover, Darwinian thinking and the theory of "the survival of the fittest" began to play an important role. Nevertheless, race thinking and racism might have disappeared, if they had not been essential to the imperialists for the justification of their acts. For them, race thinking was a major help in the continuation of their activities.

According to Arendt, there is a second reason for the development of racism, apart from the fact that it was an ideological weapon of imperialism. Race thinking and racism were understandable and spontaneous reactions of civilized people who, for the first time, came into touch with "savages". It was absolutely impossible for the imperialists to consider these "savages" as members of the same human race. (OT, III, 185) Therefore, killing these "savages" was not considered murder. Finally, all these events resulted in the abandoning of economic imperatives. These imperatives were replaced by the use of pure violence, committed by people who had discovered a new type of society, a society based on the existence of a chosen race.

Central-European countries had little hope for expansion overseas, because they were no maritime nations and consequently they felt that they had the right of expansion within the European Continent. Continental imperialism started in the homeland and was based on an increased tribal awareness, the unification of people with identical origins. The best examples of continental imperialism are the so-called Pan-movements, such as Pan-Germanism, which developed in the middle of the nineteenth century. Pan-Germanism had an affinity with race thinking and racial theories. Nazism mainly derived its ideas from Pan-Germanism rather than from imperialism. (OT III, 222–224)

Tribal nationalism arose because large groups of people did not have their domicile in their homeland at the end of the nineteenth century and the beginning of the twentieth century. They had no home, but they felt at home in their tribe. Pan-Germanism was a kind of tribal nationalism based on pseudo-mystical elements and inner qualities. Contrary to imperialistic race thinking, there was an element of divine origin and being chosen in Pan-Germanism and therefore Arendt compares Pan-Germanism with a religion. (OT III, 234)

The consequence of these perceptions is that people turn into an animal species with a hierarchical structure. Nationalistic tribal feelings were the basis for the development of a new form of anti-Semitism, which was not based on personal experiences with Jews, but which had a political, social and economical background. The reason for this was that the Jews formed a perfect model for the Pan-movements: they were also a nation without a nation-state, thus without a homeland; they also had a common origin and they belonged to a "chosen nation". However, there was one important difference with Pan-Germanism: the Jews had managed to form their own society. This is the reason why Hannah Arendt regards anti-Semitism to a large extent as a form of jealousy. (OT III, 241) After all, the Jews had succeeded, despite twenty centuries of diaspora and persecution, to keep their identity. Pan-Germanism was in fact not a party, but a movement that distrusted all parties and as such it was a precursor of Nazi-totalitarianism. It was a movement that was after the

destruction of the nation-state. The hostile attitude of Pan-Germanism towards the party system got practical significance after 1918, when the party
system was no longer a workable construction and the class system disintegrated as a result of the growth of the masses. These masses had been
completely disrupted by the events during and after The Great War. Pan-
Germanism gradually changed into its successor: Nazism. In the chapter on
the anatomy of Nazi-totalitarianism, I will go into the significance and the
role of these masses.

The Alliance Between Mob and Capital

Hannah Arendt does not provide us with a definition of the term "mob". Nevertheless, the meaning of the word in Arendt's book is somewhat different
from the usual meaning. The mob is not the people, the rabble, the lower
classes or the hopeless mass that came into being after the decline of the nation-state, but a more active and enterprising part of the superfluous labour-
ers. The mob is a residue of all classes produced by the bourgeoisie, the capital and therefore inseparably linked to it, like a parent to his or her children.
The mob is a kind of residual product of the bourgeois society, with the same
egoistic tendencies, partly criminal and prepared to do anything. The mob always shouts for a strong man or a great leader, because it hates society. Arendt
considers the unlucky alliance between gangsters and the establishment,
which was to result in the seizure of power by Hitler, symptomatic for the
strong affinity between the bourgeoisie and the mob.

Imperialism depended already on the cooperation between capital and
mob, where the latter group committed the crimes that provided a pattern for
the Nazi crimes. Racism played an important role, for not only did it provide
an excuse for their actions and a confirmation of their superiority, it also as-
sociated them as white people with the economic interests of the capitalistic
elite.

However, racism was later transformed from an economic means into an
ideology, first in South Africa, later in continental Pan-Germanism and finally
in Nazism. Although there is a connection with imperialism, we may not conclude that Nazism was a simple continuation of imperialism, since most supporters of Nazism were no criminals, but honourable members of the mass.
Mass has another meaning than mob. Masses consist of a large number of
people who are no longer part of society or of an organisation that stands up
for common interest. It is an accumulation of people, very often unemployed;
without a future, a collection of discouraged men and women. As mentioned
before, I will revert to the significance and the role of the masses in the next
chapter.

The Decline of the Nation-state

The nineteenth century concept of "nation-state" is a combination of the notions "nation" and "state". Before the nineteenth century these two notions did not usually converge. Nation-states developed in Western Europe after the French Revolution. The purpose of the state is to provide citizens with legal rights and to guarantee the protection of their common interests. The nation-state is an institute constructed by people, where people with the same roots feel at home and for which the inhabitants take responsibility. (OT III, 229–231) The nation-state was the model of society and for Arendt the French model of the nation-state was the ideal example. (OT III, 261)

However, for several groups of people in Europe it had been impossible to unite themselves in a political construction such as the nation-state. It concerned people with the same background but without roots. The Jews, who had no homeland or nation-state, formed one of these groups.

The decline of the nation-state, in particular of the German nation-state, started in fact after the outbreak of the First World War in 1914. After the armistice in 1918, Europe was flooded with political refugees and displaced persons and this was an important cause of the decline of the nation-state.

The decline of the German nation-state was caused by both internal and external factors. Internal factors were related to the ever-present tension between the state as a defender of civil rights and the idea of a nation as people with the same roots and background. This tension explains the difficult position of the Jews and other minorities in the nation-state. The tension increased with the immigration of political refugees, mainly stateless Jews, from Russia and Poland.

In her book *The Human Condition*, Hannah Arendt stresses the importance of speaking and acting as fundamental activities of human existence. However, the increasing number of refugees was deprived of the right to action and of the right to opinion. Moreover she establishes that particularly the loss of a community has been the calamity. (OT III, 296, 297)

Continental imperialism, in the form of Pan-Germanism, was an external threat to the nation-state, because Pan-Germanistic movements were looking for expansion across existing national frontiers. Summarizing we might say that the nation-state was threatened from the outside by imperialism and Pan-movements and from the inside by the appearance of minorities, refugees and stateless people.

The two characteristics of the nation-state, the guarantee of legal rights and the creation of a climate in which the inhabitants feel at home, were threatened by these internal and external factors. The national state no longer represented the people and became incapable of safeguarding its security.

Statelessness played into the hands of the Nazis in two ways. Firstly, people who have no rights and are not officially supposed to exist, are easy to eliminate. Secondly, these people might threaten society from the inside if their numbers increase, because they are forced to live as parasites.

Anti-Semitism

One of the most important and intriguing problems with regard to Nazi-totalitarianism is the question why the Jews in particular were selected as victims. For Daniel Goldhagen there is only one answer:

> Not economic hardship, not the coercive means of a totalitarian state, not social psychological pressure, not invariable psychological propensities, but ideas about Jews that were pervasive in Germany, and had been for decades, induced ordinary Germans to kill unarmed, defenceless Jewish men, women and children by the thousands, systematically and without pity. (Goldhagen, 9)

It cannot be denied that anti-Semitism played an important role, but it is questionable whether this is the one and only answer. For instance, it is a well-known fact, that anti-Semitism in France during the nineteenth century and the beginning of the twentieth century was comparable with anti-Semitism in later years in Germany. This suggests that there must have been other factors and that the whole question is more complex. Hannah Arendt's vision is more balanced. She makes a distinction between anti-Semitism, anti-Jewish feelings and religious Jew-hatred. Anti-Jewish feelings and religious Jew-hatred existed throughout the ages, but anti-Semitism appeared after 1870 and it was related to the birth of nation-states. Arendt insists that modern anti-Semitism has a political instead of a social origin. (OT III, 37, 44, 48, 87) Especially in the nation-state, the difference between Jews and the ethnical group of the nation-state was stressed. In a later stage, the Nazis used anti-Semitism as a catalyst for the formation of the organisational structure, because firstly it fitted in with the other elements of totalitarianism and secondly it was used as an argument for war and as an excuse for the Shoah. (OT III, preface, XIV)

The Nazis made use of the myth of a secret Jewish conspiracy, as described in the anti-Semitic pamphlet "The Protocols of the Elders of Zion". On the other hand, as Arendt says, the Nazis not only hated the Jews, but they also wanted to imitate them. "The Protocols of the Elders of Zion" served not only as an anti-Semitic pamphlet, but also as a textbook for the Nazis, to learn how a chosen people might dominate the world. I will revert to this subject in the chapter on Nazi ideology.

Arendt rejects two generally accepted theories about anti-Semitism: the theory of the "scape-goat" and the theory of "eternal anti-Semitism". The theory of the scapegoat not only implies that the victims were completely innocent, but also that the Jews did nothing that could possibly have a connection with the issue at stake. Moreover, the scapegoat-theory implies that the scapegoat might have been anyone else. To illustrate this, Arendt tells a joke that went round in Europe after World War I.

> An anti-Semite claimed that the Jews had caused the war; the reply was: Yes the Jews and the bicyclists. Why the bicyclists? asks the one. Why the Jews? asks the other. (OT III, 5)

The theory of eternal anti-Semitism implies that it is a permanent phenomenon and that the Jews were always hated and will be prosecuted forever. There is a common idea behind the two theories. The idea is that the Jews were not even partly responsible for the events and moreover these theories conceal the historical background. It is understandable that the Jews do not wish to discuss their share of responsibility, but Arendt states that their co-responsibility lies in the way the Jews have reacted to their political situations in the course of their history. In other words, it is a matter of political responsibility.

> Jewish history offers the extraordinary spectacle of a people, unique in this respect, which began its history with a well-defined concept of history and an almost conscious resolution to achieve a well-circumscribed plan on earth and then, without giving up this concept avoided all political actions for two thousand years. The result was the political history of the Jewish people became even more dependent upon the unforeseen, accidental factors than the history of other nations, so that the Jews stumbled from one role to the other and accepted responsibility for none. (OT III, 8)

Arendt reproaches the Jews that they escaped their political responsibility to defend their rights as Jews, which later made them a plaything of history.

The most important elements of the genesis of totalitarianism have now been described. These elements are: expansion, racism, the alliance between mob and elite, the decline of the nation-state and anti-Semitism. The crystallization of these elements into totalitarianism was not unavoidable. The synthesis of a chemical compound is only possible under specific conditions. This also applies to the crystallization of the above-mentioned elements into totalitarianism. Different conditions could have changed the course of history completely. Coincidence must have played a role as well. One single word, move, or action could have turned history in another direction.

In the third part of her book *The Origins of Totalitarianism*, Arendt gives a description of the totalitarian movement. This part is different from the other two parts of her book. This is one of the reasons why critical readers consider this book unbalanced. (initially, the three parts of the book were published separately) The first two parts are historical reviews of the origins of totalitarianism. One could be critical of minor details in her description, but in general it seems to be correct. The third part is an attempt to discover the essence of an unfathomable phenomenon, Nazi-totalitarianism. Therefore, the third part is not a historical description, but political theory or political philosophy. It is understandable that critical remarks of various scholars relate to the third part of her book. I will incorporate these remarks in the following paragraphs, in order to provide a more balanced picture of the anatomy and mode of operation of Nazi-totalitarianism.

ANATOMY OF NAZI-TOTALITARIANISM

Masses

Masses are indispensable for totalitarian movements. However, what are masses and why are they indispensable? Firstly, the word mass has a quantitative meaning. A mass is a large group of people. Totalitarian regimes require large groups of people, because totalitarianism is a destructive system that needs victims. Totalitarianism is unthinkable in a country with a limited number of inhabitants. (OT III, 308) This illustrates also why expansion was necessary: expansion means domination of new territories providing more human material.

On the other hand the word has a qualitative connotation. Masses are the result of the disintegration of classes. According to Arendt, classes are relatively stable groups of people with demonstrable common interests, while masses contain isolated "atomized" individuals. These people were "atomized" because they could not be integrated into any organisation based on common interest, into political parties, municipal governments, professional organizations or trade unions. There were two reasons for this: superfluousness and/or indifference.

Masses were a result of the disintegration of the party-system caused by the parties' inability to protect the interests of all their members. Masses consisted of lonely people, who often felt dissatisfied, frustrated and superfluous because of unemployment. Many of them were desperate, indifferent to death and lacking in "common sense". Their frustration was partly caused by the German defeat in the First World War, in particular by the Treaty of Versailles in 1919. One of the conditions of the allied forces was that Germany was to give up the compulsory military service. What happened to the millions of soldiers who returned from the battlefields in France and Belgium? We can answer this question with the help of Canetti. He makes a differentiation between open masses and closed masses. The number of people in an open mass is basically unlimited. A manifestation is a good example of an open mass. A closed mass is comparable with a rain tub. If the tub is full, no more water can be added. The ban on general military service robbed Germany of its main closed mass: the army. The prohibition of general conscription became the cradle of national-socialism because a closed mass which is dissolved by force will turn into an open mass, to which it will pass on its main characteristics; in this case drills and receiving and passing on instructions. Thus, the party, which knew no limitations within the nation, took the place of the army. (Canetti, 15, 202)

If this is true, the German army was turned into an open mass, containing millions of frustrated soldiers and this might be one of the factors in the development of masses and the national-socialist party.

All this can also be seen in the light of the loss of human plurality. Plurality is, according to Hannah Arendt, the condition for the existence of human society.

> Plurality is the condition for human action because we are all the same, that is, human, in such a way that nobody is ever the same as anyone else who ever lived, lives or will live (HC, 8)

Nevertheless, the existence of a common world is guaranteed because despite plurality, people aim for the same goal. If this common goal disappears, nothing can prevent the destruction of the common world. This destruction is usually preceded by the destruction of the many aspects in which this common world presents itself to human plurality. Plurality turns into uniformity, which is essential for totalitarian movements. This may happen in a mass society or under conditions of mass hysteria, where all people suddenly behave as though they were members of one family, each borrowing and propagating the perspective of his neighbour. Under these conditions men become solitary individuals.

> . . . they have been deprived of seeing and hearing others, of being seen and being heard by them. They are all imprisoned in the subjectivity of their own singular experience, which does not cease to be singular if the same experience is multiplied innumerable times. The end of the common world has come when it is seen only under one aspect and is permitted to present itself in only one perspective. (HC, 58)

The above-mentioned situation applies to the conditions in the years before and during Nazi-totalitarianism. According to Arendt, members of the masses were prepared to support anything that could provide them with a "home" and with new prospects.

For totalitarian leaders, sometimes originating from the mass (Himmler), but more often from the "mob" (Hitler), it was not too difficult to recruit people for their movement, offering only one new perspective: to obey the totalitarian movement and its leaders unconditionally.

There have been a lot of discussions about the motives of the members of the masses to join the Nazi party. Arendt's interpretation is that the members of the mass society, because they felt superfluous, lacked every social or political interest and only cared for their own safety. This may have been the reason for the masses to become susceptible to the Nazi ideologies, which took no interest in classes or utility.

In a certain way, mass people were victims, which does not mean that Arendt does not reproach them, because there were many amongst them who resisted the temptations of the totalitarian ideologies, which illustrates that men are capable of human reactions, despite the seriousness of the situation. However, most mass-people formed a non-differentiated aggregation of lost and lonely souls, who were prepared to accept any escape. In January 1933 six million people were unemployed and this was 25% of the total work force. Anything was acceptable to them as long as it was different from the past, and that was exactly what the Nazis promised. In his speeches, Hitler did not present a new program for the country. He only said that the political and economical situation would change and that was enough to get the active support of nearly forty percent of the German population.

> The desperate and legitimate needs of the victimized masses made totalitarianism possible. Just as the masses did not choose their misery, so they did not choose a remedy that they knew would lead to the wars and extermination camps of totalitarianism. (Kateb, 72)

Historian Carol E. Adams has criticized the theory of the disintegration of the classes into a mass. She claims that in 1920 Germany was not a mass society and also that Arendt's theory of the success of the totalitarian movement is not correct. Moreover she states that the Nazis did not only make ideological statements, but that they made substantial promises to specific groups. According to Adams, the masses were more susceptible to these promises than to the ideologies. (Adams, 34–35)

It is true that the Nazis improved certain aspects of the social and economical situation. Unemployment figures went down (however, this was on the one hand due to compulsory employment, on the other to juggling with figures); there was more public security (but not for Jews and anti-Nazis!) and the construction of motorways was seen as part of the improved national economy. A survey in 1951 showed that most Germans considered the thirties as "a nice time". This is not surprising if one realises that the preceding years were miserable: a terrible war with millions of deaths, national shame after the defeat, loss of territory, a bad economical situation, inflation, unemployment and public insecurity. (Rees, 58–61)

However, behind this visible improvement, invisible powers were hidden and this became clear during the "Kristallnacht" in 1938.[1] At that moment it was too late: the masses were caught in the ideologies of domination of the world and anti-Semitism and most Germans were of the opinion that Germany had to be cleared from Jews. Their general attitude towards the movement did not change. Many years later, after the Eichmann-trial, Arendt admits in a letter to Mary McCarthy that: "The impact of ideology may have been overrated by me". (BF, 147) Maybe the truth is in the middle: on the one hand it was the ideology that gave the atomised individuals a feeling of being part of a total (hence totalitarianism!), on the other hand it was the improvement of daily life that influenced the attitude of the population.

Eric Voegelin, like Hannah Arendt a German refugee, passed more criticism. He accepts Hannah Arendt's ideas with regard to the development of masses out of classes, but he disagrees with the reasons she gives for the reaction of the masses. According to Voegelin, the most important element in the development of totalitarianism is "the spiritual disease of agnosticism". (Voegelin, 73)

Most papers that are critical of Arendt's description of totalitarianism were published after her death in 1975. Before 1975, she seldom responded to critical papers. Voegelin's article is an exception. In her reaction she says that she does not believe that totalitarianism was a new kind of perverted religion. Totalitarian ideas were not a substitute for God, although she agrees that there could be some connection between totalitarianism and atheism, in the sense that a Christian cannot become a follower of Hitler and that morality might be in danger when people loose their faith in God. However, this does not explain the rise of Nazi-totalitarianism. (EU, 407)

In summary: Social classes disintegrated into masses. Masses contained deprived, unemployed, lonely and uprooted people; they felt redundant and superfluous, they had lost their self-respect and were frustrated by the German defeat in World War I and by the indignities they had been subjected to after the Treaty of Versailles in 1919. Some members of the masses were not politically indifferent. Hannah Arendt calls this group "the mob". We saw this group before in the chapter on imperialism; it contained criminal elements. The mob joined their creators, the elite and the capital. This group produced the first "Nazi-hooligans" as well as their leaders, including Adolf Hitler. The Nazis tried to find sympathizers and followers in the masses by means of ideological propaganda. They were successful: for various reasons the masses sympathized with the Nazi-movement and subsequently almost 40% of the German population voted for the National Socialist Party in 1933. Most members of the S.S. were also recruited from the masses. Generally these people were not criminals, but ordinary average citizens, whose actions were based on a sense of duty or on ideological motives.

Structure and Composition

Many analysts consider Nazi-totalitarianism as a modern variant of dictatorship. However, says Arendt:

> This makes them overlook the differences between the restriction of freedom in authoritarian regimes, the abolition of political freedom in tyrannies and dictatorships and the total elimination of spontaneity itself, that is, of the most general and most elementary manifestation of human freedom, at which only totalitarian regimes aim by means of their various methods of conditioning. (BPF, 96)

In order to illustrate the difference between authoritarian regimes and totalitarian movements Arendt makes use of the metaphor of the pyramid and the metaphor of the onion. The structure of the pyramid can serve as a model for authoritarian regimes. Ultimate power and authority are located at the top and descend and weaken towards the base. On the way down, power and authority are 'filtered' by the various layers of the pyramid. Each layer has a certain authority, but always less than the previous one. In this model all layers are integrated in the total structure, but they are also connected with each other as they all follow the lines laid down by the top of the pyramid. Authoritarian regimes with their hierarchical structure are the least egalitarian form of government; their principle rests on inequality and difference.

Tyrannies belong strictly to the egalitarian forms of government: the tyrant is the sole ruler, who oppresses all others, who are equal, that is to say, equally powerless. The structure of a tyranny is that of a pyramid without layers. The top of the pyramid remains suspended, supported by the edges, over a mass of disintegrated, isolated, powerless and identical individuals.

Contrary to tyrannies and authoritarian forms of government, the structure of totalitarian movements could best be compared with that of an onion. In the centre of the onion there is an empty space, where the leader is located. Whatever he does, he does from within and not, like in tyrannies, from above. The various layers of the onion represent the components of the totalitarian machine: the front organisations, the professional societies, the party members, the party bureaucracy, the elite formations and the police groups. These groups are situated in such a way that each layer forms the façade of the layer located further to the centre and the centre of the layer further to the outside. This structure has therefore the great advantage that the outside of each layer presents the picture of a normal world and the inside shows its face of radical extremism to the next layer. This can be illustrated by looking at the second layer from the outside. Let us presume that this represents the layer of the party members. For the next layer inwards, the layer of the active executors of the totalitarian system, the second layer represents the normal external world. In relation to the first layer, the layer at the surface of the onion that contains the front organizations (those who sympathized with the movement) and bystanders, the party members of the second layer not only felt different but also had the feeling that their opinions were more radical.

Another advantage of the onion structure is that the population of other countries could only see the outside layer of the onion and since this layer only contained sympathizing front organizations and the faceless millions, the first impression of the Nazi movement was not malicious and nobody was aware of what was going on in the centre of the onion. The outside layer was a kind of protective wall, which separated the party members from the outside, normal world.

> Thus the sympathizers in the front organizations, whose convictions differ only in intensity from those of the party membership, surround the whole movement and provide a deceptive façade of normality to the outside world because of their lack of fanaticism and extremism, while, at the same time, they represent the normal world of the totalitarian movement whose members come to believe that their convictions differ only in degree from those of other people so that they need never be aware of the abyss which separates their own world from that which actually surrounds it. The onion structure makes the system organizationally shockproof against factuality of the real world. (BPF, 100)

As said before, Arendt prefers the term Nazi movement to Nazi party. The goal of a movement is to organize as many people as possible and keep them in motion. In fact there was no political goal that would indicate the end of the movement. This implied that there was no party program, which is customary for a political party, and also that Nazism was amorphous, because a movement is always on its way to a new goal and hence changes shape constantly. Moreover, the ultimate goal of the movement was expansion and the destruction of real and fictitious enemies. Therefore, giving the onion the functional capacity of a macrophage could perfect Arendt's metaphor of the onion. Macrophages are cells in the human body capable of phagocytosis, the destruction of foreign and toxic substances. This is done by surrounding the toxic agent, which is possible because the phagocyte is amorphous; this means that it can take any functional and desired shape. Schematically Nazi-totalitarianism can be seen as an onion, which, depending on the circumstances, can take any shape to surround and destroy the enemy.

Although Arendt does not indicate the number of layers of the onion and their composition, we can nevertheless get a rough idea of the contents of the various layers from her description. It is almost certain that the organization of the Nazi-movement was in fact much more complicated, with layers in the layers and duplications of the various organizations, but within the framework of this review, the following scheme is sufficient.

The surface layer of the onion contained the front organizations and the faceless millions, silent bystanders who did not actively protest against the movement. These people were expected to be loyal to the movement and have confidence in its future development. The front organizations were indeed loyal to the movement. The faceless millions were neither for nor against it; they were silent. I will revert later to the role of these faceless millions, because the role of this group was probably more important than it appears to be at first sight.

Before we discuss the second layer it is important to say that, from the very beginning of the Nazi-movement, Hitler wanted the mass to be divided into party members and sympathizers. Moreover, he constantly tried to increase the number of sympathizers and to decrease the number of party members. (OT III, 366)

The second layer was the layer of a more radical and fanatical group: the party members. According to Arendt they know that the Leader is a liar and that he deceives the masses, but they respect him for it. Party members did not believe in the statements intended for public consumption. These statements were intended for the surface layer, especially for the bystanders. On the other hand they did believe in the ideologies of the Nazi movement.

The third layer is the layer of the elite, the executors of the totalitarian system: the bureaucracy, the S.S., the secret police. It was not necessary for them to believe in the ideology. They executed the orders but they were unable to distinguish between truth and falsehood and between reality and fiction or to judge the individual statement of facts. Statements of facts were immediately transformed into statements of purpose. The statement "all Jews are inferior" became "all Jews should be killed". Without such a layer, a totalitarian system is unthinkable, because it could never fulfil its ideological fiction. (OT III, 385)

There was something remarkable about this layer. All organisations in this layer were duplicated, tripled, quadrupled or even multiplied by five and power was constantly shuffled from one organization to the other, so that nobody was ever sure whether it was he who represented the will of the Leader. It was the strategy of "divide and rule". Moreover, it is clear that with the increasing number of organizations, less power was held by every individual organization. All this is the result of the realization of the principle of the Leader: no hierarchy, no restriction of freedom but elimination of freedom. It is only the execution of the will of the Leader that matters. (OT III, 398–400) In a way the internal organization was also amorphous, but that lack of a fixed shape is characteristic of movements.

Inside the layer of the executioners, was the layer of the direct subordinates of the Leader (such as Himmler, Goering, Hess, and Heydrig). These people were responsible for the functioning of the various institutions and organizations.

In the centre of the onion was the Leader, who took all the important decisions. The Leader was ultimately responsible for all the movements of the totalitarian system and he was always right. This "rightness" has nothing to do with the truth and whether he will be proved right in the end depends on the future, but since his ideas were meant for the following centuries (Hitler's thousand-year-empire), none of his contemporaries could say anything sensible about it.

It has been said that Hitler was the origin of the development of the totalitarian system, but that is a misconception. I agree with Arendt that Nazism was born in the masses. Totalitarian leaders could exert authority only because they were supported by the masses. Hitler was elected by the German population with a majority of votes in a democratic way and hence had its confidence. Moreover, the Leader and the masses made a mutual sacrifice: both parties gave up personal ambitions or the achievement of specific individual goals. This enabled them to dedicate themselves to the ideology, which, because of its historical meaning made their alliance almost inevitable: the superiority of the race.

Karl Jaspers asked the hypothetical question whether the totalitarian movement could have functioned without a dictator and he also wondered whether dictators could be interchangeable. (C, 334)

James Whitfield more or less answers this question by remarking that both Stalinism and Nazism lost their totalitarian character after the death of the leader, which demonstrates how important they were for the maintenance of the totalitarian movement. (Whitfield, 60) It is important to note that Whitfield speaks of the "maintenance" of the system and not of its "origin".

Arendt emphasizes that a totalitarian leader is basically different from a tyrant because his ultimate purpose is not the tranquillity of his own rule, but the imitation of the laws of Nature or History. Moreover the totalitarian leader does not believe that he is a free person with the power to execute his will. He is no more than the executor of higher laws.

The whole movement gave the impression of a secret society, established in broad daylight, with sworn friends and sworn enemies. These were real enemies, such as political opponents or fictitious, designated enemies such as the Jews. Originally there were only political enemies, because the Nazis realized a dichotomy: either one was in favour of the movement or one was against it. It was a division in the sense of: all the others and we and there was no room for plurality. All the others, political opponents, were successively eliminated from society and what finally remained were fictitious enemies and followers. It is also important that there were members of the elite in every layer of the movement and the alliance between these members of the elite and the mob was amazing. It is understandable that Arendt speaks of "the disturbing alliance between the mob and the elite". (OT III, 337) Members of the alliance were immediately attracted by the ideology of the totalitarian movement, while the masses had to be persuaded by means of propaganda.

IDEOLOGY

So far, we have been looking at the structure of Nazism, but by far the most important characteristics of the movement were ideology and terror, which formed its basis. Especially the ideology creates an important difference with other regimes and that is one of the reasons why it is so difficult to compare totalitarianism with other dictatorial systems. Let us focus on ideology first and on terror later.

What is an ideology? Webster's New Collegiate Dictionary gives the following definition: "an ideology is a systematic body of concepts especially about human life or culture". (Webster, 568)

Hannah Arendt has her own definition of an ideology, which is not very different but more extensive.

> An ideology is quite literally what its name indicates: it is the logic of an idea. Its subject matter is history, to which the "idea" is applied; the result of this application is not a body of statements about something that *is* but the unfolding of a process which is in constant change. The ideology treats the course of events as though it followed the same "law" as the logical exposition of its "idea". Ideologists pretend to know the mysteries of the whole historical process—the secrets of the past, the intricacies of the present, the uncertainties of the future—because of the logic inherent in their respective ideas (OT, III, 469)

The element of historicity is important, because it pretends that the ideology has a scientific and transcendent character. The mob and its leaders offered the masses an ideology that could give their existence a renewed sense. The dissatisfaction of the masses made them susceptible to an ideology with

a new order. The masses were looking for an escape out of their misery, some
kind of liberation from their isolated existence and the best liberation had to
come from a higher source. An ideology was extremely suitable for this liberation since the primary function of an ideology is: "to explain everything
and every occurrence by deducing it from a single premise . . ."(OT III, 468)
Again and again Arendt emphasizes the pseudo-scientific and pseudo-
philosophical relevance of an ideology and the attempt to know the world
with its help. It is well known that masses are susceptible to pseudo-scientific
explanations, because they make reflection unnecessary.

The power of the logic of the ideology makes the lonesome individual feel
absorbed by it; he will go with the flow and will lose, up to a point, both his
free will and his ability to judge. What is important is the manner in which
the ideological logic is used. Ideological Nazi logic was not used as a control
of thinking but rather as a movement of thought. What does this mean? Logic
as a control of thinking is looking for factual knowledge in relation to experience. Logic as a movement of thought is applied to an idea and this idea is
transformed into a premise. It pushes the individual within the idea, together
with the premise that brings the logical process into action This is the essence
of Arendt's explanation of the Nazi-ideology and it also explains its consequences: terror, total domination and genocide. Everything can be explained
by argumentation starting from the ideology. I will try to clarify this. Let us
consider a simple example of logical deduction.

When it rains, the streets get wet (premise)

It is raining (observation)

The streets get wet (conclusion)

This argumentation is valid and each time it rains and the streets get wet is
a proof that the premise is correct. Here, logic is used "as a necessary control
of thinking". However, the Nazis had an idea and transformed the idea into a
premise. The idea was not, as Arendt says, a body of statements about something that is, but rather a prophetic view of what will be. The idea was that
history was a struggle of races and that in the end the Aryan race would survive all other races. The logical reasoning of the Nazis was probably something like the following:

When time goes by, the Aryan race will survive (premise)

Time goes by (observation)

The Aryan race survives (conclusion)

Once the premise is accepted everything will be absorbed by it. The ideology serves to make the world consistent and to prove that the original
prophetic view is correct (OT III, 458)

Ideologies destroy the real world as it appears and create a fictitious world
as a substitute. Behind the real world as it appears, there would be an invisible

reality that contains a causal law, applicable to all historical events. This law, which is at the root of the all-embracing idea of the ideology, can explain the course of history—the past, the present and the future. In the Nazi-ideology world history is understood as a Darwinian struggle between races, which will inevitably lead to the destruction of inferior races and the victory of a new elite. This ideology, which has the function of a law, requires approval and, contrary to liberal democratic methods, this approval is attained from the top to the bottom or metaphorically speaking from the centre of the onion up to the outer layers. The minimum requirement was silent approval, although the movement in fact did not want approval but a confirmation of the ideology by all of the mass. This confirmation was mainly obtained by the fact that totalitarian thinking, by means of the logicality of the idea, deprives people of the possibility to consider other points of view and to reconsider ideas in the light of their effects. It is this capacity that is destroyed by ideological thinking.

> Inner compulsion by the tyranny of logicality removes the capacity to think again and to react to experience and turns men into robots, perfectly fitted for the role of executioner or of victim as required by the all-devouring process of totalitarian terror. (Canovan, 1989, 158)

The totalitarian law of the Nazis is the law of Nature and consequently totalitarianism is virtually lawless because there are no constitutional laws that indicate which human actions are allowed and which are not. With regard to the laws of Nazism, Arendt makes the following remark:

> Totalitarian lawfulness, executing the laws of Nature or History does not bother to translate them into standards of right or wrong for individual human beings, but applies them directly to the "species", to mankind. The laws of Nature or History, if properly executed, are expected to produce as their end a single "Mankind", and it is this expectation that lies behind the claim to global rule of all totalitarian governments. (EU, 340)

This was the beginning of a make-believe world, the beginning of a fictitious human existence under Nazi-totalitarian rules, where all ideological statements and explanations were directed towards a future that showed great promise for the desperate masses.

Margareth Canovan formulates a very interesting question:

> Does she [Hannah Arendt] or does she not believe that the leaders of totalitarian regimes took their ideologies seriously? (Canovan, 1989, 151)

Canovan's question relates to Stalin as well as to Hitler and the answer applies to both dictators. There are at least three possible answers to the question.

– The leaders were fanatics who believed that the ideology was based on the truth and who were willing to execute the ideology at any price.

– The leaders were cynics who used the ideology only as a means to manipulate the masses and to obtain total domination in which "everything was possible". This answer is contradictory to the first answer.

– We have seen that the Nazis tried to create a fictitious world and this gave George Kateb the idea to consider the leaders as artists.

> An alternative formulation is that totalitarian leaders show the latent murderousness inherent in estheticism: a readiness to sacrifice anything to the "consonance of their own system" or to its "beautiful" consistency. (Kateb, 79)

Margareth Canovan rejects the vision of George Kateb and I agree with her. She concludes correctly that totalitarianism, as Hannah Arendt describes it, shows two controversial characteristics: on the one hand the struggle for power and on the other a feeling of weakness. The totalitarian leader pursuits power in one respect but in the other he is the executioner of higher laws, which makes him feel powerless. On the one hand there is the belief of the leader in the omnipotence of men; on the other the superfluousness of human beings as creatures capable of handling and with a free will. This is also the reason why Arendt remarks that totalitarianism strives not towards despotic rule over men, but towards a system in which men are superfluous. (OT, III, 457)

Margareth Canovan's answer to her own question whether the leaders took their ideologies seriously, is complex:

> Hitler and Stalin were cynics to the extent of disregarding most of what ordinary Nazis or Communists would regard as articles of faith (a freedom from dogmatism symbolized by their alliance at the beginning of the Second World War), but each was also a fanatic in that he genuinely believed he had found the key to history in the endless struggle and destruction of races or classes (Canovan, 1989, 161)

Totalitarianism was a mixture of human omnipotence on the one hand and subjection to superhuman powers on the other. However, human omnipotence existed only within the frame of the ideology. Arendt clarifies this by saying that the Nazis believed doctrines such as:

> The more accurately we recognize and observe the laws of nature and life, . . . so much the more do we conform to the will of the Almighty. The more insight we have into the will of the Almighty, the greater will be our successes. (OT III, 345–346)

The masses had to be persuaded of the force of the ideology and this was done by means of propaganda, mainly anti-Semitic propaganda, but also with the help of pseudo-scientific arguments to prove the purity of the so-called Aryan race. The themes of the propaganda were not original, but prepared for them by fifty years of the rise of imperialism and desintegration of the nation-state. Here we can see the connection between imperialism and Nazism. Totalitarian propaganda did not make use of facts, because facts do not convince the masses. What does convince them is the consistency of the system the masses belonged to. Totalitarianism, as has been said before, creates a fictitious world and consequently propaganda switched from reality to fiction, from contingency to consistency. The Nazis were firmly convinced of the force of the fiction and of their ability to rewrite history again and again by adjusting the past to the politics of the present, or by removing data that did not fit in with the ideology.

The problem of the creation of a make-believe world is that it conflicts with "common sense". How was it possible that the masses fled from reality into fiction? I will revert to this at a later stage, but here it is sufficient to remark that for the atomized, disillusioned masses "common sense" did not make "sense" any more. (OT III, 352)

The most important and most effective form of propaganda was the fiction of the Jewish global conspiracy. This global conspiracy was supposed to be the origin of all misery. The content of this anti-Semitic propaganda was not at all new, original or typical for Nazism, but, as we shall see later, it got another dimension since it was situated within the framework of the ideology. The Nazis, as has been mentioned in the chapter on anti-Semitism, made use of the "Protocols of the Elders of Sion" in their propaganda. These protocols were a forgery, written around 1900 by agents of the Russian secret police in Paris. By 1919 this pamphlet had passed into oblivion, but after that escaped officers of the White Army, who had this pamphlet in their luggage, brought it to various European countries. Especially in Germany, the contents of this pamphlet fell in fertile ground, because it gave a convincing explanation of the defeat in the First World War and the painful consequences of the Treaty of Versailles. (Hadassa-Ben-Itto, 70) The "Protocols of the Elders of Sion" were a report of an invented secret Jewish conspiracy. The Jews were supposed to be the people who ruled the world behind the scenes. (OT III, 241, 358 ff)

Two years after Hitler assumed power, the Protocols became obligatory reading matter in all German schools. The interesting aspect of the Protocols is that the Nazis used the content in two ways. In the first place it was used for anti-Semitic propaganda. Global domination by the Jews was intolerable because the Jews belonged to an inferior race, which had caused social, mental and economical misery by means of its conspiracy. In the second place the Protocols were, to the Nazis, a perfect example of the way in which global domination could be attained. If the Jews, being a relatively small minority, were able to rule the world, there should be possibilities for the Nazis as well and this was the basis for their idea of future world domination. (OT III, 360)

In a clever way the Nazis transformed anti-Semitic feelings into a sense of self-respect for the masses. Anti-Semitism was, as it were, used to give the hopeless, atomised and unstable individuals, to which the masses had broken down, a new feeling of self-esteem. In this way the individuals regained their stability, which made them better candidates for membership of the organization. (OT III, 356)

Of the utmost importance was the concept of what was called "Volksgemeinschaft" (national community) based on the natural equality of all Germanic peoples and their absolute difference from and superiority to other nations. This concept of "Volksgemeinschaft" was in fact a propagandistic preparation for an Aryan racial society that was to dominate all nations. The Aryans regarded themselves as the chosen people, but the Jews did the same on the basis of their religion. It is obvious that there was no room for both.

Finally, we must realize an important thing when speaking of the Nazi propaganda. The Jews were in fact no real, that is to say political, enemies. The Nazis made them look like real enemies who conspired against them and therefore it seemed plausible to organize a counter-conspiracy as a defence.

The goal of Nazi-propaganda was to "infect" the masses with the ideology. George Kateb speaks of a "pathology" (Kateb, 52) and this qualification is in line with possibly the best description of totalitarian propaganda by Karl Jaspers in a letter to Hannah Arendt:

> It's [The Origins of Totalitarianism] like the diagnosis and symptomatology of a fungal disease that spreads and eats up everything in its path. The carriers of the disease are intelligent the way fungi are because they do instinctively what is required of them; that they are capable of what is required is also a consequence of their basic nihilism, which overcomes all human resistance. They therefore have a talent of being able to obey the law of this disease without comprehending it as a whole. The result is self-destruction of man and of these fungi themselves, which die when the body they have taken possession of dies. (C, 273)

Arendt answers:

> What you call the "fungal disease"—a wonderful parallel—is everywhere, and because . . . this disease is caused by fungi, it also attacks otherwise good and sensible people of whom I am often fond. Once one has become allergic to

fungi, one sees them in the smallest, apparently most harmless of things; and that makes communication difficult. (C, 281)

TERROR

Together with the ideology, terror[2] is the most important and also the most frightening element of totalitarian systems. A good understanding of terror is necessary to get a clear understanding of what Hannah Arendt initially called radical evil. Terror was the essential instrument of the Nazis.

> Totalitarianism is unthinkable without terror because a system that is not made to human measure, can only be forced upon men with inhuman tools (Marai, 178)

We have seen that the law of Nature was the totalitarian law of the Nazis. As constitutional laws are necessary to indicate the admissible limits of human actions in liberal and democratic societies, so is terror necessary to "translate" the laws of Nature for everyday life. Terror is not identical to violence and it appears when violence has destroyed all resisting power, so that the movement has no more enemies who can be arrested and tortured to death and when all suspicious groups have been eliminated. Thus the real political enemies of the movement, those who do not believe in the ideology and revolt against it, are eliminated by violence. We have seen that in history many times, under tyrannical, despotic and dictatorial regimes. Totalitarian terror contrasts sharply with violence because it is not mainly directed against opponents or suspects, but rather against totally innocent people, who did nothing wrong and do not understand why they are being arrested, sent to concentration camps or liquidated. This implies that the "graveyard peace" that can spread over the land under pure tyranny after the destruction of all opponents, never occurs under totalitarian rule. Terror never ends and as a matter of principle there is no peace, because totalitarian leaders assure their adherents that everything will remain in permanent flux. (EU, 298–299)

Nazism follows the law of the movement of Nature. This law selects the enemies of mankind and the ordinary mortals are deprived of the freedom to oppose this selection. The notions "guilt" and "innocence" have lost their meaning; "guilty" is the one who counteracts terror i.e. the one who, consciously or unconsciously, thwarts the movement of Nature. Nazi leaders were not wise or just, but only tools of the movement of Nature: "Terror freezes men in order to clear the way for the movement of Nature". (EU, 342)

Terror sacrifices individuals for the sake of the species, not only enemies, but if necessary all people. Terror presses people together, so that it looks as if they melt together and become one person. Human living space is diminished and there is no room or possibility for action any more. This is the reason for Arendt's statement that the essence of the human condition was affected, because she considers freedom of action an essential condition for human life. Freedom of action is connected with the human condition of plurality i.e. the fact that the earth is inhabited by people and not by man. Plurality is the "conditio per quam" of all political life. (HC, 7)

Treating people as followers of the law of Nature and not as individuals but as a species, as if people were reduced to one person, results in the increase of the pace of the movement of Nature to a level that could never be attained without help. Nazism speeds up the movement of the law of Nature and destroys everything that could slow it down, which means that terror executes the death sentences which Nature has already pronounced on unfit races and individuals[3], without waiting for the slower elimination by Nature. This is the rationalization for genocide and George Kateb remarks rightly that totalitarianism is genocide "within the frame of legal order". (Kateb, 76) This is also the explanation of the fact that the destruction of the Jews and the gypsies was not considered a crime by most of the Nazis. It was giving the movement of Nature a boost.

Everything was possible within the Nazi law, but, as we have seen before, this law was of a higher order than constitutional laws. Totalitarianism is the methodical liquidation of certain races and populations on a large scale. This liquidation is executed consciously according to a strategic plan drawn up by the rulers, whose main purpose was the destruction of target groups. This destruction took place in spite of the fact that the victims were no real enemies. They did not constitute a major obstacle for the attainment of a practical goal, and, although all properties of the victims were confiscated, it was not a matter of robbery with murder. The only possible conclusion is that the will to kill people was the most important feature of Nazi-totalitarianism. Therefore, it is understandable that Karl Jaspers wrote to Arendt that everybody was at risk and that the Jews were just the first to go. (C, 519)

Arendt remarks in many of her books that totalitarianism is non-utilitarian. At first sight this seems to be correct, although we could also say that for the Nazis the utility of the system was nothing more than the following and the acceleration of the speed of the movement of Nature. For the Nazis the whole system may have had a utilitarian character, although it was invisible, nihilistic and incomprehensible for the victims. The incomprehensibility is brought about by the fact that in a totalitarian system terror and genocide are no means to an end but means in themselves, which can lead to a climax when the totalitarian state starts to devour its own children and the executioner of today becomes the victim of tomorrow. (OV, 55)

The description of the above is a description of the stage on which the most impressive tragedy in human history is to take place. When the curtain rises, the scenario has been written, the actors have been selected and the stage setting is done. The prompter is the ideology, which tells the actors how to act. The tragedy has only one act. There is no interval. The spectators initially do not understand the essence of the tragedy, but it becomes clear when the curtain falls. Nevertheless, the tragedy remains partly incomprehensible because it crosses the border of a domain that is beyond human comprehension. The tragedy is called "Radical Evil" and it took place when Nazi-totalitarianism had reached its peak and total domination had become a fact.

TOTAL DOMINATION

In the long run, totalitarianism strives for global domination, but from the beginning it aims at total domination over people. The concentration camps are the laboratories in the experiment of total domination and this aim can be reached by the creation of a man-made hell. (EU, 240) There were about 400 concentration camps in Germany and the occupied areas, among which the six extermination camps in Poland: Auschwitz-Birkenau, Belzec, Chelmno, Majdanek, Sobibor and Treblinka.

The main principle in the concentration camps is "everything is possible", which is not the same as "everything is permitted". Not everything was permitted in the concentration camps. Of course there were starvation, beatings and torture, but all this happened according to the camp rules and S.S.-members had to stick to these rules. "Everything was possible" means that every idea or theory could be brought into practice. The idea of fabricating lampshades out of human skin was brought into practice. One can understand that everything is permitted, but the idea that everything is possible is in direct conflict with common sense.

The concentration camps show a kind of supremacy that is based on institutionalized terror, which is unique and without precedent. The prisoners are totally cut off from the external world and are not part of society any more. Labour in the camps is generally useless. In reality, the prisoners are considered "superfluous" beings and, by means of neglect, exhaustion, undernourishment and inferior sanitary facilities, transformed into "uncomplaining animals", living corpses called "Muselmänner". Eventually many died, but sometimes it took days or weeks before death occurred.

Their life is short, but their number is endless; they, the Muselmänner, the drowned, form the backbone of the camp, an anonymous mass, continuously renewed and always identical, of non-men who march and labour in silence, the divine spark dead within them, already too empty really to suffer. One hesitates to call them living; one hesitates to call their death death. (Fackenheim, 1994, 99–100)

Although there were rules in the concentration camps, there was still enough space for interpretation of the rules by the S.S. guards and this interpretation was arbitrary. The arbitrariness served as confirmation of their power. A good example can be found in an essay in Abel Herzberg's book *Amor Fati*. The essay is about the roll calls in Bergen-Belsen. When everybody was lined up, writes Herzberg, Wilhelm came to count the prisoners. If the total number was right, the roll call took one to two hours; if it was wrong it took three to six hours. It might be repeated two or three times a day, sometimes till late in the evening. Here we see an example of arbitrariness. Not a single soul, writes Herzberg, has ever understood the purpose of the roll calls, which undermined the vitality of so many people. After all, escape from the camp was impossible, but that was not the reason for the roll calls. It was not only a deliberate daily torment, but it was more. The guards counted their prey, like a miser counts his money, with sensual exaltation and excitement. The roll calls had an almost religious meaning and the roll call square was the temple. (Herzberg, 42) It is therefore that Arendt writes about an attempt of the Nazis to change the "nature", the "core" or the "essence" of human beings.

> What totalitarian ideologies therefore aim at is not the transformation of the outside world or the revolutionizing transmutation of society, but the transformation of human nature itself. The concentration camps are the laboratories where changes in human nature are tested . . . (OT III, 458–459)

It is clear what Arendt says: totalitarianism is more than an ultimate form of deprivation of freedom. In the concentration camps the Nazis have tried to change human nature, but they failed. What remained was the destruction of human beings.

According to Eric Voegelin, it is impossible to change human nature; changing human nature is a contradiction because "nature" is a philosophical concept; it denotes that which identifies a thing as a thing of this kind and not of another. Tampering with the "nature" of a thing means destroying it. (Voegelin, 74)

In her book *The Human Condition* Arendt goes into detail about human nature. Human nature is not the sum of all human activities and capabilities, because without them human existence might still be possible. Neither can the conditions of human existence explain what or who we are. The question of human nature—who we are—seems unanswerable in both its individual psychological sense and its general philosophical sense. We are incapable of determining human nature, and attempts to define human nature almost invariably end up in the construction of a deity, which may cast suspicion upon the very concept of "human nature". (HC, 10–11)

The disintegration of man as an individual occurs in phases. The first phase is the arbitrary arrest by which the legal person is destroyed, since the arrest stands in no relation to actions or opinions of the arrested person. In the concentration camps there are no legal rules either. The second phase is the destruction of the moral person caused by the isolated location of the concentration camps. No information from the camps reaches the outside world; even the death of the prisoners is anonymous. All reminders of the existence of the prisoners are erased. Martyrdom is useless under these circumstances. The third phase is total subjection and reduction to 'a bunch of conditioned reactions' and the final phase is the destruction of the physical person.

It is obvious that for the people who were sent directly to the extermination camps, the second and third phase were lacking. For most of them total domination resulted in immediate destruction of the physical person.

Arendt emphasises that this kind of total terror destroys the dialectic interpretations of political strategies. These interpretations rest on the belief that something good could originate from evil. This dialectic was more or less plausible as long as murder was the worst thing people could do to each other. Since the existence of total terror, with its concentration camps and extermination camps, we must realise that murder is a lesser evil. Murder is a concept we are familiar with, it is within the pattern of society and murderer and victim have a relation to each other on which the dialectic is based. The murderer leaves a corpse behind and he does not pretend that his victim never existed. If he wipes out traces, they are his own and he does so to avoid recognition, but he does not wipe out memories of the victim held by the people who have loved him or her. However, the Nazis destroyed all traces of their victims and pretended they had never existed. Instead of saying that the Jews were "murdered" I prefer to use Sándor Márai's expression. He says "they disappeared in the labyrinths of the descent into hell". (Márai, 156)

The Dutch poet Gerrit Achterberg also uses the word "disappearance" in his poem "Auschwitz":

> Chalk marks made by foreign hand[4]
> Sentence you coldly
> To disappearance in a distant land.
>   (Achterberg, 622)

The victims are simply untraceable; they do not exist any more, have never existed and thus have no history.

A very important point that has been mentioned before is the fact that the concentration camps and the extermination camps were non-utilitarian and this is one of the reasons why the totalitarian system is difficult to fathom. The camps were, considered from a normal point of view, absolutely useless, they served no purpose, not even the personal benefit of the rulers. Considering the fact that the Nazis carried on a war on more than one front for the sake of expansion, one could state that the energy spent on the concentration camps and extermination camps was not only unproductive, but also harmful.

> Our common sense, trained in utilitarian thinking for which the good as well as the evil makes sense, is offended by nothing so much as by the complete sense-lessness of a world where punishment persecutes the innocent more than the criminal, where labour does not result and is not intended to result in products, where crimes do not benefit and are not even calculated to benefit their authors. For a benefit to be realized in centuries can hardly be called an incentive, especially not in a situation of great military emergency. (EU, 241)

We must conclude from this that the main purpose of the totalitarian leaders was to follow the law of Nature and that direct expansion could be sacrificed for it. Despite the fact that Arendt constantly points at the uselessness of the camps, she also says that this uselessness was only semblance and that these camps were the most essential instruments of the movement. Without these camps it would have been impossible for the leaders to turn the members of their elite troops into fanatics, or to bring a total nation into a state of apathy. After the initial excesses, the leaders and the oppressed population would have returned to a normal daily life with humane laws. (OT III, 456)

In the camps, especially in the extermination camps, says Arendt, something has happened that ought not to have happened and for which the criminals can be neither punished nor forgiven. A radical evil appeared that had been unknown before. This evil appeared at the moment when the impossible was made possible, because after all, the motto in the camps was that everything was possible.

RADICAL EVIL IN NAZI-TOTALITARIANISM

One might call Nazi-totalitarianism as a political movement a radical evil in its totality. One of the reasons could be that the Nazi ideology together with terror inevitably results in genocide. Nevertheless, there are arguments to restrict the term "radical evil" to what happened in the concentration—and extermination camps. Arendt indicates this in the introduction of the first edition of *The Origins of Totalitarianism* by saying that an absolute evil appeared during the last stages of Nazism and it is obvious that she refers to the events in the camps.

However, there is another argument. Arendt says:

> But let us assume for the moment that the racial theories could have been convincingly proved. For it cannot be gainsaid that the practical political conclusions the Nazis drew from these theories were perfectly logical. Suppose a race could indeed be shown by indubitable scientific evidence, to be inferior; would that fact justify extermination? (MD, 29)

A definitive step is necessary to bring theory into practice.

> There is an abyss between the men of brilliant and facile conceptions and men of brutal deeds and active bestiality which no intellectual explanation is able to bridge. (OT III, 183)

The gap between theory and practice had to be bridged and by bridging this gap a limit was passed that ought not to be passed and moreover a domain was entered that is difficult to enter for the human intellect, which seeks an explanation for everything. When entering this domain another gap appears, namely the gap between language on the one hand and events and experiences on the other. Paul Ricoeur states that all sensible actions of human beings can be expressed in words. (Ricoeur, II) However, the events in the concentration camps and the extermination camps had nothing to do with sensible actions and accordingly Sarah Kofman says that words, speaking and language are inadequate to describe the senseless and useless extermination in the camps and if one tries it can only be done in a stifled voice. (Kofman, 45)

> The facts are: that six million Jews, six million human beings, were helplessly and in most cases unexpectedly, dragged to their death. The method employed was that of accumulated terror. First came calculated neglect, deprivation and shame, when the weak in body died together with those strong and defiant enough to take their own lives. Second came outright starvation, combined with forced labor, when people died by the thousands but at different intervals of time, according to their stamina. Last came the death factories—and they all died together, the young and the old, the weak and the strong, the sick and the healthy; not as people, not as men and women, children and adults, boys and girls, not as good and bad, beautiful and ugly—but brought down to the lowest common denominator of organic life itself, plunged into the darkest and deepest abyss of primal equality, like cattle, like matter, like things that had neither body nor soul, nor even a physiognomy upon which death could stamp its seal (EU, 198)

These events, this evil, which is so difficult to fathom and for which we cannot even find an adequate word, is called radical or absolute evil by

Arendt. It is radical or absolute, unpunishable and unforgivable, because it cannot be explained and understood by evil motives such as self-interest, greed, covetousness, resentment, lust for power or cowardice. She also draws the conclusion that this radical evil has emerged in connection with a system in which all men have become equally superfluous. (OT III, 459)

Nevertheless, Arendt has a problem with the term "radical evil". This becomes obvious when she states that, in our philosophical tradition, we cannot conceive of a radical evil. This is true for Christian theology as well as for Kant, the only philosopher who must have suspected the existence of a radical evil, but he immediately rationalized it in the concept of a "perverted illwill", which could be explained by comprehensible motives (OT III, 459)

Both Arendt and Kant use the term "radical evil". The question is if there is a connection between the interpretations of radical evil of the two philosophers. Does "radical evil" have the same meaning or is there a difference between their interpretations. To answer this question, we shall first have a look at Kant's view on radical evil.

NOTES

1. Kristallnacht (Crystal Night, Night of broken Glass, November Pogrom). In the night of 9–10 November 1938, members of the Nazi party destroyed more than thousand synagogues and Jewish owned shops, while about four hundred Jews were killed.

2. Terror comes from the Latin word "terrere", which means "to frighten". The best-known example of terror in European history is La Terreur (The Terror) during the French Revolution. The king and twelve hundred aristocrats were sent to the guillotine, not for what they had done, but for who they were. The Terror, the revolutionairies' decision to kill the king and, subsequently, to annihilate the nobility, introduced a policy based on mass murder. The Terror foreshadows Hitler's annihilation of the Jews. (Dwork & van Pelt, 13–14)

3. Unfit individuals were: schizophrenics, mentally handicapped, manic-depressives, hereditary epileptics, the blind, the deaf and alcoholics. All these were to be sterilized or castrated. The Nazis estimated that some 400.000 people would be sterilized or castrated as a result of their measures (Dwork & van Pelt, 73)

4. The final destination of the goods wagons, which served as means of transport for the Jews, was written on the outside of the doors in chalk letters.

Chapter Two

Kant's View on Radical Evil

KANT'S THEORY

During his study of human actions and human freedom, it was inevitable that Immanuel Kant would come across evil. In his study of evil Kant did not take the prevailing prejudices as a starting point. He did not take the side of the Christian doctrine, which told him that man had become evil after the Fall; nor did he take the side of the philosophers of the Enlightenment, who believed that man was basically good.

According to Karl Jaspers, Kant had the courage "to look into an abyss", an abyss that was overlooked by esthetical humanism. Kant wanted to find the essence of evil and his starting point was the moral law that exists in all human beings. This moral law is the categorical imperative, which tells people how to act morally correctly. Categorical means that the law is unconditionally valid and hence requires unconditional observance by all reasonable beings in all circumstances. The best-known version of the categorical imperative is as follows:

> It is morally necessary to act in such a way that the maxim of one's acting could become, through one's will, universal law. (KPV, par 7, 310 [31])

To avoid misunderstandings, it is important to say that Kant did not "invent" a moral principle. It is not Kant who offers the categorical imperative to mankind. Kant investigates the functioning of our practical reason and concludes that its general principle is the categorical imperative. Everybody is able to detect the same principle as Kant's categorical imperative, on condition that he listens to his conscience and is willing to find its basic principle. From the wording of the categorical imperative it is immediately clear that it only concerns the form of the act and not the content. The categorical imperative indicates that acts should only be performed on the basis of maxims (fundamental principles) that have universal validity and this is only the case if there is no question of contradiction. For that reason, lying can never be a universally valid principle, because it would make communication between people impossible and hence would lead to an intolerable society. Karl Jaspers states that Kant's categorical imperative forces human beings to ask themselves what kind of world they would want to create, if this were within their power.

Man is not forced to act according to the categorical imperative, but he ought to abide by the law on moral grounds in order to become a better person. However, if we ought to abide by the law, we must also be able to do so and therefore Kant says: "we ought to become better men . . . hence this must be within our power. . ." (Rel., 56 [49–52])

The question why Kant wants us to become better persons will be discussed in a later paragraph.

We all know that human beings not only act according to the categorical imperative. Besides moral acts we see many immoral or evil acts and this leads us to the existence of evil and also to the question of the origin of evil.

To explain the existence of evil, Kant assumes that mankind has three predispositions to doing good in his nature.

– The predisposition to animality in man. This is important for self-preservation, for the propagation of the species and for community with other men i.e. the social impulse. It concerns the physical self-preservation of man. The danger of the animal nature is that it can degenerate in rudeness, voracity, voluptuousness or lawlessness.

– The predisposition to humanity in man. Man is a social and thinking being. We are considering the comparative self-love of man, which Kant regards as positive and which may not be confused with self-conceit or amour-propre. Self-love means that man can consider himself as happy or unhappy, compared to others and it can also give him a certain value in relation to other people. This predisposition could degrade into rivalry, jealousy, envy, ingratitude or spitefulness.

– The predisposition to personality in man. Man has the gift to form his personality, in other words to become a reasonable and responsible person. This means that man, by nature, has the motivation to respect the moral law of his own free will and also that he is responsible for his own actions.

These three natural predispositions are not only good in themselves, but they promote the good and they are original because they are essential for the existence of human beings. (Rel., 29–33 [15–19]) However, besides the tendency to doing good, Kant also speaks of a natural inclination to doing evil.

Hence we can call this a natural propensity to evil, and when we must, after all, ever hold man himself responsible for it, we can further call it a radical innate evil in human nature (yet none the less brought upon us by ourselves). (Rel., 39 [27–28])

Because man has a free will, he can either include the moral law into his maxim or he can decide not to. Therefore, Kant speaks of a good or evil character and with respect to the latter he distinguishes three successive steps or levels.

– The first level of doing evil is the level of weakness, the frailty of the human heart. Human beings are no angels and good intentions are sometimes weaker than wrong inclinations. This means that we have the intention of doing good, but we are unable to do it, because adverse motives are stronger. (Rel., 34 [21–22]) Moral weakness means nothing else than to be open to the temptation to give preference to self-interest over the moral law.

– The second level of evil is the impurity, i.e. mixing unmoral with moral motives. (Rel., 34 [21–22])

– The final level is the level of wickedness of the human nature. It is the propensity to adopt evil maxims. At this level the moral law is made subordinate to motives of self-interest. (Rel, 35 [22–24])

About the third level, Kant makes the following remark:

It may also be called the perversity (perversitas) of the human heart, for it reverses the ethical order [of priority] among the incentives of a free will; and although conduct which is lawfully good (i.e. legal) may be found with it, yet the cast of mind is thereby corrupted at its root (so far as the moral disposition is concerned), and man is hence designated as evil. (Rel, 35 [22–24])

What we see here is that, according to Kant, it is a matter of the intention of the act and not of the final result. An act performed on wrong moral grounds is always reprehensible, even if the outcome is good. In Kant's view being good or evil is a question of establishing priorities.

Hence the distinction between a good man and one who is evil cannot lie in the difference between the incentives, which they adopt into their maxim (not in the content of the maxim), but rather must depend upon subordination (the form of the maxim), i.e., which of the two incentives he makes the condition of the other. Consequently man (even the best) is evil only in that he reverses the moral order of the incentives when he adopts them into his maxim. (Rel, 44, [34–35])

Man must always act according to the moral law and not on the basis of the wrong priorities. Because man has a free will he is also free in establishing priorities. Therefore evil is not situated in the passions, desires or instincts, because these are in the human nature and thus morally indifferent. Evil is in the human will, i.e. in the possibility of our free will to let one motive prevail over another, in the way in which the motives are ordered and in the way in which the motives are each other's conditions. This implies that men are always responsible for their actions and may be called to account. This is the reason why Kant speaks of guilt.

> This innate guilt (reatus), which is so nominated because it may be discerned in man as early as the first manifestations of the exercise of freedom and hence can be imputed. . . (Rel, 46 [36–38])

Kant speaks of "radical evil" when he speaks of the inclination of human beings to do evil. Why is evil "radical"?

> This evil is *radical* because it corrupts the ground of all maxims; it is, moreover, as a natural propensity inextirpable by human powers, since extirpation could occur only through good maxims, and cannot take place when the ultimate subjective ground of all maxims is postulated as corrupt; yet at the same time it must be possible to overcome it, since it is found in man, a being whose actions are free. (Rel., 45 [35–36]).

Evil is radical because it affects the ground of our maxims and because it is a natural inclination and therefore cannot be destroyed, but only conquered. Finally, Kant rejects the possibility of a diabolical will, which means that a person performs evil deeds as a result of an evil reason and an evil will. Kant precludes this possibility, since in that case the fight against the moral law is a motive in itself and consequently the person would be a diabolical being. I will revert to this in a later paragraph on diabolic persons.

> . . . a reason exempt from the moral law, a malignant reason as it were (a thoroughly evil will), comprises too much, for thereby opposition to the law would itself be set up as an incentive (since in the absence of all incentives the will cannot be determined), and thus the subject would be made a devilish being. Neither of these designations is applicable to man. (Rel., 42 [31–32])

In summary Kant's view on radical evil is the following. Man has three predispositions to doing good: his predisposition to animality, his predisposition to humanity and the predisposition to personality i.e. to become a reasonable and responsible person. Besides the predispositions to doing good, man also has an inclination to do evil. Kant distinguishes three levels of evil. Man does evil as a result of his weakness, by mixing moral and unmoral motivating causes and finally, in case of wickedness, when the moral law is neglected. Being good or evil is a question of establishing priorities and man is free in doing that because he has a free will. In fact, evil is the consequence of a free will and that means that man is responsible for it. Kant speaks of radical evil, because it affects the ground of our maxims and because it cannot be destroyed but can only be conquered. Finally Kant denies the possibility of a totally malicious will: man cannot basically be a devil.

Some aspects of the above will be further discussed in the following paragraphs: the essence of evil, conquering evil, diabolical people and finally I will say something about the development of man and the function of evil in this development. I will also come back to Kant's remark that we must become better persons.

THE ESSENCE OF EVIL

Karl Jaspers goes more deeply into this point in his article "Kant's view on radical evil". Jaspers' question is "What is radical evil?" and with this question he does not ask about the origin of evil but about its essence.

Kant speaks about a moral law, about the reversal of the relation between the moral law and unmoral motives, such as egoism, jealousy and lust for power. However, there is no question of a tangible presence of evil, which as such could be contended.

> The decisive principal characteristic of radical evil is that I cannot see it as an object. (Jaspers, 1958, 112)

Jaspers illustrates this by saying:

> Evil is, like the good, no existence that can be investigated, it is no natural phenomenon with universally valid properties. (Jaspers, 1958, 113)

Evil is no subject for discussion in psychology, because, says Jaspers, in psychology evil does simply not exist. We have also tried to understand evil by giving it a metaphysical reality. However, evil cannot appear as one or another mode of being, as a substance or as a result of the deficiency of something else. The first idea can be found in Hegel's philosophy. He regards evil as something negative that is inextricably bound up with the development of mankind; the second view is presented by Plotinus, who regarded evil as a deficiency of the good, a way of thinking that was later found in the works of many philosophers.

All these efforts failed in making evil a tangible object and the reason is that it never came to anyone's mind to look for the drive for doing evil in man himself. According to Jaspers, this is the great merit of Kant. Kant is not looking for the origin of evil in a naturalistic, psychological or meta-physical dimension, but in the intelligible (i.e. rationally knowable) dimension of our existence and therefore it can be found in the field of human freedom.

> It is the reversal of the relation between obedience to the moral law and the longing for happiness. The result is that in the maxim the unconditional is put under condition of the conditional. (Jaspers, 1958, 116)

The unconditional is the moral law, which is put under condition of the natural inclinations (the conditional), while it must be the other way round to permit good actions.

There is another problem. The categorical imperative is a general formal law, which does not indicate anything about the content. This general indefinite law must become transparent for man in the form of certain specifically defined laws. The question is how man can implicate the categorical imperative. Jaspers states rightly: "The jump from general law to defined law is the big question mark. How can it be made?" (Jaspers, 1958, 117)

This question is not new and Augustine already raised the problem. The moral law of Kant, the unconditional, is Augustine's love for God and the conditional is the love for the world. Augustine tells us that, in order to find happiness, we are to put our love for God before our love for the world, while Kant tells us we have to act according to the moral law by establishing the proper priorities. The unconditional love for God and Kant's unconditional moral law are in fact identical, but they are no more than directions and indications for our actions and therefore radical evil remains for man, at least in Jaspers' opinion, a more or less invisible opponent.

CONQUERING EVIL

Karl Jaspers' second question is the following: "Do we have the power to free ourselves from the 'reversal', from the suffocation of evil?" (Jaspers, 1958,118)

In order to be able to answer this question, Jaspers repeats, in a few words, Kant's view on the inclination to do evil.

> The inclination to do evil is not inborn like a natural tendency, but it is incorporated in the awareness of our basic principles [maxims], as if it belonged to the "nature" of our reason, which is tied up with our sensual existence. Therefore, this inclination to do evil—although freedom, therefore action and hence accountable—is, as Kant says

. . . inextirpable by human powers, since extirpation could only occur through good maxims and cannot take place when the ultimate subjective ground of all maxims is postulated as corrupt. (Jaspers, 1958, 118)

I should like to point out an apparent contradiction between Jaspers' remark that the inclination to do evil is not inborn and Kant, who talks about a "radical, innate evil". (Rel, 39 [27–28])

In my opinion this contradiction occurs because the terms "inborn" and "innate" have different meanings for Kant and for Jaspers. For Jaspers "inborn" is related to heredity and little can be done against an inborn error. Therefore, Kant's remark that radical evil is inborn, but nevertheless submitted to our will, seams strange to us. During Kant's life, concepts like genes, chromosomes and heredity were unknown. When Kant speaks of innate or inborn, he does not refer to heredity but rather to a character trait, which is present in all men, but which does not necessarily become manifest.

When we get to the core of Kant's line of reasoning, says Jaspers, we cannot understand how someone who is evil by nature can transform himself into a good person. Nevertheless, Kant indicates that this is possible, because he says that we ought to become better men, hence this must be within our power. According to Kant this cannot be done by means of a simple decision, but only by a total change of the will. Kant compares such a metamorphosis with a rebirth. (Jaspers, 1958, 119)

According to Jaspers this is a tremendous problem, because man is able to know the legality of his actions, but never the moral state of his character. Man can never know how or who he really is, in other words, if he is a really good man if his actions are good. According to Jaspers, evil remains mysterious, also in Kant's theory. In the first place, the origin is incomprehensible. Why are our maxims corrupted by the propensity to evil, while we do it ourselves? We know nothing about our natural qualities. In the second place it is absolutely unclear how an evil person can become a good person by means of an inner revolution. (Jaspers, 1958, 125–126)

Jaspers concludes:

Kant's philosophy of "radical evil" is disappointing, if one expects to gain a clear understanding of the possibility of performing better actions, so that I am able to make the general terms a starting-point for the decision on the content of my actual actions. (Jaspers, 1958, 132)

For Jaspers radical evil remains an invisible opponent. I do not fully agree with him. Karl Jaspers was a psycho-pathologist before he became a philosopher. As a psycho-pathologist he knows that our mental activities are difficult to fathom. One cannot expect from Kant or anybody else to give precise directives for our actions. The origin of evil was unclear and is still unclear. Maybe the propensity to evil is located in particular genes, in some specific molecular compounds, or it might be a result of specific biochemical reactions. We don't know yet, but Kant made us aware of the fact that evil is not something outside man, but that it is located in man himself and particularly that it is the consequence of our free will. We know that we have a choice, that we can establish priorities and that nobody can say: "I can't help it, it's just the way I am".

DIABOLICAL PEOPLE

According to Allison, to Kant the fact that man cannot be a devil is an a priori, which is a result of his thesis that man always ought to act according to the categorical imperative, even if he doesn't meet the moral law. The inclination not to act according to the categorical imperative does not mean that the law is totally rejected, because this is incompatible with the predisposition to the good.

> Man (even the most wicked) does not, under any maxim whatsoever, repudiate the moral law in the manner of a rebel (renouncing obedience to it). The law rather forces itself upon him irresistibly by virtue of his moral predisposition. (Rel, 43, [32–34])

This means that sometimes self-interest prevails over the moral law, without repudiating that law. This concept of radical evil, says Allison, is the logical consequence of two essential characteristics of the theory of the free will.

The first characteristic is that inclinations alone are not enough for a free subject to act, but the inclination should also be incorporated in the maxim. This characteristic means that the subject is responsible for actions that are based on heteronomy or on adverse inclinations and it explains also that evil is rooted in our will and not in our nature.

The second characteristic is the reciprocal connection between the moral law and a free will. This second characteristic precludes the possibility of a diabolical will, understood as a will that explicitly denies the authority of the categorical imperative, since it rules out the possibility of such a denial. If the moral law is the law of the free will in the sense that it provides the ultimate standards on which our actions are based, a free rational agent can never reject the moral law without undermining his own agency.

Combining these two characteristics, we arrive at the result that evil must be rooted in the free choice to act against the law (as a kind of inner voting in favour of the inclination towards evil) while the authority of the law is still recognized and respected.

For some scholars, like John Silber, says Allison, this conclusion is in flat contradiction to perceptible facts and it seems that Kant's concept is vulnerable, because evil can take such a form that the open denial of the moral law, which Kant excludes, is obvious. According to John Silber, Napoleon and Hitler are historical examples, as well as fictional characters like Melville's captain Ahab in *Moby Dick*. Perhaps even better examples are Cathy Trask in John Steinbeck's *East of Eden* and above all James Claggert in Melville's *Billy Budd*. About James Claggert Melville says:

> . . . Claggert, in whom was the mania of evil nature, not engendered by vicious training or corrupting books, but born with him and innate, in short "a depravity according to nature". (Melville 35–36)

For these characters, evil could not be understood as the contrast between the moral law and self-interest and a prevalence of the latter.

Allison refutes this criticism on Kant's concept by pointing at the fact that John Silber's examples need not be persons who do evil for the sake of doing evil. We must be careful when qualifying incomprehensible evil (such as captain Ahab's determined and obsessed hunt for Moby Dick or Napoleon's unrestrained megalomania) as evil that is done for the sake of evil only. There may be other explanations. Moreover, Allison states, Kant had to reject the possibility of a diabolical will in order to create the conditions for moral accountability. In order to be accountable and hence have the possibility to make a choice between good and evil, it is necessary to recognize the validity of the moral law. Someone who lacks the capacity to recognize the moral law and thus lacks the consequent feeling of respect, cannot have a diabolical will because a being like that has no will at all. It could be considered as a monstrosity of nature, a non-person, because it lacks the characteristic property of a person. Allison concludes:

> Thus, the very condition, which makes morality possible at all, also rules out the possibility of a genuinely diabolical will (Allison, 177)

The question whether men can be devils remains a very difficult problem. In Kant's opinion it is impossible because he departs from the three dispositions to doing good, which make a being a human being. A being that lacks the third disposition, in other words a being that lacks the disposition to recognize and respect the moral law, is, according to Kant, no human being. This could be Allison's non-person or a monster. It is questionable whether such a being exists i.e. a being that has the appearance of a human being, but in fact is not.

THE DEVELOPMENT OF MAN AND THE FUNCTION OF EVIL

Kant's opinion that we ought to become better persons is a direct result of his view on history. Mankind ought to aim at "the highest good" and this is a result of Kant's view that only the moral law must determine the will. However, the tendency to do evil is a disturbing factor, because man is not only a spiritual but also a natural being. There is a constant struggle between the moral law and the tendency to do evil. The "highest good" will be reached when the will is completely in accordance with the moral law. At that moment man is holy. Nobody will ever reach this stage and therefore this process is endless. The ultimate goal will probably never be reached, but we must aim at it. (KPV, 430, 122)

Kant departs from the idea that the first men lived like animals. They were unaware of good and evil. Evil tendencies (envy, greed, lust for power) crept into man when he started to live with others. (the formation of communities, societies and states) Ever since, man has had to put up an inner fight, but as he got into this situation through his own fault he must do everything to free himself from the power of evil tendencies. The good principle must triumph, but this can only be realized by forming a community that is exclusively based on the laws of virtue. Kant speaks of an "ethical commonwealth" or an "ethical state". (Rel., 118–120 [127–130])

It is not man's duty to aim at an ethical state, but it is the duty of mankind, despite the fact that we do not know if it is within our power. The problem of an ethical state is the legality of the laws of virtue. In a legal state the population makes the laws, but this is not possible in an ethical state, since here the inner morals are at stake. There must be another legislator and this leads to the idea of God as a moral legislator. An "ethical commonwealth" can only be imagined as a people of God that lives according to His laws of virtue. Reaching the formation of an ethical state is hampered by the sinful human nature and Kant rightly sighs: "How indeed can one expect something perfectly straight to be framed out of such crooked wood?" (Rel., 129 [140–142]) The foundation of an ethical state must be expected from God, but man should not only sit by and watch:

> Rather must man proceed as though everything depended upon him; only on this condition dare he hope that higher wisdom will grant the completion of his well-intended endeavours. (Rel, 129 [140–142])

In this process of bringing man to perfection, the struggle between good and evil has a function. It is the motive for the transition from the state of nature to civilisation. The struggle is the engine and also the condition for progress. Man must first get to know evil before he can aim at the good. From evil we have to learn how not to do things and the good can only be reached via evil. (ApH, 288 [329–330])

We will return to Hannah Arendt. She also speaks of radical evil. The question is whether her radical evil is identical to Kant's radical evil or whether it has its own identity.

Chapter Three

Hannah Arendt's View on Radical Evil

First, I should like to make a remark about the definition of the term "evil". Neither Kant, nor Arendt gives a definition of evil. In his book *The Roots of Evil*, Erwin Staub gives a definition of evil, which to a large extent applies to Arendt's description of totalitarian radical evil.

> Evil is not a scientific concept with an agreed meaning, but the idea of evil is part of a broadly shared human cultural heritage. The essence of evil is the destruction of human beings. This includes not only killing but also the creation of conditions that materially or psychologically destroy or diminish people's dignity, happiness and capacity to fulfil basic material needs. (Staub, 25)

In 1945, shortly after the end of the Second World War, Arendt wrote an article for the magazine *Partisan Review* titled "Nightmare and Flight". The article is a critique of the book *The Devil's Share* by Denis de Rougemont. Arendt reproaches De Rougemont that he escapes from reality by attributing totalitarian evil to the devil. By doing this, De Rougemont avoids the question of the responsibility of man for his actions, because the Nazis were ordinary men who have shown what man is capable of. This is the real nightmare and therefore, said Arendt, the problem of evil will be a fundamental problem for the coming years. (EU, 134)

After a remark like that, one would expect that Arendt, at some moment in her life, would have held a discourse on the problem of evil. However, she never did this, although one gets the impression from her books that she was planning to do so. Nevertheless, we can say that the question of evil has been a fundamental one. Elisabeth Young-Bruehl writes that Arendt was still struggling with it when writing her last book *The Life of the Mind*. Words, phrases and passages on evil can be found regularly in all her books and articles but

she never draws up a consistent theory. It is like looking for the pieces of a
jigsaw puzzle, a puzzle that will never be completed because there are pieces
missing. Very often it is not even clear what the precise meaning is of certain
expressions like "absolute evil", "radical evil" or "the banality of evil". In this
chapter I shall try to understand the meanings of "absolute evil" and "radical
evil". I will refer to the "banality of evil" in the next chapter.

To get an understanding of the exact meaning, it is necessary to review the
history of the two expressions chronologically.

In 1948 Arendt writes an article for *Partisan Review* entitled "The Concentration Camps". This article was adapted and revised for incorporation in
the first edition of *The Origins of Totalitarianism* in 1951 and later revised
again for the second edition in 1958. When comparing the two versions, the
various phases of her thinking become apparent. In the original article "The
Concentration Camps", she writes the following:

> Murder in the camps is as impersonal as the squashing of a gnat, a mere tech-
> nique of management as when a camp is overcrowded and is liquidated—or an
> accidental by-product, as when a prisoner succumbs to torture. Systematic tor-
> ture and systematic starvation create an atmosphere of permanent dying, in
> which death as well as life is effectively obstructed. The fear of the *absolute evil*,
> which permits of no escape, knows that this is the end of dialectical evolutions
> and developments. It knows that modern politics revolves around a question
> which, strictly speaking, should never enter into politics, the question of all or
> nothing: of all, that is a human society rich with infinite possibilities; or exactly
> nothing, that is, the end of mankind (CC, 748)

In the introduction of the first edition of *The Origins of Totalitarianism* she
writes:

> And if it is true that in the final stages of totalitarianism an *absolute evil* appears
> (absolute, because it can no longer be deduced from humanly comprehensible
> motives), it is also true that without it we might never have known the truly rad-
> ical nature of Evil. (OT 1, VIII-IX; my italics)

In the "Concluding Remarks" of this first edition, Arendt says:

> Until now the totalitarian belief that everything is possible seems to have proved
> only that everything can be destroyed. Yet in their effort to prove that everything
> is possible, totalitarian regimes have discovered without knowing it that there
> are crimes which man can neither punish nor forgive. When the impossible was
> made possible it became the unpunishable, unforgivable absolute evil, which
> could no longer be understood and explained by the evil motive of self-interest,
> greed, covetousness, resentment, lust for power, and cowardice; and which

therefore anger could not revenge, love could not endure, friendship could not forgive. Just as the victims in the death factories or the holes of oblivion are no longer "human" in the eyes of their executioners, so this newest species of criminals is beyond the pale even of the solidarity of human sinfulness. Difficult as it is to conceive of an *absolute evil* even in the face of its factual existence, it seems to be closely connected with the invention of a system in which all men are equally superfluous. The manipulators of this system believe in their own superfluousness as much as in that of all others, and the totalitarian murderers are all the more dangerous because they do not care if they themselves are alive or dead, if they ever lived or ever were born. The danger of the corpse factories and holes of oblivion is that today, with populations and homelessness everywhere on the increase, masses of people are continuously rendered superfluous if we continue to think of our world in utilitarian terms (OT 1, 433; my italics)

The "Concluding Remarks" were deleted in later editions. The above-mentioned text was incorporated in her discussion of "Total Domination", but after the first paragraph, cited above, she added the following sentences:

It is inherent in our entire philosophical tradition that we cannot conceive of a "radical evil", and this is true both for Christian theology, which conceded even to the Devil himself a celestial origin, as well as for Kant, the only philosopher who, in the word he coined for it, at least must have suspected the existence of this evil even though he immediately rationalized it in the concept of a "perverted ill will" that could be explained by comprehensible motives. Therefore, we actually have nothing to fall back on in order to understand a phenomenon that nevertheless confronts us with its overpowering reality and breaks down all standards we know. There is only one thing that seems to be discernible: we may say that radical evil has emerged in connection with a system in which all men have become equally superfluous (OT 2, OT 3, 459)

After the appearance of the first edition of *The Origins of Totalitarianism*, Hannah Arendt wrote in a letter to Karl Jaspers:

Evil has proved to be more radical than expected. In objective terms, modern crimes are not provided for in the Ten Commandments. Or: The Western Tradition is suffering from the preconception that the most evil things human beings can do arise from the vice of selfishness. Yet we know that the greatest evils or radical evil has nothing to do anymore with such humanly understandable sinful motives. *What radical evil is I really don't know,* but it seems to me it somehow has to do with the following phenomenon: making human beings as human beings superfluous (not using them as means to an end, which leaves their essence as humans untouched and impinges only on their human dignity; rather, making them superfluous as human beings). This happens as soon as all unpredictability—which in human beings is the equivalent of spontaneity—is eliminated. And all this in turn arises from—or better goes along with—the delusion of the omnipotence (not simply with the lust for power) of an individual man. (C, 166, my italics)

What can we conclude from these paragraphs?

– We see that Arendt initially uses the term "absolute evil", but later speaks of "radical evil". I assume that these two expressions have the same meaning and hence are synonyms. Nevertheless, it is confusing that Arendt uses two different expressions. Especially the use of "radical evil" is confusing, because of Kant's use of this term. By using the term "radical evil" she creates the impression that the evil she describes is identical to Kant's radical evil, which is absolutely not the case. It would have been better if she had stuck to "absolute evil".

– That Arendt's radical evil has another meaning than Kant's radical evil can be concluded from her remark that Kant's radical evil can be rationalized into a perverted ill will, while Arendt's evil cannot be rationalized or explained by humanly understandable motives. In Kant's theory the word "radical" is related to the inclination to do evil, while Arendt uses "radical" for evil itself.

– Nowhere she gives the impression that evil was done by monsters or demons. On the contrary, she says that the real terror did not begin until the S.S. took over the management of the concentration camps from the S.A.

The camps were no longer amusement parks for beasts in human form, that is for men who really belonged in mental hospitals and prisons; the reverse became true: they were turned into "drill-grounds" . . . on which perfectly normal men were trained to be full-fledged members of the S.S. (CC, 758)

Margareth Canovan says that Hannah Arendt, considering the way in which she describes the mechanism of Nazism, can never have thought of monsters and demons. (Canovan 1992, 24, note 30) and Elisabeth Young-Bruehl writes, that after the Eichmann trial:

. . . Arendt rejected the concept she had used in *The Origins of Totalitarianism* to point at the incomprehensible nature of the Nazis—"radical evil". As she did this she freed herself of a long nightmare; she no longer had to live with the idea that monsters and demons had engineered the murder of millions. (YB, 367)

So, what exactly did Arendt mean by "radical evil"? A keyword that keeps coming up in many of her books is "superfluousness". Radical evil, she states, appeared in connection with a system in which all people became superfluous in the same way. She does not give a clear explanation of the connection between superfluousness and radical evil and it is therefore understandable that some scholars have been looking for this connection. Two of these scholars are Richard J. Bernstein and Richard L. Rubinstein.

Richard Bernstein states, as we saw in the first chapter, that the feeling of being superfluous has played an important role in the decline of the nation-state. Especially the stateless refugees had a feeling of superfluousness. Bernstein's most important remark is that the phenomenon of superfluousness is characteristic for totalitarian regimes.

> . . . totalitarianism was the deliberate attempt to make human beings *qua human* superfluous, to transform human nature so that what is essential to live a *human* life—plurality, spontaneity, natality and individuality—is destroyed. (Bernstein 1996, 144)

In history we have seen mass murder, genocide, torture and terror. However, totalitarianism is something different because it tries to destroy typically human qualities and it is therefore that Arendt speaks of "crimes against humanity". Bernstein continues by saying that:

> Radical evil differs from the main traditional Western understanding of evil because it has nothing to do with humanly understandable "evil motives" . . . indeed it has nothing to do with *human* motives at all. (Bernstein 1996, 145)

It is still not absolutely clear what Arendt meant by "radical" or "absolute" evil. Maybe Bernstein provides the definitive answer by saying that Arendt does not use a normative concept of human nature as the basis for her idea of radical or absolute evil.

> Rather, it is more perspicacious to say that Arendt's own thinking was deeply affected by the traumatic experience of witnessing what had seemed to be impossible—that an unprecedented totalitarian movement could arise whose ideology was based on the principle that "everything is possible", including the transformation of the human species into something less than human. And, what is even more frightening, totalitarian regimes sought to prove this 'principle' in the laboratories of the concentration camps. The spectre that haunted Arendt, the spectre of totalitarianism, was one in which human beings would become superfluous, and even the concept of humanity itself would be obliterated. (Bernstein 1996, 147)

I think we may conclude that this spectre is Arendt's radical or absolute evil.

Richard Rubinstein states that the word "superfluousness" has a cognitive, a social and a political meaning. People are unemployed, they feel uprooted and finally they get a feeling of not belonging to the human world any more.

There is no longer place for them. Totalitarianism can be interpreted as a rational and resolute answer to this crisis, as far as a non-normative measure at the lowest cost can be considered a rational answer. Rubinstein paraphrases Goya, when he states that "the dreams of reason bring forth monsters". (Rubinstein, 117) Human superfluousness provokes the rise of totalitarianism, as we saw in the first chapter and racism was an ideological aid with an easy, simple message:

> Only those who share our roots can hunt with our pack. All others are prey, first those within our borders and later on the others, for the earth is not big enough or rich enough for all of us. Such a program requires a totalitarian regime that will not be impeded by legal abstractions from uprooting the alien enemy in our midst. (Rubinstein, 117)

Rubinstein indicates that totalitarianism or the Nazis did not start the process of superfluousness. What the Nazis did was: "to cut aside the hypocrisies and commit themselves to radical action on thoroughly consistent bourgeois premises". (Rubinstein, 118) It has struck me that Rubinstein uses the word "radical". Arendt may have been thinking something of the kind, which is that the Nazis were looking for a radical solution by means of radical methods and that consequently totalitarian evil is radical. If Nazism was rational, we may not forget that there is an essential difference between this functional rationalism and humanity. Rubinstein points to the fact that we have to regain our humanity and not our rationality and he concludes with a question and a warning:

> Can we find a credible basis for community that will count no man or woman superfluous? If we cannot, the totalitarians may very well win the day in the long run. (Rubinstein, 119)

So far Arendt's radical evil. The next chapter is about one of the most sensational events after World War II: the trial of Adolf Eichmann. We will see that during the trial Arendt switched from radical evil to "the banality of evil".

Chapter Four

Eichmann in Jerusalem: the Banality of Evil

ADOLF EICHMANN

For a good understanding of the Eichmann-trial, which finally would lead to Arendt's concept of "the banality of evil", it is necessary to say a few words about Eichmann's background.

Adolf Eichmann was born in 1906 in a middle-class family. He was offered the possibility of getting a good education, but he did not make use of this opportunity. He did not finish high school and became a miner in his father's company. In 1925 his father found him a job in the sales department of the Upper Austrian Electricity Company where he worked until 1927 and from 1927 to 1933 he was a representative for an oil company, a job he obtained with the help of family connections.

In 1933 he joined the Nazi-party. During his civil career he only worked for his family or in jobs obtained with the help of his family. In fact he was a failure, a residual product and as such he belonged to "the mob", a group of people crying for a strong man. Eichmann always wanted to belong to a specific group and therefore he joined youth movements like "Wandervögel" (Wanderers).

From 1933 he was given military training in SS camps for two years. However, military life did not appeal to him and therefore he applied for a position at Himmler's Sicherheitsdienst (Security Service). It is not sure whether or not he knew exactly what the task of the Sicherheitsdienst was. In the beginning he was asked to gather data about the Freemasons. He found this task very boring and when he was offered a job at the Jewish Department he accepted it immediately, mainly to be released from his first task.

The first assignment in his new job was reading the book *The Jewish State* by Theodor Herzl. However, he did much more than just reading it. He made an extensive study of Zionism and became an expert in Jewish affairs. He was promoted to sergeant major and gradually gained the confidence of the Gestapo (Secret State Police). It was during this period that he helped many German Jews to emigrate to Palestine. He did not do that out of affection for the Jews. He merely executed his superiors' orders to the best of his ability. It is not known what exactly were his feelings towards the Jews, but whatever these feelings may have been, they were always subordinate to the Nazis' objectives.

We know that the Nazis' attitude towards the Jews changed considerably in the following years. All measures against the Jews were in fact directed towards the "Endlösung" (final solution) and Eichmann cooperated in the development and execution of these measures doing the job as best he could. In the beginning the measures appeared to have a friendly face, like the formation of Jewish Councils to provide the Jews with so-called help. At a later stage it became obvious that the purpose of the formation of the Jewish Councils was a completely different one. More radical was the enforced emigration (banishment is a more adequate word) of 150.000 Austrian Jews in 1939 after the "Anschluss" (the alliance between Austria and Germany). The way in which he executed this assignment showed in particular how well he was trained as a bureaucrat. This is the reason why Hannah Arendt compared Eichmann to a colonial imperialistic bureaucrat: punctual, inflexible and never corrupt. It has never been proven that Eichmann was cruel. In fact he was deaf to the requests of his victims. He only tried to translate his superior's general instructions into orderly procedures.

Until 1939 Eichmann was a bureaucrat, but not yet a totalitarian bureaucrat. Arendt states that The Nazi regime became truly totalitarian and openly criminal after the outbreak of the war on September 1, 1939, because this date was also the start of the extermination of certain population groups by the so-called "Einsatzgruppen" (SS-groups with a specific task). Eichmann was never a member of one of these groups, although he always hoped to be selected.

In 1941 Eichmann still believed that the words "evacuation" and "final solution" just meant emigration of all the Jews of the Third Reich to another area. He was engaged in three different projects: a Jewish enclave in Poland, evacuation to Madagascar and a third idea that was realised in the model concentration camp of Terezin (Theresienstadt). About Theresienstadt Hannah Arendt said ironically that Eichmann believed that this would be: "a Jewish homeland, a gathering-in of the exiles of the Diaspora". (EJ, 80)

In the meantime Eichmann became more and more capable as a totalitarian bureaucrat. He learned how the Jewish victims themselves could help him and also how to set one group of Jews against another in order to obtain information; he was able to play different roles and he also developed his own bureaucratic vocabulary such as "emigration" for expulsion and "special treatment" for execution.

In 1941 Heydrich told him that the Führer had announced the extermination of all Jews. During a trip to Chelmno[1], Eichmann saw what his work, sending trainloads of people to the East, resulted in. At that moment Eichmann almost completely met Arendt's criteria for a totalitarian bureaucrat. Nevertheless, his conscience spoke for the last time when he sent a transport of 25.000 German Jews to Lodz, instead of to Minsk and Riga where they would have been executed immediately after arrival. He knew that execution of so many people would be impossible in Lodz, because of lack of facilities. His conscience spoke only for four weeks because after attending the Wannsee conference, where the Final Solution was proclaimed, he worked day and night at the organisation of the deportations, without conscientious objections. From being an expert in "forced emigration", he now became an expert in "forced evacuation". His devotion to totalitarian bureaucracy was now complete. Eichmann executed orders without asking questions, without considering the consequences, without thinking and consequently without judging.

The apotheosis of his contribution to the Final Solution was reached with the deportations of the Hungarian Jews in 1944. His complete department was transferred to Budapest. However, at Himmler's orders, a few changes were made. Besides the "radical" orders from Eichmann's superiors Müller and Kaltenbrunner new rules and regulations were now issued by a more "moderate wing". According to these new rules Jews could be used as a means of exchange, which resulted in negotiations about "Jews against material": one million Jews against ten thousand trucks. Eichmann did not take the initiative for these negotiations, but initially he was involved in them. In fact, he never joined the moderate wing. On the contrary, Eichmann undermined Himmler's orders as much as possible, because he felt protected by his superiors.

It is beyond doubt that Eichmann did his utmost to execute the Final Solution under all circumstances and this resulted in the deportation of 434.000 Hungarian Jews in two months. The gas chambers in Auschwitz were hardly capable of handling such an enormous amount of people in such a short period.

Finally, Eichmann lost his fight against Himmler's moderate wing. The deportations were stopped and Eichmann was dismissed from his position at the Jewish Department. After the capitulation Eichmann travelled in Germany under a false name, but nevertheless the Americans arrested him. In a camp for SS-members he was interrogated several times, but his real identity was not revealed. In January 1946 he escaped en went to the Lünenburger Heide, where he worked as a lumberjack under the name of Otto Heninger. With the help of ODESSA, an organisation of former SS-members, he escaped to Italy via Austria. From a Franciscan priest, who knew his real identity, he got a passport and help to escape to Argentina. In Argentina he obtained a work permit and identity papers in the name of Ricardo Klement, catholic, stateless, unmarried, 37 years of age, seven years younger than his real age.

On May 11, 1960, three members of the Israeli secret service arrested him. He immediately declared that he was Adolf Eichmann. His arrest may have been a relief to him. He had the choice between execution on the spot or a trial in Jerusalem. Eichmann chose for the trial in a personal declaration and allowing the world to be a witness to one of the most fascinating trials in history. For Hannah Arendt this trial resulted in her statement about 'the banality of evil', which caused considerable controversy. In the next paragraph I shall focus on the trial.

THE TRIAL

The trial against Adolf Eichmann started on April 11, 1961. He was accused of 15 crimes, including crimes against the Jewish people and crimes against humanity. His answer to the question whether he felt guilty was always the same: "Not guilty in the sense of the indictment". His lawyer, Robert Servatius, answered the question in a press interview: "Eichmann feels guilty before God, but not before the law", but this answer was never confirmed by Eichmann himself. Eichmann declared that the indictment for murder was wrong. He had never been involved in the killing of the Jews. He had never killed a Jew or any other person. He had never given an order to kill a Jew, but there seemed to be little doubt that he would have killed his own father, if he had been ordered to do so. According to him he could only be convicted for his assistance in the extermination of the Jews and according to his own declaration in Jerusalem, this had been one of the major crimes in history. What he had done was only a crime in retrospect. He had always been a law-abiding citizen. Hitler's orders had possessed the force of law in the Third Reich, even stronger: Hitler's orders were the laws of the Third Reich.

During the hearing half a dozen psychiatrists had declared Eichmann to be "normal". Whatever this means, Eichmann was not mentally deficient, neither in a moral, nor in a legal sense. After the trial, the president of the court, Gideon Hausner, declared in an article in The Saturday Evening Post, that he disposed of information which had not been brought forward during the trial. According to this information, Eichmann was "a man obsessed with a dangerous and insatiable urge to kill" and "a perverse, sadistic personality".

(EJ, 26) If this had been the case, says Arendt, he would have belonged in a mental hospital According to the psychiatrists, Eichmann was not only a normal person, but he had also nothing against the Jews. Alas, says Arendt, nobody believed this, mainly because the judges did not believe that a normal person could be perfectly incapable of telling right from wrong. The judges concluded that he was a perverse liar and in doing so they missed the essence of the matter. They assumed that a normal person must have been conscious of the criminal character of his deeds. Eichmann was "normal" insofar that he was no exception during the Nazi regime. Under the circumstances of the Third Reich only "exceptions" were able to think "normally" and this created a dilemma for the judges, which they could not resolve.

Already at the beginning of the trial a number of Eichmann's character traits became apparent. He was a boaster, only interested in his own career and absolutely incapable of entering into someone else's views. The way he spoke was extremely boring because officialese was his only language. He was unable to utter a single sentence that was not a cliché. He only uttered empty phrases but the judges thought that the emptiness was feigned. However, the truth was that he was incapable of speaking otherwise. His inability to speak, says Arendt, was closely connected with his inability to think, or more precisely: to place himself in someone else's position. In the next chapter we shall see that this quality is essential in order to arrive at a sound judgment. His inability to think made communication with him impossible, since he was unable to see the reality. (EJ, 49)

Important for the rest of this story is that, according to Arendt, Eichmann's attitude was mainly based on self-deception and this also applied to the majority of German society.

Eichmann was not a calculating liar or a monster. Arendt felt he looked more like a clown. However, this thought would have been fatal for the trial. Moreover, the idea would hardly have been sustainable in view of the sufferings he had caused to millions of people. Therefore, his worst clowneries were hardly noticed and seldom reported. It is remarkable that many years after the trial, Arendt's husband, Heinrich Blücher found the following passage in Bertold Brecht's play *The Resistible Rise of the Man Arturo Ui.*

> The great political criminals must be exposed and exposed especially to laughter. They are not great political criminals, but people who permitted great political crimes, which is something entirely different. The failure of his enterprises does not indicate that Hitler was an idiot and the extent of his enterprises does not make him a great man. If the ruling classes permit a small crook to become a great crook, he is not entitled to a privileged position in our view of history. (YB, 331)

In an interview, Arendt cited Brecht's words and she added that in assessing Hitler c.s. it is important to realize that: "no matter what he does and if he killed ten million people, he is still a clown". (YB, 331)

An important matter during the trial was the question of conscience, not only Eichmann's, but the conscience of all concerned: Nazis, symphatizers, bystanders and even victims. Was there a decisive moment in the lives of people who lived in a totalitarian society, a moment of choice, a moment when the voice of the conscience could no longer be ignored?

For Eichmann this moment came when he visited Chelmno and saw what happened to the Jews. He almost fainted, but nevertheless continued his work. The process that made him a totalitarian bureaucrat had reached the point of no return. For Eichmann it was a crucial moment because from thereon he chose not to act as a human being, but as a totalitarian robot. According to Arendt it would have been possible for him to pull out without serious consequences.

After attending the Wannsee conference, of which he wrote an account, Eichmann was a completely totalitarian bureaucrat. He said that he did his duty; he not only obeyed orders, but he also obeyed the law. He used the word "Kadavergehorsam" (rigid discipline), but there was more to it, for to everyone's surprise, Eichmann declared that he had lived according to Kant's moral precepts and in particular to a Kantian definition of duty, all his life. At first sight this seemed to be outrageous and incomprehensible, since Kant's moral principles are closely related with man's faculty of judgment, which excludes blind obedience. Apparently this was not the end of Eichmann's knowledge of Kant because he came up with an approximately correct definition of the categorical imperative when he said that the principle of his will must always be such that it can become the principle of general laws. (EJ, 136)

In the Introduction I said that Eichmann's appeal to Kant was not a complete mistake from Fackenheim's point of view. I shall try to explain why. Kant's categorical imperative can be summarized as follows:

   – It is morally necessary to do one's duty for duty's sake.
   – It is morally necessary to act in such a way, that the "maxim" of one's acts could become, through one's will, universal law.
   – It is morally necessary never to treat humanity as a means only, but always as an end as well.

The last definition is the heart of Kant's categorical imperative and it is clear that Eichmann defied this principle, but what about the others? Let us first consider the second principle. There is no doubt that Eichmann obeyed this principle, because the "maxim" of his acts was to make, through his own will, the Führer's will into universal law. His idea of law was of course different from Kant's. Kant's universal law is law and universal only if it makes no distinction and treats all as equals, but Eichmann's universal law discriminates between Aryans and non-Aryans. However, the philosophical question is: where is it written that all are equal? (Fackenheim, 1982, 270–272)

A possible answer to this question could be that people are not equal, but that they are of equal value, but in fact this does not solve the problem: how are we to decide if Hitler has the same value as mother Theresa?

Eichmann's law was Hitler's law. The Führer was the legislator of the Third Reich, the Führer's orders had force of law and therefore it was not necessary to put them on paper. In fact the orders were laws, because they were not limited in time and space, which is the case with orders. After all, it all concerned the "Thousand-Year Empire on Earth". Eichmann acted according to the categorical imperative of the Third Reich, as formulated by Hans Frank: "Act in such a way that the Führer, if he knew of your action, would approve it". (Frank, 15–16) Frank called this "the version of Kant for the household use of the common man". In Kant's philosophy the source on which our actions are based is practical reason; in Eichmann's household version it was the law of the Führer (EJ, 136)

We have not looked at the first principle yet. There is no doubt that Eichmann obeyed this principle; he was a dutiful, idealistic mass-murderer. Law was law and duty was duty, without exceptions. From that perspective it becomes clear why Eichmann went through with the deportations of the Hungarian Jews against the orders of the "moderate wing": from his point of view these orders were illegal. His "conscience" explains his attitude and compromises were impossible. It also explains the transport of the Jews to Lodz instead of to Riga in 1941. He obeyed the Führer's law and at that moment there was no order for extermination. It is therefore doubtful whether these actions were a result of fanaticism; he probably only did what he considered his duty.

The Führer's law changed the First Commandment from "Thou shalt not kill" into "Thou shalt kill".

> Evil in the Third Reich had lost the quality by which most people recognize it— the quality of temptation. Many Germans and many Nazis, probably an overwhelming majority of them must have been tempted *not* to murder, *not* to rob, *not* to let their neighbors go off to their doom (for that the Jews were transported to their doom they knew, of course, even though many of them may not have known the gruesome details), and not to become accomplices in all these crimes by benefiting from them. But, God knows, they had learned how to resist temptation. (EJ, 150)

Rarely, has anyone been so harsh in her judgment on her compatriots. The judges in Jerusalem did not know what to do with the accused. The public prosecutor, Gideon Hausner, was unable to understand a mass murderer who never killed a man himself and probably did not have the courage to do so. He continuously tried to accuse Eichmann personally of murder, but that was an impossible task. He also called Eichmann a perverse sadist and considered him the greatest monster that the world had ever seen. Of course it would have been much easier to believe that Eichmann was a monster, but the problem with Eichmann and many others was that they were not perverse, not sadistic, but "terribly and terrifyingly" normal. Eichmann was neither a monster nor a hero but he had done his duty. He was a normal person, "stinknormal" (thoroughly normal), as Arendt expressed it and the whole trial taught her the lesson of the fearsome, word- and thought-defying "banality of evil". (EJ, 252) Evil had manifested itself as banal and superficial, not as heroic, demonic, profound or radical and its origin seemed to be an incapability to think and to judge.

This statement was the cause of one of the controversies that arose after publication of the book *Eichmann in Jerusalem.* In the epilogue of the book, Arendt stresses the point that the book is not a theoretical treatise on the nature of evil. The expression "banality of evil" was only based on what she had heard and seen. With the "banality of evil" she tried to put into words a phenomenon, which stared one in the face during the trial. With the exception of the motive for his own career, Eichmann had no motives at all.

> He *merely,* to put the matter colloquially, *never realized what he was doing. . .* He was not stupid. It was sheer thoughtlessness—something by no means identical with stupidity—that predisposed him to become one of the greatest criminals of that period. And if this is "banal" or even funny, if with the best will in the world one cannot extract any diabolical or demonic profundity from Eichmann, that is still far from calling it commonplace (EJ, 287–288)

In 1945 Hannah Arendt wrote that it would be impossible to try any Nazi for his crimes, because so many Germans were involved that it would be impossible to separate the guilty from the innocent (EU, 121–132) After the Eichmann trial she changed her opinion. It was not relevant whether Eichmann had been a minor or a major cog in the machine of the "Final Solution". He took an active part and all cogs in a criminal machine are guilty of the crime and must therefore be condemned. She refuted the idea that small cogs in the machine would not be responsible for their acts by saying:

> If the defendant excuses himself on the ground that he acted not as a man but as a mere functionary whose functions could be carried out by anyone else, it is as if a criminal pointed to the statistics of crime—which set forth that so-and-so many crimes per day are committed in such-and-such a place—and declared that he did only what statistically was expected, that it was mere accident that he did it and not somebody else, since after all somebody had to do it. (EJ, 289)

Eichmann was guilty of and responsible for his actions and therefore he was hanged. Arendt's report of the trial left us two expressions, which have been subject to discussion for many years: "thoughtlessness" and "the banality of evil".

THE BANALITY OF EVIL

Hannah Arendt's switch from "radical evil" to "banal evil" was caused by Eichmann's behaviour during the trial. The expression "the banality of evil" implies that evil has no greatness, nothing special, but on the contrary, seems to be ordinary and vulgar and is caused by ordinary, thoughtless people. What exactly did Arendt mean by "the banality of evil"?

I mentioned already that Arendt said that *Eichmann in Jerusalem* should not be considered as a treatise on the nature of evil. In the book she uses the expression "the banality of evil" only once and this may indicate that it was an impulsive thought rather than a scientific theory. In *Eichmann in Jerusalem* Arendt does not give any explanation for the use of the expression apart from the indication that there was a strong connection with "thoughtlessness". Seven years later she returns to the subject in the introduction of the chapter Thinking in her book *The Life of the Mind.* She states that behind "the banality of evil" there was no thesis or doctrine, although she knew that it was contradictory to our tradition of thought about the phenomenon of evil. She made the remark "willy-nilly". (LM, I, 3)

The concept so far was that evil is something demonic and evil men act out of envy, like the envy of Cain, who slew Abel or out of hate or covetousness. Eichmann did not act out of envy, hate or covetousness. It was something completely different that manifested itself during the trial.

> However what I was confronted with was utterly different and still factual. I was struck with a manifest shallowness in the doer that made it impossible to trace the uncontestable evil of his deeds to any deeper level of roots or motives. The deeds were monstrous, but the doer—at least the very effective one now on trial—was quite ordinary and the only notable characteristic one could detect in his past behaviour during the trial and throughout the pre-trial police examination was something entirely negative: it was not stupidity but *thoughtlessness*. (LM I, 4)

The obvious question is: what did Arendt mean by "thoughtlessness"? Her answer is:

> In the setting of Israeli court and prison procedures he functioned as well as he had functioned under the Nazi regime but, when confronted with situations for

which such routine procedures did not exist, he was helpless, and his cliché-ridden language produced on the stand, as it had evidently done in his official life, a kind of macabre comedy. Clichés, stock phrases, adherence to conventional standardized codes of expression and conduct have the socially recognized function of protecting us against reality, that is, against the claim on our thinking attention that all events and facts made by virtue of their existence. If we were responsive to this claim all the time, we would soon be exhausted; Eichmann differed from the rest of us only that he clearly knew of no such claim at all. (LM I, 4)

It cannot be expressed more clearly: he simply did not think about the things he saw and heard and not even about his own actions.

Arendt's bosom friend Mary McCarthy did not completely agree with the use of the word "thoughtlessness". In a letter of June 9, 1971, she says that she objects to the use of the word in this context, because it does not express exactly what Arendt wants to say. She says that it is wrong to use a keyword in such an important book in a meaning that it does not normally have, even if the reader would understand what Arendt wanted to say. However, without a doubt there will be readers who will interpret the word "thoughtlessness" as forgetfulness or inattentiveness. McCarthy preferred synonyms, for instance a synonym that was mentioned by Arendt herself: "an inability to think, namely, to think from the standpoint of somebody else". (EJ, 49) Moreover it is not clear to Mary McCarthy what the difference is between "thoughtlessness" and "stupidity". She would prefer to describe Eichmann as "profoundly, egregiously stupid" and this is not the same as a low I.Q. She agrees with Kant, who states "stupidity is caused not by brain failure but by a wicked heart". (BF, 296)

From Arendt's observations and writings during and after the Eichmann trial the following conclusions can be drawn.

Eichmann was neither a sadistic monster, nor did he possess a satanic greatness. On the contrary, what struck one most were his commonness, his triviality, his superficiality and his normality. His motives were mainly ambition, a desire to please his superiors, obeying orders and doing what he thought was his duty, which means compliance with the law, the law of the Führer and subsequently the law of the Third Reich.

What was incomprehensible was his apparent inability to think and to judge. How was it possible that an apparently normal person was unable to differentiate between good and evil? All he said were "idle words" and the reason was that he had nothing to say. There was no profundity in his words; there was only triviality and superficiality. The "banality of evil" and the concomitant "thoughtlessness" were new phenomena in a new type of mass murderer.

We may find it almost impossible to imagine how someone could "think" (or rather not think) in this manner, whereby manufacturing food, bombs or corpses, are "in essence the same" and this can become "normal", "ordinary" behaviour. (Bernstein, 1996, 170)

THE ARGUMENTS FOR AND AGAINST
THE BANALITY OF EVIL

The expression "the banality of evil" is the origin of one of the controversies that came up after publication of the book. There were many who sympathized with Arendt's view or even agreed with it. However, the number of opponents was also considerable and they made no secret of their criticism. Their main reproach was that Arendt, in using the term "the banality of evil", made the Shoah a trivial event and also that she made Eichmann much more sympathetic than he was.

In this chapter I will present the most important remarks with regard to the expressions "the banality of evil" and "thoughtlessness". In the next chapter I shall comment on these remarks.

Gershom Scholem wrote Arendt a letter saying:

After reading your book I remain unconvinced by your thesis the "banality of evil"—a thesis, which, if your sub-title is to be believed, underlies your entire argument. This new thesis strikes me as a catchword: it does not impress me, certainly, as the product of profound analysis—an analysis such as you gave us so convincingly, in the service of a quite different, indeed contradictory thesis, in your book on totalitarianism. At that time you had not yet made your discovery, apparently, that evil is banal. Of that "radical evil", to which your then analysis bore such eloquent and erudite witness, nothing remains but this slogan—to be more than that it would have to be investigated, at such a serious level, as a relevant concept in moral philosophy or political ethics. I am sorry—and I say this, I think, in candor and in no spirit of enmity—that I am unable to take the thesis of your book more seriously. I had expected, with your earlier book in mind, something different. (JP, 245)

Arendt's reply is very important:

In conclusion, let me come to the only matter where you have not misunderstood me, and where indeed I am glad that you have raised the point. You are quite right: I changed my mind and I do not speak of "radical evil". It is a long time since we last met, or we would perhaps have spoken about the subject before. (Incidentally, I don't see why you call my term "the banality of evil" a catchword or slogan. As far as I know no one has used the term before me; but that is unimportant). It is indeed my opinion now that evil is never "radical", that it is only extreme, and that it possesses neither depth nor any demonic dimension. It can overgrow and lay waste the whole world precisely because it spreads like a fungus on the surface. It is "thought-defying", as I said, because thought tries to reach some depth, to go to the roots, and the moment it concerns itself with evil, it is frustrated because there is nothing. That is its "banality". Only the good has depth and can be radical. But this is not the place to go into these matters seriously; I intend to elaborate them further in a different context. Eichmann may very well remain the concrete model of what I have to say. (JP, 250–251)

As a result of this letter, J. Glenn Gray wrote to Hannah Arendt that he interrogated hundreds of Nazi functionaries and that Eichmann seemed to fit well into their mold. However, that evil would have no metaphysical reality or depth might be true for Eichmann, but probably not for a man like Goebbels. (YB, 370)

Karl Jaspers had similar objections, because first he writes:

Now you have delivered the crucial word against "radical evil", against gnosis! You are with Kant who said: man cannot be a devil, and I am with you. But it's a pity that the term "radical evil", in a very different sense that was not understood even by Goethe and Schiller, comes from Kant. (C, 525)

However, a few weeks later he says:

I think it's a wonderful inspiration and right on the mark as the book's subtitle. The point is that *this* evil, not evil per se, is banal. I wasn't altogether happy with your phrasing of this point in your response to Scholem. *What* evil is stands *behind* your phrase characterizing Eichmann . . . Your answer in your letter struck me as too combative and too weak at the same time. (C, 542)

Arendt herself may have had second thoughts, since, during a conversation with Mary McCarthy, she said that she considered Reinhardt Heydrig, according to her the real planner of the Final Solution, as the personification of absolute evil. (YB, 370)

In his letter, Scholem states that the two expressions "banality of evil" and "radical evil" are contradictory. Hannah Arendt confirms this in a letter to Mary McCarthy on September 20, 1963:

. . . the very phrase "Banality of Evil" stands in contrast to the phrase I used in the totalitarianism book, "radical evil". This is too difficult a subject to be dealt with here, but it is important. (BF, 148)

In chapter 6 I will come back to the meaning of "radical evil" and "banal evil".

During the process there were two psychiatric reports that contained opposite diagnoses. Six psychiatrists made the first diagnosis prior to the hearing. This diagnosis stated that Eichmann was "normal", in other words not mentally disturbed.

The second diagnosis was made by the Hungarian psychiatrist Leopold Szondi, with the help of a test developed by him, the Szondi-test. The test is a projective technique based on a person's reactions to a series of 48 photographs of psychiatric patients. The photographs were chosen in accordance with the principle of genetic relationship, that is, the person assumedly selects a photograph which portrays a psychiatric disorder also inherent in the subject's own familial genealogy. The outcome of the test indicated that Eichmann was "a man possessed by a dangerous and insatiable urge to kill, arising out of a desire for power" and "a perverted, sadistic personality". In his report Szondi wrote that during his 24 years of practice, he had never seen such convincing results.

Imre Kertész' reaction is the following:

> Herewith all theories about a "deskmurderer" have been refuted. Killing out of bloodlust—the usual cliché. Eichmann could not have been replaced by anyone else, like everybody—including me—thought, to the greater glory of dynamic Nazism. What remains is a miserable theory: they were criminals who assumed power and wielded it in a criminal way. The cowardice, blindness and greed of the population and the pragmatism of life did the rest. How banal this is! It is difficult for me to resign myself to the thought that such trivial causes brought me to Auschwitz. (Kértesz, 2003, 194)

The political psychologist Alford states that Arendt did not take the possibility into consideration that both diagnoses could be correct.

> One was a description of his behaviour and words, which were indeed "normal"; the other was an explanation of what must lie behind their flatness, behind the utter incommensurability between word and deed, behind the total failure of empathy. (Alford, 22)

Alford continues by saying that there was a kind of interaction between Eichmann's obsessive behaviour and the Nazi ideology: the ideology and the bureaucracy enhanced his defense mechanism against this obsession by arranging that this defense mechanism fitted in a normal behavior. Alford is convinced of the correctness of the result of the Szondi-test and states that Eichmann's obsessive urge to kill was steered in the "right" direction by the Nazi ideology. Alford concludes:

> If it is only the interaction of unintegrated rage with evil ideologies and policies that causes evil, if in other circumstances neither Mengele nor Eichmann would

have become evil men, then where does evil lie? In man? Evil ideologies or policies? Or in a few men, such as Hitler? I have answered "in man", though of
course it is not that simple (Alford, 24)

An interesting reaction to "the banality of evil" comes from Lionel Abel,
one of the sharpest critics of Arendt's work. In his article of 1963 "The Aesthetics of Evil", he states that Arendt's judgment on Eichmann is not a political or moral judgment but an aesthetic one. By an aesthetic judgment, Abel
means a judgment that is based on external characteristics and on the pattern
of behaviour of a person. Abel wonders whether a mass killer like Eichmann
can be judged in this way instead of on moral or political grounds. Abel points
at the trial against Laval in France, which contains aspects similar to the Eichmann case. Pierre Laval was Minister of Foreign Affairs during the Pétain
government and he became the most important vassal of the German occupiers of France. He was tried and consequently executed on October 15, 1945.
Simone de Beauvoir wrote that the Laval during the trial was not the same
person as the Laval at the height of his power. The person one wants to punish has, in a sense, escaped. The same goes for Eichmann, since 16 years had
passed between the end of the war and the beginning of the trial.

Instead of depicting Eichmann as an adherent to the ideology of the Third
Reich (otherwise he could never have reached his position), Arendt presents
him as a comic, average, dutiful servant of Hitler, who did nothing but respect
the law. Arendt's picture of Eichmann, says Abel, is the picture that Eichmann
showed in Jerusalem. These were the only tactics he could employ, because
he could not, morally or politically, justify his actions. If we judge Eichmann
on moral and political grounds, says Abel, it is obvious that Gideon Hausner's
judgment, that Eichmann was a moral monster, was a valid and intelligent
judgement and that Arendt's judgment was perverse and arbitrary. If one
judges Eichmann on aesthetical grounds, he may not look like a monster, but
this is no reason to consider him insignificant. According to Abel it is impossible to judge people's morals by their looks, except in the painting in *The
Picture of Dorian Gray* by Oscar Wilde. To his dismay, Dorian Gray saw his
painted face change after every evil deed and finally become the face of a
hideous monster. However, the face of the real Dorian Gray did not change
and remained attractive and unaffected. Eichmann said that he would jump
laughing into his grave, because the fact that he had the death of five million
Jews on his conscience gave him extreme satisfaction. (EJ, 46) This is sufficient for Abel to consider him as a monster, while Arendt can only see it as
plain boasting. It is quite possible, says Abel, that Eichmann was a clown, but
is this contradictory to the fact that he was also a moral monster? Iago and
Richard III were also comic moral monsters. (Abel, 1963, 211–230)

Walter Laqueur's tone in his article "Footnotes on the Holocaust" is much softer than Abel's, although in fact he says the same thing.

> Eichmann cut a sorry figure at the trial, which induced miss Arendt to develop her theory of the banality of evil. But Hitler himself would not have emerged as a hero in similar conditions. Once they cease to inspire fear, dictators and their servants are bound to become pathetic creatures and it is difficult to understand in retrospect how anyone could ever have been overawed by them. Miss Arendt's appraisal of Eichmann, in brief, is too much influenced, I feel, by his performance in Jerusalem. Men tend to be banal in prison. (JP, 255)

Gertrude Ezorsky approaches the problem in a different way in her article "Hannah Arendt's View of Totalitarianism and the Holocaust". She states that Hannah Arendt's portrait of Eichmann is a paradox: his triviality is set against the enormity of his deeds and this paradox is a challenge to "common sense". In general one does not judge a person without looking at his deeds. Ezorsky discusses in great detail the psychiatric data based on the results of the Szondi-test that were published by Gideon Hausner in the Saturday Evening Post after the process in 1962. Hannah Arendt said that, according to these data, Eichmann should have been in a mental hospital. This is wrong, says Ezorsky, because sadists and killers are not sent to mental hospitals by a court of law. If the accused is legally sane, he stands trial. Moreover, Ezorky reproaches Arendt that she did not inform the readers of the New York Post of the results immediately, but only later in her book. As a scientific researcher, it was her duty to present this information to her readers, despite the fact that it challenged her own opinion. Ezorsky also discusses the fact that Eichmann suggests he was neither a Jew-hater, nor a member of the Nazi movement out of conviction, or as an adherent of the ideology. He probably only did this to defend himself and keep up a false appearance. Nevertheless, says Ezorsky, Arendt's picture of Eichmann's entry into the Nazi party may not be entirely wrong. Someone can be attracted to fulfilling a particular role in a political movement, because it means something to him and gives him satisfaction, but this attitude is not an alternative to political conviction. Especially these people, says Ezorsky, are in need of arguments that justify their membership. Ezorsky's third point of discussion is Eichmann's statement that all he did was comply with the laws of the Third Reich. She refers to the question of the Hungarian Jews. According to the court in Jerusalem Hitler gave permission for the emigration of a few thousand Jews, on condition that Horthy would hand over all the others to the Germans. About the fact that Eichmann did not accept this offer she says:

> This is the man whom Arendt sketches as a law-abiding citizen, loyal out of conscience, to Hitler, but free of hatred for Jews. But the real Eichmann was a killer,

ready to take the initiative even against Hitler's order, so that no Jews should live. Arendt's tale that Eichmann was without fanatical hatred of Jews seemed initially implausible and turns out to be plainly false (Ezorsky, 68)

Ezorsky concludes that Eichmann's paradox—the contradiction between his character and the nature of his deeds—is not in accordance with the facts. One cannot separate a man from his actions, because in that case one denies that the life he leads is his own. What Arendt did not see is that the various roles that Eichmann assumed influenced him. Like Lionel Abel, Ezorsky also points out that Eichmann in Jerusalem was a different person than Eichmann during the war. His mediocrity and his banality are partly feigned, but they are in any case symptoms of an instantaneous picture and inconsistent with his deeds during the Nazi regime. She refers to a passage of Hilberg's book, *The Destruction of the European Jews.* Hilberg writes that the Jews were encouraged to write postcards to their relatives and friends after their arrival at Auschwitz-Birkenau. After the victims were killed, the postcards were sent off in small batches in order to create the impression that the senders were still alive. From Eichmann's letter to the Foreign Office about the Slovakian Prime Minister's intention to inspect one of the camps we may conclude that Eichmann played an active part in this charade.

To counteract the fantastic rumors circulating in Slovakia about the fate of the evacuated Jews, attention should be drawn to the postal communications of these Jews with Slovakia, which are forwarded directly through the advisor on Jewish affairs with the German Legation in Bratislava (Wisliceny) and which, incidentally, amounted to more than 1000 letters and postcards for February-March this year. (Hilberg, 470–471)

Ezorsky concludes:

Had Arendt reflected on this communication, she might have concluded, that its author, Adolf Eichmann, exemplified not the banality of evil, but the *cunning* of evil. (Ezorsky, 71)

In an article "Can Evil be banal?" Nathan Rotenstreich went even further. The philosophical point that he disputes is that evil can never be banal because it presupposes deliberation and planning. It is not an immediate expression of urges overcoming the evildoer. There are no evil deeds that are not grounded in awareness of acts and their results. Thus, in doing evil, a person is not or not any more banal and the deeds take him out of the "grey" sphere of banality. Rotenstreich discusses a number of points that all have the purpose of demonstrating that evil never can be banal.

– He wonders whether Arendt's supposition that evil had become a day-to-day routine for Eichmann is a valid reason to call it banal. Perhaps we should look at it from another angle. If someone is involved in a routine of this kind, it is likely that he adjusts himself to a continuous series of crimes to such an extent that he loses his sensitivity to evil. The fact that Eichmann never made decisions, but only executed orders, does not mean that the evil was banal. The making of a decision does not imply that the act is done on one's own initiative. Here again it can be said that routine participation can be a sign of the involvement and adaptation to evil without assuming that the actor is the beginner of a series of acts.

– Eichmann was an adult person, also in the respect that in his involvement in the execution of the Final Solution, he must have been aware of his actions and their consequences, at least of the direct and immediate consequences. Again, this goes beyond the description of routine.

– If the nature of the total crime is not banal, those who participate in it are not banal either, even if their other qualities are trivial or trite.

– Eichmann declared at a particular moment that he accepted that he could no longer control his actions and that he was unable to change this, as he had to obey orders. This implies that he was aware of the relation between the acts and his own decisions. How can we call a person who confesses his dilemma banal, and to what extent can a person say that his inclination to obey orders is a situation that he is unable to change?

– Even if Eichmann only took minutes of the Wannsee Conference, he could understand what it meant that the Jews "had to be handled in a proper manner". If we say that Eichmann was a cliché type of person this indicates that he was not very original, but it does not mean that he did not understand the contents of his own minutes.

– The complexity of the whole situation does not in any way justify the use of the word "banality". Banality is a term invented by Arendt, but it is not a qualification of the subject matter.

The Nazis' actions were planned and were not a result of sudden urges or egoism. Planning implies that one calculates the consequences of the deeds. There is a relationship between planning and being aware of the consequences. The Nazi criminals found the motives for their actions in the ideology of the Third Reich. Everybody who was involved in these planned actions committed a crime that cannot be considered as banal or normal, because the deeds were not a result of urges, but of convictions and "worldviews". All this, says Rotenstreich, leads us to Kant's conception of evil. Arendt's notion of "radical evil" may be disregarded, because this term is essential for Kant's view. Nevertheless, he thinks that totalitarian evil can be explained with the help of Kant's theory, because inherent in evil is the violation of the moral law. Finally, says Rotenstreich, perhaps the word "ba-nal" should not be used in the context of ethical considerations at all. I will revert to this question in chapter 6.

COMMENTS

In this chapter I discussed: Adolf Eichmann, the trial, the banality of evil and arguments for and against the banality of evil. I shall now enter into the major elements of these subjects.

Eichmann: Normal or Mentally Disturbed?

The question whether Eichmann was normal or not was a major point of discussion. The main question is: when is a person normal? The Dutch psychiatrist prof. Rümke provided a surprisingly simple and practical answer to this question. According to Rümke a person is normal if he considers himself normal and if his partner, children, friends and colleagues also consider him normal. In general, a person is normal if he behaves normally in society. This has nothing to do with his character. Serial murderers can behave normally for years.

The difficulty with Eichmann was that there were no partners, children, friends or colleagues to be consulted. In fact there was nobody in the court who had ever met Eichmann before and therefore the diagnosis about the normality of Eichmann had to be made with the help of other methods. One of these methods was the Szondi test. The result of the test indicated that Eichmann possessed a perverted, sadistic personality. This outcome was in contrast with the diagnosis of six psychiatrists who said that he was a normal person. I want to make two remarks with regard to the Szondi test. First I do not quite understand why the president of the court, Gideon Hausner, could not bring out the result of the test during the trial. Was the result of the test that positive? Was there a test at all? My second remark is that I do not know how reliable the test is. What is the percentage of false positive results? Alford's opinion that both diagnoses could be correct is another possibility. As I said above behaviour and personality are two different things.

The judges in Jerusalem made the assumption that a normal person must be aware of his criminal deeds, but, says Arendt, in the totalitarian system of the Nazis, Eichmann was considered normal. A person who acted normally according to the standards of the judges in Jerusalem, was an exception during the Nazi regime! Arendt's point of view is of the utmost importance in understanding the essence of the process. Bruno Bettelheim clarifies this in his essay: "Eichmann, The System, The Victims".

Bettelheim, who was an ex-prisoner of Dachau and Buchenwald, states in his essay that our yardsticks for normality cannot be applied to the behavior of people in a totalitarian society. What became obvious during the trial was the incompatibility between our concept of life and the bureaucracy in a totalitarian state. Our imaginative powers, our frames of reference and our feelings are incapable of fathoming the discrepancy between Eichmann's banality and the fact that someone like him could be responsible for the destruction of millions.

> Had he been more of a man, his humanity would have kept him from his evil work; had he been less of a man, he would not have been effective at his job. His is exactly the banality of a man who would push the button when told, concerned only with pushing it well, and without any regard for who was pushed by it to his death, or where. (Bettelheim, 260)

Everything he did seemed to be legal in the totalitarian state and therefore the qualification "murderer" that we know was not applicable to him, because it is a qualification that belongs in a normal society. What the judges, unlike Arendt, did not realize was that it was not Eichmann as a person who was in court, but Eichmann as the personification of totalitarianism. It was totalitarianism that was brought to trial in Jerusalem, but it is impossible to punish a system; Eichmann, however could be sentenced and therefore the judges chose to consider him as a sadist, a liar, a murderer, a fanatic and above all a monster. He was in fact a monster, but only as part of a monstrous system and not as a person. Of course he was aware of the fact that the Jews were gassed; he never denied it. The judges constantly hammered away at his conscience, but in a totalitarian society there are no voices from the outside that appeal to someone's conscience. The metaphor of the totalitarian onion-structure may clarify this. Eichmann was probably situated in the third layer from the inside. If he looked around he saw the direct co-workers of the Führer in the inside layer, while the outside layer contained the party-members. (for him the "normality")

> This is what makes living in a totalitarian society so desperate, because there is nobody to turn to for guidance, and there are no voices from the outside. (Bettelheim, 263)

Conscience

An important question was the question of conscience, not only Eichmann's conscience, but the conscience of all who had either actively or passively supported the Nazis. Wasn't there a moment that their conscience was roused?

According to Bruno Bettelheim too few Germans listened to the voice of conscience when Hitler came to power. For some this moment came after the proclamation of the euthanasia program; for more in 1938 after the Kristall-nacht and for still more after the lost battle of Stalingrad in 1943. Such a moment came for every prisoner in a concentration camp, when the problem arose whether one would support the SS or not. The moment also came for many Jews, especially for the Jewish leaders and for members of the Jewish Councils.

> My thesis is that if one does not stand up to one's experience in accordance with one's values, if one takes the first step in cooperating with the totalitarian system at the expense of one's convictions and sentiments, one is caught in a web that tightens with each step of cooperation until it becomes impossible to break free. (Bettelheim, 271)

However, the problem of taking the first step in cooperating with a totalitarian system is complex. Imre Kertész, winner of the Nobel Prize for literature 2002 and former prisoner of Auschwitz and Buchenwald, makes this clear. After his return to Budapest he asks his neighbours what they did during the German occupation. They say that they tried to stay alive and Kertész remarks that this means that, all that time, they took the necessary steps. The neighbours do not understand his answer and Kertész tries to clarify his remark. He says that a freight train can contain an average of three thousand persons. The selection of a person takes one or two seconds. A person who was situated in the middle of the row on the platform in Auschwitz, like Kertész, had to wait ten to twenty minutes before he arrived at the spot where it was decided whether he was to go to the gas chambers immediately, or was given a chance to stay alive. Meanwhile the row moved forward and everyone took, with regular intervals, a bigger or smaller step, depending on the speed of the selection. What Kertész wants to make clear is that things do not only overcome us, but that we also take the necessary steps. (Kertész, 1994, 237, 238)

From Kertész' remarks we may conclude that, with the exception of those who actively resisted the totalitarian regime, everyone cooperated to a greater or lesser extent, actively or passively. Even those who resisted cooperated at the very moment they were killed. If 14–year old Imre Kertész had not taken the necessary steps on the platform, the SS would have shot him, but at that moment he would, in a way, have cooperated with the system, because the final goal of the Nazis was the production of corpses. It reminds one of *Sophie's Choice* or the Antigone's tragic conflict: whatever you do seems to be morally wrong, but who on earth would not have taken the necessary steps if he had been in Imre Kértesz' situation?

Going back to Eichmann, we may state that Eichmann's conscience did not force him to query the decision on the execution of the Final Solution. This raises the question: what is the relation between conscience of the individual and politics? According to Arendt, broadly speaking, conscience cannot play a major role in politics, since political actions may sometimes have nasty consequences. (CR, 60, 64, 82, 92; HC, section 33) Considered from this angle, one cannot reproach Eichmann. He was undoubtedly a model-citizen of The Third Reich who performed his task conscientiously, but it was this conscientious interpretation of his task, which made him a criminal. Nevertheless, it remains an intriguing question, why his conscience did not make him realize that his deeds were wrong, because he executed, indeed "conscientiously", a criminal task. Arendt answers this question by saying that conscience is indeed a private matter, but that it does not operate independently from the world. Conscience activates in man an inner discussion in order to determine whether a particular action is right or wrong. Conscience also sets the standards and decides whether human actions do or do not come up to the standards. However, these standards are to a large extent determined by the society one belongs to and are therefore not objective, but subjective. Eichmann's problem was that in his immediate surroundings there was no one who was against The Final Solution, so there was nothing or no one to activate his conscience into warning him that he was doing the wrong thing. According to Bruno Bettelheim this was the problem of living in a totalitarian society: there were no protesting voices from the outside. Nevertheless, there is an argument against Arendt's opinion. There are universal crimes, which are intolerable under any circumstances. Extermination of completely innocent individuals is one of these crimes.

> Every culture has a concept of murder, distinguishing this from execution, killing in war and other "justifiable homicides". (C. Kluckhohn, 663–677)

But, if this is true, the question arises once more why Eichmann and all others did not oppose the Final Solution. One of the possible answers is that the Nazis did not consider the Final Solution as murder of an innocent population, but rather as a "justifiable homicide" and a logical consequence of the ideology. However, this brings up another question. If the Nazis did not consider it as murder, why were the extermination camps built in very remote areas? With the exception of Auschwitz-Birkenau[2] and Majdanek[3] all sites (Belzec, Chelmno, Sobibor and Treblinka) are, even today, very difficult to find. Moreover the Nazis tried to obliterate any evidence of their criminal activity after the liquidation of the camps, with the exception of Majdanek.[4] The only explanation possible is that, although the Nazis did not consider their activities as a crime, they must have been aware that the majority of people would consider them as premeditated murder of a few million innocent individuals.

The matter of the conscience has another aspect. We have heard that Eichmann soothed his own conscience by appealing to Kant. He had done his duty by complying with the laws of the Third Reich. However, as Arendt states, Kant's moral theory excludes blind obedience. The main principle of the moral law is practical reason, which is intelligible (intellectually knowable). Kant assumes that everybody has the faculty of practical reason and that it is radical, which means that it is not reducible to another principle. But Kant says also that a moral principle must be independent of other factors. Kant agrees neither with Mandeville, who said that moral principles were determined by law, nor with Montaigne, who considered education as the source of moral principles. (KPV, 324, [40])

However, man is a rational being and therefore he must consider himself the source of his moral principles. In other words, moral law does not only govern rational beings, but they also make this law. Man is his own legislator. The source of Eichmann's moral principle was not Eichmann himself, but the law of the Third Reich and according to Kant, state laws can never be the source of moral principles.

Aesthetic Judgment

Abel and Laqueur have their doubts about Arendt's final opinion that Eichmann's evil was banal. Her opinion was based on her presence at the trial and the study of the interrogation reports. The banality was a phenomenon that stared her in the face during the trial and one gets the same feeling watching the recently made documentary film of the trial. It is of course possible that she was wrong or partly wrong. On the other hand, it is very doubtful whether Eichmann was able to play a role during the full year of the trial, without ever revealing his true self. More intriguing is the question whether he was the same person at the trial as during the deportations. In the case of Eichmann this is very difficult to determine because he did his work behind his desk. The witnesses in the trial had never seen Eichmann at work and even if they had, a reliable judgment would have been extremely difficult. Practically all witnesses were Israeli citizens and survivors of the concentration- and extermination camps. Arendt calls them "background witnesses", because all these witnesses had personally experienced the consequences of Eichmann's activities, but none of them had ever met him. The only witnesses who could possibly have given a sound judgment on Eichmann's personality during the Third Reich were his co-workers and superiors. However these witnesses could not come to Israel, because they would have been arrested immediately.

The fact that there were no witnesses for the defence was also the major problem of the counsel for the defence, dr. Servatius. It is one of the reasons why Arendt argued in favour of a trial in a neutral country and in an international court of justice.

Finally, concerning the banality of evil, Richard Bernstein states that a distinction has to be made between the conceptual issue of the banality, which means that persons can commit evil without traceable evil motives and the question whether Eichmann fits in this issue. Arendt was rather sceptical about the ability of people to look into someone else's heart and to know the motives for his deeds. It is therefore a little extreme to state that Eichmann, apart from his personal advancement, had no motives at all. Some of Eichmann's actions, like the deportations of the Hungarian Jews, indicate that he was probably more fanatical in the execution of his duty than Arendt wants us to believe. (Bernstein, 170)

Totalitarianism in Court

It has already been said that it was, in fact, the totalitarian system that was brought to trial in Jerusalem. Eichmann was the personification of totalitarianism. It was the system that was devilish, but its components, the perpetrators, seem to be in general ordinary and banal. This was Arendt's opinion, but her vision was not always accepted. The judges tried to separate Eichmann from the system and this was the reason for the occurrence of the paradox of Gertrude Ezorsky, who stated that his devilish deeds were not in accordance with his banality. She speaks of "the cunning of evil" and tries to illustrate this with a number of examples.

However, in my opinion there is no paradox at all. Consciously or unconsciously, Arendt has been looking for the origin of evil, applying Kant's method. Everyone agreed that Eichmann's deeds were terrible, but for Arendt that was not the essential point. Like Kant, she was interested in the intentions that resulted in Eichmann's actions and she came to the conclusion that these intentions were not present in Eichmann as a person, but in Eichmann as a part of the totalitarian system. Considering it from this point of view, the question of the postcards from Auschwitz can be seen as part of the system and the execution of an order. It goes without saying that camouflage was used to hide the truth, but this doesn't change the banality of evil. Bruno Bettelheim states that:

> . . . Eichmann had to be tried as a person. But to do so required that he be viewed as a man of extraordinary qualities; that is as a monster. This Eichmann certainly was, but as part of a monstrous system; as a man, he was blatantly not.

and goes on to say:

> Arendt tries to show the full horrors of totalitarianism, which go very far beyond those of anti-Semitism. A more complete understanding of totalitarianism requires that we see Eichmann as basically a mediocrity whose dreadful importance is derived from his more-or-less chance position within the system. (Bettelheim, 264–265)

Hans Morgenthau also stresses the point that Eichmann's deeds have to be considered in connection with the totalitarian system:

> The evil is not in the deed itself but in the logic, in the persistent consistency of the philosophies underlying the actions. And so Arendt could coin that phrase, which has become a part of the language, "the banality of evil", suggesting there exists no correspondence between the evil done and the evildoer. The evildoer can be a minor figure in a bureaucratic machine believing in the presuppositions of the doctrine. He executes almost mechanically, bureaucratically, the mandates of that doctrine. The evil he commits has its roots of reasoning but not in an evil of intent. (Morgenthau, 129)

We cannot see Arendt's vision on Eichmann apart from her remark in *The Origins of Totalitarianism* that the totalitarian movement mainly consisted of normal, isolated individuals, men in the crowd. Ezorsky says that Arendt's vision on Eichmann fitted in her theory and that is absolutely true. However, she also said that Arendt's portrait of Eichmann was actually contradicting the facts, suggesting that Arendt made Eichmann fit into her theory of the totalitarian movement. (Ezorsky, 79) This seems to me an unkind and incorrect insinuation.

Planning and Deliberation

Rotenstreich brings a number of arguments under discussion, which had to demonstrate that Eichmann's evil couldn't be called banal. Upon closer consideration it appears that all arguments are derived from one basic argument: all his actions were based on planning and deliberation; he was an adult person and therefore this evil cannot be called banal. The question that arises is whether Rotenstreich has understood the exact meaning of Arendt's "banality of evil". When reading his article, one gets the impression that he considered banality a harmless property, but that was not Arendt's intention. Banality is "thoughtlessness", an incapability to think and to judge and above all the incapability to place oneself in someone else's position. In a political system like Nazism, this can be an extremely dangerous property. Rotenstreich also, like many others, mistakenly considers Eichmann as an individual and an autonomously deciding person in the totalitarian system. He does not take into consideration that Eichmann was part of a system, in which he could not make any substantial decision, but only decisions that were in line with the laws of the Third Reich. He hardly recognizes this connection and he completely ignores Bruno Bettelheim's view that it was totalitarianism that stood trial in Jerusalem. The only connection, in Rotenstreich's view, is that Eichmann, as part of the totalitarian system, couldn't be banal because Nazism was not banal, but this is a curious argumentation. Parts do not always determine the whole and vice versa. It is possible to build an architectonic monster from marble or a beautiful building from paving bricks.

The Meaning of the Word "Banality"

The Oxford Dictionary gives the following synonyms of "banality": "commonplace" and "triteness"; Websters Dictionary gives "commonplace", "vulgarity" and "lack of originality". Some dictionaries translate "banal" with "ordinary" or "nothing special" and also "boring" or "dull". It is obvious that Hannah Arendt experienced Eichmann's behavior in this way: it was ordinary, commonplace, nothing special, his language was shallow, he sounded like a cliché, there was no originality in his replies. The way he spoke was "boring" or "dull".

Arendt has "willy-nilly" extended the banality of Eichmann's personality to "the banality of evil". It is understandable that many protested against this description. Eichmann had to be the personification of the devil, but Arendt described him as a mister Average. This description suggests that Eichmann acted in the "usual way", in other words not very different from the way most people would have acted if they had been in his shoes. This interpretation brings Arendt close to the statement that Eichmann's weaknesses, although they were considered crimes, were only human and that everybody probably has an identical potential for evildoing and also that Eichmann was nothing special or extraordinary as a person. In chapter 3 we saw that, according to Kant, there is basically a potential for evildoing in every person: the propensity to evil. Although we all have this propensity, we are also able to suppress it. In other words, the banality of his actions does neither clear Eichmann of the charge, nor does it reduce its importance.

What about "thoughtlessness"? In fact this fits in with banality, for, how many people reflected on their position and their actions during the Nazi-regime? Eichmann adopted ideas and ideologies of others without reflection and without trying to understand them. He did not reflect on the consequences of his actions, but who did in the Third Reich? What made Eichmann unique was his position in the totalitarian machinery, his ambition and his excessive talent for self-deception, but apart from this, he was the norm and not the exception. Arendt confirms this by saying:

> Nothing proved easier to destroy than the privacy and private morality of people who thought of nothing but safeguarding their private lives. (OT 3, 338)

As I have said before, the people involved in the genocide were no sadists, but ordinary, "banal" people, whose only vice was that they had a passion for survival and success. People who had a feeling of responsibility for society and who were interested in the public domain, were transformed into "bourgeois", who only valued private life, without any sense of public responsibility.

Universalisation of Banal Evil

We have seen that Bernstein and Jaspers wonder whether all evil is banal. Jaspers states that Eichmann's banality of evil does not imply that all evil is banal. Bernstein reverses things by saying that banal evil may exist, but that it is questionable whether Eichmann's evil was banal. Is all evil banal or are there other types of evil? I will revert to this question in chapter 6.

It is obvious that Hannah Arendt asked herself after the Eichmann trial what might be the role of thinking in the origin of evil. If she states that Eichmann's crimes are a consequence of his thoughtlessness, she suggests not only that thinking might have a role in the origin of evil, but also that thinking, in one way or another, might prevent evil. This is the main reason for Arendt to go into the subject of the activities of the mind: thinking, willing and judging. The result of her studies can be found in her book *The Life of the Mind,* the subject of the next chapter.

NOTES

1. Chelmno (Kulmhof) is the first camp built solely for the purpose of extermination, established in December 1941 at a site 60 kilometers from Lodz. Approximately 300,000 Jews were killed at Chelmno, primarily by firing squad and by asphyxation in mobile gas vans. (Laqueur, 2001, 115)

2. The extermination camp Auschwitz-Birkenau is only a few miles away from Oswiecim (Auschwitz)

3. Majdanek is situated in a suburb of Lublin, a town of 200,000 inhabitants. The camp was built in 1941 as a concentration camp, but later it was also used as an extermination camp.

4. There was no time to destroy the camp, because of the rapid approach of the Russian army.

Chapter Five

The Life of the Mind

THINKING

Introduction

Hannah Arendt considered the field of the activities of the mind the domain of the "philosophers" or, according to Kant, of the "professional thinkers". Arendt did not consider herself a philosopher, but an expert in political theory. The immediate cause for entering into this domain was Eichmann's "thoughtlessness" and the "banality of evil". This expression was contradictory to the philosophical and theological tradition of the problem of evil. In this tradition, says Arendt, we have learned to consider evil as demonic. The incarnation of evil is Satan. We were told that evil men acted out of envy (Kain, Richard III), out of weakness (Macbeth) or out of pure hatred for the sheer goodness of others (Jago's hate for the Moor and Claggert's hate for the innocence of Billy Budd). In Eichmann's case there was no envy, weakness or hate, but rather the opposite: an incredible shallowness. Eichmann's main characteristic was "thoughtlessness": he was commonplace and totally helpless without routine procedures.

Clichés, stock phrases and conventional attitudes have the function to protect us against reality because reality constantly claims our thinking attention and if we would respond to this claim all the time we would soon be exhausted. Eichmann, however, did not pay attention to reality at all. It is this absence of thinking that struck Arendt during the entire process and this provoked a number of questions. Would ill-nature (in the literal meaning: an ill nature, an evil character) not be a necessary precondition for evil doing? Is thinking in one way or another connected with our ability to distinguish good from evil or right from wrong? The most important question of all is whether the activity of thinking, the habit of examining everything that attracts our attention, makes men abstain from evil doing or "condition" them against it. (LM, I, 5)

In order to answer this question, we must first find an answer to a preceding question: What is thinking? This question was not raised in her book *The Human Condition*. Arendt preferred to call it *Vita Activa*, because the book describes the physical activities of men: acting, work and labour. Thinking does not belong to the "vita activa", but to the "vita contemplative". According to Plato, thinking is a kind of inner dialogue between me and myself. When we think, we open the eyes of the mind. Thinking may be considered as the actualisation of the division between the "I" and the "Self". However, there are other questions such as: "What are we doing when we are thinking?" and "Where are we when we are thinking?" At first sight, these questions seem to belong to the field of "metaphysics", but according to Arendt, "metaphysics" has fallen into discredit. We have done away with the ancient idea that everything that is not phenomenal—like God or Plato's Ideas—would be more real than anything perceptible. We have abolished Plato's "real world", but according to Nietzsche, we have abolished the world of appearances as well, because these two worlds are inseparably connected. The framework that used to form the basis for our thinking does not exist any more. Nevertheless, human ability to think is not lost. We are still thinking beings and we do not only use our ability to think for knowing and doing. (LM, 10–12)

Arendt points out that since ancient times, there has been a distinction between philosophers and "ordinary" people and even to day many philosophers are considered as people who live in their own world. Their world is not the world of appearances, the world of things we see around us, but a world that is only accessible for them. However, says Arendt, if the ability to distinguish right from wrong or good from evil is linked with our ability to think, we may not only expect this from philosophers, but from every "ordinary" person, because all human beings, intelligent or not, are capable of thinking.[1]

Important in this respect is Kant's distinction between "Vernunft" and "Verstand", reason and intelligence. Reason is connected with thinking and meaning; intelligence with knowing and knowledge. Reason is not interested in truth but in meaning and these are not identical. Although Kant made this distinction between thinking and knowing, he never studied the activity of thinking and that is exactly Arendt's purpose.

In the first part of *The Life of the Mind*, Arendt goes extensively into thinking. Her editorial classification is not always systematic and she sometimes mixes questions about thinking with reflections about willing and judging. In this chapter I shall restrict myself to a summary of her ideas on thinking. Remarks on willing and judging are incorporated in the next two chapters. For systematic reasons, I shall use the following questions as a guideline.

- what is thinking and how does it "appear"?
- what is the function of thinking?
- what makes us to think?
- what is the final result of thinking?
- does thinking play a role in the prevention of evil?

What is Thinking and How Does it "Appear"?

Together with willing and judging, thinking belongs to the fundamental activities of the mind. Although they share certain characteristics, such as the absence of physical activity, they are completely different. The necessity to think is, according to Kant, a kind of inner impulse. Thinking is an autonomous activity and characteristic for thinking is its invisibility and inaudibility, not only for the outside world but also for the thinking ego. The thinking person has withdrawn into himself. He enters into a discussion with himself and seems to be in another world. The question is whether thinking can appear or remains hidden from everyone and forever.

All things in this world appear and if something appears and we observe it, we say that it "is". This presupposes an observer: nothing exists unless somebody observes it.

In contrast to the opinion in ancient times, appearances are not any longer considered as "secondary qualities". The world of appearances was supposed to be different from the "real" world behind the appearances. Today it is of more importance how things appear to us, than what things really "are" and the same goes for men: their inner life is less important than their appearance. Man is judged by his deeds, not by his thoughts. This implies that thinking would be useless if the thoughts do not, in one way or another, "appear" to the outside world. The most important instrument for this purpose is language. By means of words we let others know what we think. Words make the invisible "visible" and thus thinking becomes part of the world of appearances. Thinking beings have an urge to speak, because thoughts cannot appear without speaking.

The main problem with words is that they are sometimes inadequate. We all know the expression: "Words fail me", which means that we cannot find the proper words to express our feelings or thoughts. With words we speak in symbols, analogies or metaphors to provide a reality for abstract thoughts. Words try to bridge the gap between the invisible and inaudible and the visible and audible, the gap between thinking and being.

However, besides the fact that words do not always adequately express our thoughts, we have the choice between putting our thoughts into words as precisely as we can and choosing our words in such a way that their meaning differs form our thoughts, in which case we do not say what we think. More-over, human beings have the capacity to manipulate their thoughts and thus to deceive.

"Verscheinung" (appearance) and "Schein" (semblance) play an important part in Kant's writings. Kant also speaks of "Das Ding an Sich" (the thing in itself). The "thing in itself" exists but is not knowable or visible. We only know the thing as it appears to us, mainly as an optical picture The thinking ego may be compared with "the thing in itself": it exists, nobody can perceive it and it only appears to us in words.

Arendt's motive to start her study of the faculty of thinking was the Eich-mann process. It is therefore understandable that for her the most important question is whether the semblances are inauthentic or authentic ones, in other words, whether the semblances are based on dogmatic beliefs (such as the dogma of the Nazi ideology) or inherent to the fact that words are sometimes inadequate to express our thoughts.

What is the Function of Thinking?

Kant has provided the best answer to this question. Kant's expression for thinking is "Vernunft" (reason) to distinguish it from "Verstand" (intelli-gence). Intelligence stands for knowledge and truth, reason for understand-ing. Reason tries to fathom the meaning of our daily observations. However, although Kant said that reason was not suitable for the acquisition of knowl-edge, he could not give up the idea that the ultimate goal of thinking was the acquisition of knowledge and truth. We shall see in one of the following para-graphs that Arendt disagrees with Kant when he says that knowledge could eventually be the result of thinking.

What Makes Us Think?

Many philosophers have tried to answer this question and one of the first to do so was Plato. According to him, thinking is the result of an admiring won-dering about the invisible harmonious order of the cosmos. In this wonder there is no place for disharmony, ugliness and evil. According to Arendt no Platonic dialogue deals with the question of evil[2], but she does mention *Par-menides,* where Plato shows concern for the consequences that the undeniable existence of evil could have for his doctrine of the Ideas. However, it would be absurd to think that there would be Ideas of ugly and evil things. (LM I, 150)

The next philosopher is the Roman Epictetus, who wants to withdraw com-pletely from reality. All that is present becomes absent and reality disappears by pretending that it is nothing but an impression. The applied method is the concentration on the perception of the object and not on the object itself. The object loses its impression on the observer. A tree is no longer a tree, but becomes an impression. This escape from reality can already be found with Cicero. He applied this method of thinking in order to compensate for the frustrations of politics and life itself. (LM I, 160)

The absolute climax of this way of thinking was reached five hundred years later with Boethius. Boethius not only put reality "into perspective", like Cicero and Epictetus, but he made it "disappear" completely. Boethius applied this way of thinking to the question of evil and his argumentation is the following:

God is the final cause of everything, but since he is also "the highest good" he cannot be the cause of evil. Since everything must have a cause, evil does not exist. What about the evil things we see around us? We only think that these things are evil. They are not, because all that exists must be good, since it is created by "the highest good". Evil is an illusion and you can make it disappear by thinking. (LM I, 161)

We may conclude that the Greek answer to the question: "what makes us think", is exactly the opposite of the Roman answer. According to Greek philosophy it is wondering about the harmonious order of the cosmos; for the Romans it is the horror of the fact that men are thrown into a hostile world. On the other hand, there is a similarity between the two answers. In both cases thinking makes men withdraw from the world of appearances. It is an escape from reality. Moreover, while thinking, one is not conscious of the body and the self. The theories of the Greeks and the Romans about the power of mind over body are contradictory to our daily experience. According to Arendt, the reason why these theories are unrealistic is that philosophers have given the answer to the question what make us think. Philosophers separate the question from the facts of everyday life and consequently they come up with vague and general answers, which are totally unpractical. It is better to put the question to a practical instead of a professional thinker and this leads Arendt to Socrates.

Although Socrates can be found in every book on philosophy, he is, according to Arendt, not a philosopher because he never developed concepts or theories and he never put anything on paper. He asked questions, but never gave an answer, because he had no answers. His dialogues are aporetic, which means that they have no conclusions. One of the questions he asked himself was what was the use of thinking, but he had no answer to this question either. He used the wind as a metaphor for thinking: it is invisible, but nevertheless we can perceive it. Thinking is part of life and as such it is a continuous quest for meaning. For Socrates thinking is Eros, a longing for wisdom and understanding, a kind of desirous love and therefore only lovable things can be the objects of thought. Evil is excluded from thinking because it is considered as the absence of good. Evil does not exist in itself; it has no roots of its own and therefore Socrates could not accept that somebody would do evil on purpose.[3] Arendt concludes that, according to Socrates, the connection between thinking and evil is: people who are not interested in beauty, justice and wisdom are incapable of thinking and those who can think cannot do evil.

What is the Result of Thinking?

There is a persisting misconception, says Arendt, that thinking and the quest for meaning would finally provide us with specific concepts. Thinking does not result in a concept that survives the activity of thinking. Does this mean that thinking does not provide us with concepts at all? Arendt's answer is that thinking questions the correctness of all concepts and is comparable with the result of Penelope's weaving: what was woven during the day was undone in the night. It looks as if thinking is a useless activity but that is not the case. If we were unable to think we would be robots or sleepwalkers.

According to Socrates, thinking is like flute playing, which means that it has an end in itself and that it does not leave a lasting result. On the contrary, thinking has a destructive, undermining effect on "frozen thoughts" and on all established criteria, values and moral rules. Thinking unsettles all our certainties.

Thinking also has disadvantages, as it constantly asks for meaning. Doctrines, values and convictions are analyzed by the thinking ego. If these values, convictions and norms loose their validity, they are replaced by other, sometimes contradictory and even negative values and convictions. The danger is in man's desire to find ultimate convictions that make thinking superfluous. Thinking is also dangerous for any religious conviction, because it does not supply a new creed. However, the greatest danger of thinking is, that what seems to be a meaningful thought often turns out to be meaningless the moment one wants to apply it to daily life. Thinking often provides nonpractical ideas and convictions, which means that it is often unavoidable to take up a new standpoint.

All these disadvantages provoke the question whether it would not be better not to think at all. However, non-thinking is much more dangerous, because this means that people stick to the accepted and established rules, concepts and values of a particular society, without ever thinking about their meaning. This may be not dangerous in itself but non-thinking persons can easily be persuaded to accept new morals or ethics and, according to Arendt, for many non-thinking people this is no more difficult than changing their table manners.

The ease with which such a reversal can take place under certain conditions suggests that everybody was fast asleep when it occurred. (LM I, 177)

Arendt alludes to what happened in Nazi-Germany. The commandment "Thou shalt not kill" was in no time reversed to "Thou shalt kill".[4]

Does Thinking Play a Role in the Prevention of Evil?

We have seen that Plato ignores evil. It is no subject for the thinking ego. sand, the Romans simply make evil disappear by thinking about it. Both theories are unacceptable for Arendt.

Socrates says that only people who are interested in beauty, justice and wisdom are able to think. If that is the case, it seems logical to state that people who think can never do evil, because thinking people are not interested in evil. However, we have seen that, according to Arendt, all people are able to think, whether they are intelligent or not, because thinking is an autonomous function. Also Socrates, who constantly entered into discussions with many different people, must have taken for granted that everybody was able to think, in the sense of "having an inner dialogue with oneself". If evil is no subject for thinking people, the conclusion must be that if there is something in thinking that prevents people from evil-doing, it must be in the activity of thinking itself and not in the objects of thought.

Socrates had no concepts, theories or answers to questions. He restricted himself to questioning and let people draw their own conclusions. There are only two exceptions: he made two positive statements. The first statement was that it would be better to be wronged than to do wrong. The second was that he would prefer people disagreeing with him to contradicting himself. (LM I, 181) What is the meaning of these two statements?

When thinking, we split ourselves up into two persons, who start a dialogue like a dialogue between two individuals. These two imaginary persons may have different or even contradictory opinions, but the ultimate goal of the inner discussion is that the two come to an agreement. They must end up as friends and not as enemies. This is why it is better to be wronged than to do wrong, because one can be a friend of a victim, but it is much more difficult to be a friend of an evildoer. Who wants to be a friend of a murderer, says Arendt, not even another murderer!

In the *Nicomachean Ethics* Aristotle writes something similar. When speaking about friendship he says that "your friend is another self", which indicates that you can have a dialogue with a friend as with your self, because the self is also a friend. He also says that inferior people are "at variance with themselves" and that wicked people "do not rejoice or grieve with themselves; for their soul is rent by faction". (Aristotle, 228–229 [1166]

Arendt illustrates this with the following passage from Shakespeare's *Richard III*:

> What do I fear? Myself? There's none else by;
> Richard loves Richard: that is I am I.
> Is there a murderer here? No, Yes I am:
> Then fly: what from myself? Great reason why:
> Lest I revenge. What! Myself upon myself?
> Alack! I love myself. Wherefore? For any good
> That I myself have done unto myself
> O! no: alas! I rather hate myself
> For hateful deeds committed by myself.
> I am a villain. Yet I lie, I am not.
> Fools, of thyself speak well: fool do not flatter.
> (Shakespeare, 617)

The subject of this extract is conscience. Conscience is the "name" of the other person in the inner dialogue of thinking. Conscience is related to consciousness. For a long time the English language used one word for the two concepts and in some languages there is still one word, like in French the word "conscience". Consciousness makes us aware of something while conscience has a moral and legal connotation because it tells us in a very general way what to do and more precisely what not to do.

For religious people conscience is the inner voice of God and for non-believers it is Kant's inner moral law. Conscience or the moral law is always present just like consciousness, but there are people who do not listen to their conscience and in that case there is no inner discussion. In other words: they do not think. They couldn't care less whether they contradict themselves or not and consequently they do not want to be responsible for their deeds. They can commit crimes because they are capable of forgetting them the next day. Wicked people do not regret their deeds, says Arendt.

Thinking, we have learned, is an ability of all human beings. Nevertheless, says Arendt, we all have the possibility not to make use of this ability and some people do this. However, if thinking is an autonomic function, how is it possible not to think? The answer is that there are two ways of thinking. The first is what Arendt calls non-cognitive or non-specialized thinking. Perhaps we can call it "free-floating" thoughts: we become aware of things around us, but everything remains superficial. It is a well-known phenomenon in long distance runners. One is aware of the surroundings but one does not think about them specifically. This non-cognitive thinking is an ever-present faculty in all people, runners and non-runners.[5] Cognitive or specific thinking is also an ever-present faculty but people have the possibility not to make use of it. It is not true that this is only the case in less intelligent people; it is a possibility for everybody, intelligent and well-educated people not excluded.

It is possible for people to lead a life without cognitive thinking but it is meaningless. Arendt compares these people to sleepwalkers. They let themselves be led by others without thinking and that is especially dangerous in the case of a political crisis. People who think about the situation attract the attention because they do not unthinkingly follow others. In these situations, says Arendt, the purging component of thinking is political by implication because the consequences of inadequate existing values, theories and convictions are demonstrated and destroyed. Destroying existing values and convictions has a liberating effect on the most political mental capacity of human beings: judging. It is the faculty that assesses specific situations without fitting them in general rules. (LM I, 192)

Let us now have another look at Shakespeare's Richard III, who was incapable of loving and therefore was to become a crook that does not live in harmony with himself. The reason why Richard III could not bear to be alone with himself is fear. It is impossible for him to start a dialogue with himself, because he is not his own friend. On the contrary, he is his own enemy and fears himself.

I think Shakespeare's Richard III and Adolf Eichmann and many others in the Third Reich are comparable because they all feared the inner dialogue and thus their conscience. They were all "thoughtless" in the sense of cognitive thinking and consequently they were unable to judge, which created the conditions for doing evil.

Summarizing: Thinking may be regarded as the silent dialogue between me and myself, or in other words between me and my conscience. It is an inner impulse, an autonomous function and part of life. Nevertheless, we may choose not to think i.e. to refrain from cognitive thinking. The products of thinking, thoughts, are invisible, but they can be made "visible" to others by means of language. The function of thinking is to understand the meaning of all the things we see around us. Thinking does not provide us with concepts, convictions or theories. On the contrary, thinking has a destructive effect on existing values and convictions, but it has a liberating effect on another mental capacity: judging; according to Arendt the most political mental function. Without thinking we are unable to judge and it becomes simple to exchange existing values for others under the influence of malicious agitators. Thinking may play a role in the prevention of evil, not in a direct manner but indirectly, because thinking is the condition for judging, the ability to distinguish beauty from ugliness, right from wrong and good from evil. If there is any faculty that can prevent evil, it must be judging.

I shall go back to judging in a later paragraph, but first I shall focus on the second part of Arendt's book: "Willing".

WILLING

Introduction

An interesting and important difference between thinking and willing is the time factor. According to Arendt thinking is always "out of order", which means that it interrupts our daily activities. Thinking takes place in the present, but willing is the mental faculty for the future. Willing is related to events to come, events that have not yet taken place and have never occurred before. It is also connected with our plans and projects for the future, a future that is basically undetermined.

The necessary condition for existence of the will is that it is free, because an unfree will is a contradiction. A free will implies that all our plans for the future are contingent, because if we accept that our will is free we have the choice between carrying out our plans or not.

The Greeks, Aristotle in particular, were convinced of the fact that the future was nothing more than a result of the past. However, if the past determines the future, a free will is useless and therefore a free will was unknown to the Greeks. The notion of "freedom" had a limited meaning for the Greeks, because it only indicated that one was free to go from one place to another. Freedom meant in fact freedom of movement. Only in the first century, Paul discovered the free will and freedom of action. This indicates that the origin of the free will is in theology and not in philosophy.

In modern times the interest in free will as a mental capacity to determine the future has increased enormously as a result of our belief in progress and a "makable" world.[6] Nevertheless, philosophers have always had their doubts about the existence of a free will. They have a number of arguments for their objections.

– The existence of a free will is an illusion. The future is determined by causality and hence by the past.

– There is not necessarily a connection between the will and freedom.

– A free will implies contingency and that is inconsistent with the laws of all-embracing universal philosophical systems.

– A free will implies that man is capable of starting something new, while tradition only knew freedom of choice between two established possibilities, the so-called "liberum arbitrium".[7]

These four objections led Arendt to the supposition that philosophers, or as she used to call them "professional thinkers", preferred necessity to freedom.

Moreover, their suspicion against the free will was enhanced by the fact that evil is closely related to the existence of a free will.[8]

In the chapters on Kant and on Thinking I said a few words about the manner in which the classical philosophers tried to explain the existence of evil. What follows is a more extensive historical, although not chronological, review.

Ontological dualism of good and evil (Mani); evil as a deficiency of the good (Augustine); evil as a disturbance of the original harmony (stoa; Leibnitz); evil as an optical illusion (Boethius); evil not caused by God, but allowed for testing mankind (St. Thomas Aquinas); evil as a consequence of human anthropology which leads to unavoidable rivalry and class struggle (Hobbes); evil as God's punishment for disbelief and finally evil and suffering as a punishment for sinning. (Houtepen, 95) The idea of the existence of a free will and the possibility for men to do evil is in contradiction with all these theories.

How is the relation between thinking and willing? It seems that willing and thinking are antagonists. Arendt gives five essential differences between these two mental faculties.

– Thinking concerns the present or the past, while willing is only directed towards the future.

– Thinking is an end in itself, but willing is not satisfied with willing itself. Willing is looking forward to the end of willing when it results in action.

– Willing is related to action; thinking to rest and silence.

– Thinking often concerns memories and events of the past, which we cannot change; willing looks ahead to things that we would like to change without knowing if our ideas can be realized.

– Thinking and willing both happen in their own frame of mind: serenity when thinking; tension when willing.

The editorial set-up of "Willing" is totally different from "Thinking". In "Thinking", Arendt emphasizes the analysis of thinking; in "Willing" she describes the historical development of the will. Because of this difference and the very nature of willing, this subject cannot be approached in the same way as thinking. I shall first give a summary of the history of the will and then try to answer the question of the role of willing in the prevention of evil.

The Historical Development of the Will

Many centuries after the moment that man became conscious of his capacity to think, he became aware of his free will. An important question is whether man is capable of developing new mental capacities and if so, why this happens. In order to answer these questions Arendt started a historical investigation into the origin and development of the will. She reviewed the ideas of a number of philosophers and theologians about the will.

According to Aristotle action, in the sense of how people want to be and to appear, requires a kind of mental exercise. He called it "proairesis", which means making a choice between two or more alternatives. Desire and reason are often in conflict and the decision is a question of preference and deliberate choice. Proairesis, the possibility to make a choice, may be considered as the precursor of the will. However, the space for freedom of choice is extremely limited and in fact we talk about the means to an end that has already been determined and cannot be chosen. The Latin word for the possibility to choose between two or more alternatives is liberum arbitrium, a kind of referee who makes the final decision but who is unable to start something new. Proairesis and liberum arbitrium are therefore no autonomous faculties, determined by their own nature and obeying their own laws. (LM II, 55–63)

The apostle Paul says that complying with God's law does not always come naturally, because the will to comply with the Law provokes a counter-will. In fact Paul does not speak of two wills but of two contradicting laws: the law of the mind and the law of the body. God's Law demands voluntary obedience and this led to the discovery of the will. It is the will that decides whether man obeys the Law or not. None of the classic peoples—Jews, Greeks and Romans—were aware of this possibility of choice. The will is split up in a will that wants the good and a counter-will that has evil in mind. These two equal opponents start an inner fight and the winner decides what kind of action will be taken. However, the fight never comes to a definitive end. If the will to obey the Divine Law is the victor, the counter-will continues to protest and he who decides not to obey the Law will always keep the desire to obey God's Law. The will is impotent, says Paul, because the will hinders itself. (LM II, 63–70)

The Roman Epictetus was a contemporary of Paul. He agreed that the will provoked a counter-will but his opinion about the nature of the will was the opposite of Paul's. He regarded the will not as impotent but as supreme. The will is the mental faculty that commands and everything is subordinate to the will, reason included. The will cannot change the factual world, but the will is able to reproduce the real world in another phenomenon, deprived of its reality.[9] On a mental level the will is supreme, but in the real world it remains impotent.

With Augustine there is a breaking point in thinking about the will. For the first time in philosophical history we see a glimpse of something that looks like Kant's free will. Liberum arbitrium is partly replaced by a relatively free will. In Augustine's works the will is related to the fact that man is something special. Man comes into the world as a new beginning, but this beginning is also the beginning of the end. Contrary to animals, man is conscious of the fact that his life is limited. Therefore, animals only have a physiological, but no mental beginning and end. Because man is a being that consciously lives toward the end of his life, God endows him with a will. This is also in accordance with the fact that man was created after God's image. However, since man is only temporary and not eternal like God, his will is only directed towards the future. If Augustine had drawn the full consequence of his theory, says Arendt, his definition of the will would not have been based on the liberum arbitrium, but it would have been almost similar to Kant's free will. This is not the case because Augustine positions the freedom of the will between the opinions of the Greeks and Kant. Augustine's will is only relatively free: the will can only influence the causality, which means the sequence of events, but the will is incapable of starting something new, because this property would make man more powerful than God. According to secular thinkers like Arendt and Kant, starting something new is possible, because a free will, resulting in freedom and spontaneity is part of the human condition. (LM II, 110)

Thomas Aquinas lived eight hundred years after Augustine and his idea of the will is quite different from Augustine's. He is not specifically interested in the will as a separate mental power, but rather in the connection between reason and intellect on the one hand and the will on the other. The most important question for him was which of the two has the primacy and hence is the most important. Thomas is an adept of Aristotle's concepts so it is not surprising that he follows the *Nicomachean Ethics*. Important in Aristotle's theory is the end and the means to achieve it. The end is apprehended by the intellect. After determination of the end follows deliberation about the means and finally there is the desire for the means. (LM II, 117) The will is a kind of superior appetite that must eliminate all lower appetites. Is Thomas' will a free will? The answer is: yes and no. The will is free in so far that it is free in the choice of the relevant means to the determined end. This means that with Thomas there is still a liberum arbitrium. In contradiction to Augustine, Thomas considers the intellect to be superior to the will and this may be explained by considering the ultimate question: what does man's last end and happiness exist of? For Augustine the answer to this question was: the love for God and this love can be obtained by the will; for Thomas the ultimate happiness was to know God by means of the intellect.

The step from Thomas Aquinas to Duns Scotus is only one generation, but his conception about the will was totally contradictory to Thomas' view. Thomas said that the will was an executive capacity of the intellect, whereas Duns Scotus asserted that the intellect was subordinate to the will. The intellect supplies the will with knowledge and ends. A remarkable and possibly necessary consequence of this is that Duns Scotus' will is free. He clearly distinguishes the liberum arbitrium, which can only select means to an already existing end, from his own will, because Duns Scotus' will is free to choose ends for their own sake. (LM II, 132) The consequence of a free will is contingency, but surprisingly enough, Duns Scotus believed in contingency. For Duns Scotus there was nothing wrong with contingency, contrary to many other philosophers, who were of the opinion that contingency conflicted with the laws of causality.

> By contingent, said Scotus, I do not mean something that is not necessary or which was not always in existence, but something whose opposite could have occurred at the time that this actually did. That is why I do not say that something is contingent, but that something is *caused contingently.* (LM II, 138)

This is of course grist to the mill of Hannah Arendt, as it is the causal element in human affairs that makes them contingent and unpredictable. Arendt points to the fact that the two world wars have, over and over again, been explained by causality. Every theory uses another cause as a starting point for its elaborations, though it is much more plausible that the two wars were the result of accidentally coinciding factors.

In her journey through the history of the will, Arendt makes a jump of many centuries from Duns Scotus to Nietzsche. Nietzsche paid a lot of attention to the will. According to him there is a continuous battle between a "willing I" and a "resisting I". The will derives its power from this battle: if there was no resistance the will would be powerless. The "willing I" tells the "resisting I" what has to be done or in other words, the "willing I" commands and the "resisting I" obeys in the end and does as it is told. To be conscious of the superiority of a "willing I" over a "non-willing I" that must obey, means that Nietzsche's will is free. Nietzsche's remark that the will can never "will backwards" is very important. This seems obvious, but it had never been said before. In fact Nietzsche says: I should like to make things of the past undone, but I can't. The will is incapable of changing or removing events of the past and according to Arendt our legal punishments are based on this incapability. Therefore, in a way, the will is impotent and Nietzsche's explanation of the nature of evil is based on this impotency. There is sometimes resentment and frustration about the past, as well as feelings of revenge and destruction. However, since the past cannot be destroyed and the current situation always incorporates a past, our destructive feelings are directed towards the present.[10] (LM II, 178)

One of the important philosophers who are missing in the historical review of the will is Kant. According to Arendt Kant does not fit in the review because Kant did not consider the will as a separate mental faculty, but rather as a part of thinking. Kant's willing is practical reason and he calls it "Vernunftwille" (the will of reason). Kant's will is nothing more than the executor of the decisions of practical reason.[11]

In general, philosophers are suspicious with regard to a free will, because a free will implies contingency and this unsettles all philosophical concepts. Philosophers, says Arendt, have discussed the philosophy of the will, and philosophers are professional thinkers and no actors. Philosophers interpret the world, but, with some exceptions, they do not want to change it.[12] They find systematic necessity more appealing than the freedom to start something new. However, changing the world can only be done by acting, by starting something new spontaneously. Philosophers have considered the will as the "principium individuationis", the source of the specific individual character of each person. This individualisation is the cause of the problem of the freedom of the will, i.e. the idea that everyone differs from everyone else and is therefore capable of acting individually and is also individually responsible for his actions. This shakes man's belief in necessity, resulting in the alarming realisation that the world is not as it ought to be. Contingency is the price of a free will and for some this price is too high.

For people who want to change the world, willing is inextricably bound up with freedom of action and this takes us from philosophical freedom to political freedom. Philosophical freedom is only relevant for hermits. However, citizens are no hermits. They live in political structures, in communities with laws that restrict freedom. In general citizens possess restricted political freedom, which enables them to start something new. Political freedom has to do with plurality. If we use our freedom to change the world we must cooperate with others. Only by cooperation can we create something new, but there is an abyss between the old situation and the new one. The end of the old political order is not automatically the beginning of a new order. There is no continuity but there is a gap between the two.

Arendt refers to the American Revolution. The founders of the republic, the Founding Fathers, were well aware of the difference between liberation of oppression and constitutional freedom and the hiatus between them. The Founding Fathers could only bridge this gap with the conviction that the new order would be better than the old one. Arendt compares this to the birth of a new human being and not to creativity. Human beings are born and not created and therefore a new baby is free, whether he or she likes it or not. Making use of our freedom may cause problems, but in that case there is another mental faculty that can help us: judging. Judging is the faculty that helps us make a difference between things we like and things we dislike.

Does Willing Play a Role in the Prevention of Evil?

Philosophical freedom, the freedom of the will, has nothing to do with action and has therefore no political significance. Since we deal with political evil we can disregard philosophical freedom. Political freedom is connected with freedom of action, the possibility to start something new, which may result in a fresh turn of history. Political freedom, the will to change the world, is restricted by our dependence on others, which limits our freedom of action and therefore political freedom is closer to "I can" than to "I want to". Moreover, the will itself does not decide what must be done. The will is not involved in decision-making, but in creating the possibilities for acting. It is the spontaneity of acting that enables men to start something new and give history a new direction that was not pre-determined. Our conclusion must be that the will itself is of limited significance in the prevention of political evil.

If both thinking and willing only play a subordinate role in the prevention of evil, there is only one mental function left that might play a role: judging.

JUDGING

Introduction

Unfortunately, Arendt did not live long enough to write the third part, about judging, of *The Life of the Mind*. Nevertheless, her *Lectures on Kant's Political Philosophy*, which were published after her death, give us a fairly clear idea of the possible contents of the book. These lectures were based on Kant's *Kritik der Urteilskraft (Critique of Judgment)*. Arendt considered these lectures as "Kant's unwritten political philosophy". I shall not go into the question whether this remark is correct or not, but it is a fact that the Kant lectures give a good insight in Arendt's understanding of judging. In her book *Between Past and Future* and particularly in her essay "The Crisis in Culture" Arendt elaborates on certain parts of her Kant lectures.

We have seen that thinking is the inner dialogue between the "I" and the "Self" or between the "I" and the conscience. It is important that these two remain friends and do not contradict each other. Thinking does not provide results in the form of theories or concepts, but it has a liberating effect on the faculty of judging. Arendt summarizes this faculty as follows:

> The faculty of judging particulars (as Kant discovered it), the ability to say, "this is wrong", "this is beautiful", is not the same as the faculty of thinking. Thinking deals with invisibles, with representations of things that are absent; judging always concerns particulars and things close at hand. But the two are interrelated in a way similar to the way consciousness and conscience are interconnected. If thinking, the two-in-one of the soundless dialogue, actualizes the difference within our identity as given in consciousness and thereby results in conscience, then judging, the by-product of the liberating effect of thinking, re-

alizes thinking, makes it manifest in the world of appearances, where I am never alone and always much too busy to be able to think. The manifestation of the wind of thought is no knowledge; it is the ability to tell right from wrong, beautiful from ugly. And this indeed may prevent catastrophes, at least for myself, in the rare moments when the chips are down. (TM, 446)

In a lecture in the United States in 1973, during a congress of the American Society for Christian Ethics, she gave a further explanation of her interest in Kant's *Kritik der Urteilskraft (Critique of Judgment)*.

> . . . And once you are empty in a way, which is difficult to say, you are prepared to judge. That is without having any book of rules under which you can subsume a particular case, you have got to say "this is good", "this is bad", "this is right", "this is wrong", "this is beautiful" and "this is ugly". And the reason why I believe so much in Kant's Critique of Judgment is not because I am interested in aesthetics, but because I believe that the way in which we say "this is right, that is wrong", is not very different from "this is beautiful, this is ugly". (YB, 452)

What is Judging and How Does it Become Visible?

Kant makes a difference between determinant and reflective judgments. Determinant judgments subsume particulars under given universals. The universals are rules, principles or laws. These determinant judgments also play an important role in practical reason. Individual actions are subsumed under and determined by the categorical imperative. Reflective judgments differ from determinant judgments. Here the particular is given and it has to be decided to which universal it belongs. Aesthetical judgment of a work of art is an example of a reflective judgment.

In her lectures on Kant's Critique of Judgment, Arendt does not differentiate between determinant and reflective judgments. She usually speaks of "judgment" and sometimes about "reflective judgments" or "aesthetical judgments". She makes the following remark about this:

> Judgment is no practical reason; practical reason "reasons" and tells me what to do and what not to do; it lays down the law and is identical with the will, and the will utters commands; it speaks in imperatives. Judgment, on the contrary, arises from "a merely contemplative pleasure or inactive delight". (LK, 15)

We may conclude from this that Arendt situates judging in the contemplative sphere and that it does not belong to the actor. Kant's Critique of Judgment is a discussion on reflective judgments. Contrary to the faculty of thinking, the purpose of reflective judging is not to be in harmony with oneself, but rather to keep one's own interest, concern or point of view at a distance and to consider everything from a universal, impartial position. Taking the viewpoints of others into account and putting ourselves in the place of the other man contributes to the impartiality. Kant speaks of "eine erweiterte Denkungsart" (enlarged thought). (KU, par. 40, 146, [159])

Reflective judgment is a reflection on human affairs. Man must be capable of taking up a general point of view.

> This general viewpoint is closely connected with particulars, with the particular conditions of the standpoints one has to go through in order to arrive at one's own "general standpoint". (LK, 44)

One could say that someone who reflects upon a particular event imagines how others would judge this. Modifying one's own judgment with the help of as many other judgments as possible, one can finally arrive at an "impartial" judgment.

This general point of view or judgment is the standpoint of the spectator. For Kant, the spectator exclusively determines the significance of an event. It is absolutely necessary that the spectators' judgment is proclaimed openly. According to Kant, the spectators' reactions are an indication for the morals of the nation. This surprising role of the spectator is, according to Arendt, not originally Kant's idea. It is an old philosophical view that the significance and importance of an event can only be seen by those who refrain from action. The actor can never have an impartial judgment, because he is by definition partial and moreover the actor strives for honour and sometimes for power. However, the actor must know the opinion of the spectators, because the success of his actions depends on it. The actor is not autonomous, he does not listen to the voice of reason, but he acts,

> . . . in accordance with what spectators would expect of him. The standard is the spectator. And this standard is autonomous. (LK, 55)

A good example is the French Revolution. Arendt concludes from Kant's remarks on the French Revolution that,

> . . . what counted in the French Revolution, what made it a world-historical event, a phenomenon not to be forgotten, were not the deeds and misdeeds of the actors, but the opinions, the enthusiastic approbation, of spectators, of persons who themselves were not involved.[13] (LK. 65)

Kant said that he only understood man's capacity of judgment after his study of the taste. His conclusion was that judging could be derived from taste and he had two arguments for this conclusion. His first argument was that only taste and smell observe the particular as particular, whereas all objects presenting themselves to the objective senses share their properties with other objects, in other words, they are not unique. His second argument is that in taste the feeling of "it pleases me" or "it displeases me" is overwhelmingly present. (LK, 66)

However, it has always been said that taste is beyond the domain of politics and reason. The reason is obvious: taste is arbitrary and extremely subjective, because there can be no dispute about taste (de gustibus non disputandum est) and this is, without a doubt, true for certain private feelings. The disadvantage of taste is that it is very difficult to communicate with others about it. This problem can be solved by transforming private taste, feelings or judgments into a general judgment and for this transformation man has two additional capacities: imagination and reflection.

Imagination is men's capacity to give presence to what is absent. We are able to call up acquired impressions by means of imagination. We can think about these imaginations or representations of impressions and this is the operation of reflection. Reflection is the real judgment on situations, events and impressions.

> Only what touches, affects one in representation, when one can no longer be affected by immediate presence—when one is uninvolved, like the spectator who was uninvolved in the actual doings of the French Revolution—can be judged to be right or wrong, important or irrelevant, beautiful or ugly, or something in between. One then speaks of judgment and no longer of taste, though it still affects one like a matter of taste, one now has, by means of representation, established the proper distance, the remoteness or uninvolvedness or disinterestedness, that is requisite for approbation, for evaluating something at its proper worth. By removing the object, one has established the conditions for impartiality (LK, 67)

Representation and reflection make judgment impartial. By closing our eyes and looking with the eyes of the mind, we are able to see the totality, which gives the particular its meaning. This capacity to judge enables man to get an understanding of things from the perspective of others and to orient himself towards the public domain and the common world, an understanding that was already known to the Greeks. It was called "phronesis" and they considered this capacity the most important virtue of a statesman, as wisdom was for the philosopher.

The question is what we can do with our judgment. What is the criterion of reflection? The answer is that generally we want to tell others about our judgment. We want to bring our judgment out into the open. Thus, the criterion is communicability and the way to put this to the test is by using a third capacity of man: sensus communis or common sense. The sensus communis explains the political importance of reflective judgment. Sensus communis is a kind of sixth sense that incorporates us into the community; it is a specifically human quality because the most important communicative instrument of men, language, depends on it. Kant says the following about the sensus communis:

> However, by the name sensus communis is to be understood, the idea of a public sense, i. e., a critical faculty which in its reflective act takes account (a priori) of the mode of representation of everyone else, in order, as it were, to weigh its judgment with the collective reason of mankind. . . This is accomplished by weighing the judgment, not so much with actual, as rather with the merely possible judgment of others, and by putting ourselves in the position of everyone else, as the result of a mere abstraction from the limitations, which contingently affect our own estimate. . . Now it seems that this operation of reflection is too artificial to be attributed to the faculty which we call common sense. But this is an appearance due only to its expression in abstract formulae. In itself nothing is more natural than to abstract from charm and emotion where one is looking for a judgment intended to serve as a universal rule. (KU, 40, 214 [157])

The importance of the sensus communis becomes obvious in Hannah Arendt's description hereunder:

> Common sense—which the French so suggestively call the "good sense", *le bon sens*—discloses to us the nature of the world insofar as it is a common world; we owe to it the fact that our strictly private and "subjective" five senses and their sensory data can adjust themselves to a nonsubjective and "objective" world which we have in common and share with others. (BPF, 221)

About the maxims of the sensus communis, Kant says the following:

> While the following maxims of common human understanding do not properly come in here as constituent parts of the critique of taste, they may still serve to elucidate its fundamental propositions. They are these: 1. thinking for yourself; 2. thinking from the standpoint of others; 3. thinking consistently. The first is the maxim of unprejudiced thought; the second that of enlarged thought and the third that of consistent thought. (KU, 40, 214–215 [158])

As mentioned earlier, the purpose of "enlarged thought" is not to remain friends with yourself, but rather to remain friends with the opinions of others. It is an imaginary dialogue between "me" and "the others". One must try to come to an agreement with the others, free from subjective feelings. The final judgment should transcend our own subjective opinions. It is of course impossible to incorporate the opinions of all other people and therefore the final judgment can never possess a universal validity. It remains restricted to the opinions of those others, in whose place the judging person has put himself. According to Kant, it is the only way to communicate with each other. If we do not try to understand the opinion of others, we shall never make contact with others and we shall never be able to speak in a manner that is understandable for others.

Because of our capacity of thinking from the standpoint of others, reflective judgment is, according to Arendt, the most political faculty of man. Political thinking is representative thinking. Arendt explains why reflective judgment is so important for the public domain. Judgments based on taste have in common with political judgments that they can convince people. The judging person can urge others to arrive at the same judgment by means of persuasion only. The Greeks applied this method in politics. Persuasion was the weapon for the citizen in the polis to change the judgment of others and persuasion was preferred to violence. This judgment is always somewhat subjective, although we try to make it as objective as possible and this decision

> . . . also derives from the fact that the world itself is an objective datum, something common to all its inhabitants. The activity of taste decides how this world, independent of its utility and our vital interests in it, is to look and sound, what men will see and what they will hear in it. (BPF, 222)

It is obvious that, in order to persuade others of the correctness of his judgment, the spectator must make his judgment knowable to others. Therefore Arendt says:

> The importance of the occurrence (Begebenheit) is for him [Kant] exclusively in the eye of the beholder, in the opinion of the onlookers, who proclaim their attitude in public. Their reaction to the event proves the "moral character" of mankind. Without this sympathetic participation, the "meaning" of the occurrence would be altogether different or simply nonexistent. (LK, 46)

Arendt emphasizes the importance of the capacity of judgment of the spectators. It seems that the spectator is even more important than the actor. This does not do justice to political action and the political actor, says Hans Achterhuis, while both were praised in her book *The Human Condition.* (Achterhuis, 99) In her essay "The Crisis in Culture" she tries to combine the actor and the spectator, acting and judging.

> Culture and politics, then, belong together because it is not knowledge or truth that is at stake, but rather judgment and decision, the judicious exchange of opinion about the sphere of public life and the common world, and the decision what manner of action is to be taken in it, as well as how it is to look henceforth, what kind of things are to appear. (BPF, 223)

Although Arendt combines political action and judgment, she does not solve the problem. A certain tension between actor and spectator remains. I will refer to this in my reflection on thinking, acting and judging in the Third Reich in chapter six.

Criticism of Arendt's Theory of Judgment

Arendt's theory of judgment was the subject of discussion much more frequently than her reflections on thinking and willing. Arendt's interpretation of Kant's *Critique of Judgment* contains so many contradictory elements, that criticism and discussions were inevitable. It is quite possible that part of the discussions would not have taken place if Arendt had lived long enough to finish the third part of *The Life of the Mind.* The Kant lectures are in fact no more than a reflection on and an interpretation of Kant's aesthetical judgment. Her own ideas about the capacity of judgment were never expressed clearly. We presume that, if she had written the part on judgment, this part would have fitted in with the other two and with her other work and that many of the contradictory or supposedly contradictory elements would not have appeared.

In an additional explanatory essay about Arendt's lectures on Kant's political philosophy Ronald Beiner compares Arendt's view with Aristotle's theory on judging and he points out a number of problems and questions. (Beiner, 131–144) The most important question is whether judging belongs to the actor, to the spectator, or to both. Other matters of discussion are the absence of wisdom and perception in judging, the purpose of judging, the role of rhetoric in the political judgment, the fact that Arendt's judgment is noncognitive and finally the reliability of reflective judgments.

All these questions are the consequence of the fact that Arendt transforms Kant's theory of aesthetical judgment into a theory of political judgment. In doing so she runs the risk of exchanging a value judgment on political events for an unfounded aesthetical judgment. In this respect it might have been preferable if she had used Aristotle as a basis for a theory on political judgment, because he connects judging with the purpose of political deliberation, rhetoric and community.

Beiner presumes that Arendt did not look for a political judgment in Kant's theory but for a theory about judging in general. She was looking for one faculty of judgment that could be used in all situations—in political events, when judging a work of art or describing a historical event—and not for a separate faculty of political judgment. It is always a matter of "it pleases me" or "it displeases me".

This is contradictory to the statement in her essay "The Crisis in Culture", where she said that the capacity of judging is a specifically political property.

(BPF, 221) This essay also gives the impression that judgment is a capacity that belongs to political deliberation and political action, thus to the actor. In chapter six, I shall demonstrate that this is also a problem in her description of Eichmann's behaviour.

One of the most important questions is whether judging belongs to the vita activa (the actor) or to the vita contemplativa (the spectator). On the one hand it belongs to the vita activa, as a function of representative thinking of political actors, on the other hand judging takes place in the vita contemplativa of the spectator. Arendt seems to have given preference to this last concept, although judging is more or less stuck between the actor and the spectator, which makes her concept of judging rather narrow.

In this connection Beiner wonders why Arendt chose Kant for her concept and not Aristotle. Arendt agrees that Aristotle offers an alternative theory for judging. (BPF, 221) Her preference for Kant could be explained by her conception that politics is a matter of judging about phenomena and not about ends. This is one of her most important reasons for relating political judgment to Kant's aesthetical judgment. Her interpretation of Kant is a very personal one and she uses Kant's texts to clarify her own ideas. Karl Jaspers made the following remark about this:

> There are two kinds of Kantians: those who settle forever in the framework of his categories and those who, after reflecting continue on the way with Kant. (Jaspers, 1962, 152)

However, Beiner has another explanation for Arendt's choice of Kant. He refers to the only passage in *The Human Condition* that refers to judging.

> Where human pride is still intact, it is tragedy rather than absurdity, which is taken to the hallmark of human existence. Its greatest representative is Kant, to whom the spontaneity of acting, and the concomitant faculties of practical reason, including force of judgment, remain the outstanding qualities of man, even though his action falls into the determinism of natural laws and his judgment cannot penetrate the secret of absolute reality (the Ding an Sich). (HC, 235, note 75)

The tragedy in our judgment is that it confronts us with a reality that can never be understood completely, but which we have to live with. This explains why the spectator's point of view is so important and why judgment is primarily a task for the spectator. Political judgment gives us hope, so that we remain active even if we are confronted with tragic barriers. Only the spectator is in a position to offer this hope, as can be concluded from Pythagoras' remark:

> Life . . . is like a festival; just as some come to the festival to compete, some to ply their trade, but the best people come as spectators [theatai], so in life the

slavish men go hunting for fame [doxa] or gain, the philosophers for truth. (LK, 55)

Does Judging Play a Role in the Prevention of Evil?

One is inclined to say, that if thinking and willing do not play a major role in the prevention of evil, it must be judging. One thing is certain: if judging is to play a role in the prevention of evil, it is absolutely necessary that our judgment be proclaimed in public, because it can only be put to use if it is generally known. Arendt is somewhat vague, as we saw at the beginning of this chapter.

> The manifestation of the wind of thought is no knowledge; it is the ability to tell right from wrong, beautiful from ugly. And this indeed may prevent catastrophes, at least for myself, in the rare moments when the chips are down. (TM, 446)

Arendt reviewed this passage from a lecture in 1971 and incorporated it in "Thinking".

> The manifestation of the wind of thought is no knowledge; it is the ability to tell right from wrong, beautiful from ugly. And this, at the rare moments when the stakes are on the table, may indeed prevent catastrophes, at least for the self. (LM I, 193)

The expressions "when the chips are down" and "when the stakes are on the table" have the same meaning: "when it's really important" or "when things get serious". "Myself" has been replaced by "the self", which means that Arendt changed a personal statement into a general statement. Judging might prevent an inner catastrophe by keeping one's self-interest at a distance, by thinking from the standpoint of others and above all by thinking consistently. Could the spectators in Germany have prevented the catastrophe if they had openly protested against the rise of Hitler and his Nazi-party? The truth is that their judgment was no protest but an approval based on self-interest and frustration. I will refer to this again in the next chapter.

NOTES

1. If Arendt says that all human beings are able to think, irrespective of their intelligence, it is obvious that her term "thoughtlessness" cannot be similar to "inability to think". Her own alternative was "inability to think from somebody else's standpoint".

However, this is not an inner discussion between the "I" and the "Self" and it is therefore questionable whether it may be called thinking.

2. Arendt ignores the dialogue about evil in *Theaetetus*. In this dialogue Socrates says:

> The elimination of evil is impossible, Theodorus; there must always be some force ranged against good. But it is equally impossible for evil to be stationed in heaven; its territory is necessarily mortal nature—it patrols this earthly realm. That is why one should try to escape as quickly as possible from here to there. (Plato, 72–73)
>
> This suggests that Plato saw the battle against evil as continuous, rather than one that can ultimately be won.

3. Socrates' idea about evil coincides with Arendt's reply to Gershom Sholem's letter. (see chapter 4) In her answer Arendt says that evil has no depth and that it is thought- defying, because when you think about it and try to get to its roots, there is nothing.

4. See also chapter 4.

5. The Dutch European champion all-round skating, Mark Tuitert, said during an interview: "Before an important tournament I eliminate some mental functions. I drop everything I consider unimportant. There is nothing to it." (Haarlems Dagblad, February 9, 2004)

6. Since we do not have a way of measuring progress it is better to speak of change or transformation.

7. Liberum arbitrium is a Latin expression. Liberum means free; arbitrium comes from ad (to) and bitere (to go). Liberum arbitrium means "free to go" or free to move from one place to another.

8. See chapter 2: Kant considered evil as a consequence of the existence of free will.

9. See also chapter 5 on thinking.

10. See chapter 1: One way of explaining the Nazis' urge to destruct is that it was born from the masses' frustration with the past, which was mainly caused by Germany losing the First World War.

11. See also chapter 5.

12. One of the exceptions was Karl Marx.

13. For comparison: the millions of bystanders made Hitler's success possible.

Chapter Six

Reflection

TOTALITARIANISM

Introduction

Hannah Arendt did not consider herself a "professional thinker" or a "professional philosopher". In an interview with Günter Gaus, broadcasted on the German television on October 28, 1964, she said that she was not a philosopher but that she occupied herself with political theory. (EU, 1–23) Although she had studied philosophy, she had parted with it once and for all. She also avoided the term "political philosophy", because there is a tension between politics and philosophy, between man as an acting and as a thinking being, a tension that does not exist in philosophy of nature. Acccording to Arendt everyone, including the philosopher, can be objective to nature, but since Plato it has been absolutely impossible for the philosopher to be objective with regard to politics. The main reason is that politics, contrary to nature, deals with people. In the Gaus-interview Arendt says that philosophers, with a few exceptions, have an aversion to politics. One of the exceptions is Kant.

Despite the fact that she did not consider herself a philosopher, many people, including myself, do consider her a philosopher, even though she certainly was not an analytical philosopher. Neither did she belong to any of the contemporary movements. The tone of her language is often pessimistic and in many of her texts threat and danger make themselves felt. Had she been a painter, she would no doubt have been an impressionist. Looking at a painting of Sisley, one sees an impression of a landscape, not the detailed picture of the real forms. Looking at the picture through a magnifying glass, one will undoubtedly detect many irregularities and going through Arendt's writings with a fine-toothed comb one will encounter inaccuracies, especially with regard to historical data. This is why Stephen Whitfield quotes a remark of George Lichtheim who said that Arendt: "to put it mildly, was no historian." (Whitfield, 53)

However, somebody who searches Arendt's writings for inaccurate details —and we shall see that Jacob Robinson did this with her book about the Eichmann trial—can be compared with somebody who listens to a pianist exclusively to hear how many mistakes he makes. This is not the proper way to read Arendt's work and Stephen Whitfield remarks rightly:

> Given a choice Arendt would rather have been original than right. . . Had she merely been right, she could not have had such an impact, nor could she have teased so many stunning perceptions from the stuff of history (Whitfield, 255)

She wasn't lacking in originality. *The Origins of Totalitarianism* offers a surprising view on a new phenomenon in history. The book fascinates until the last page and therefore George Kateb calls her rightly a "shocking writer." However, because of her subjective and impressionist style of writing, it is obvious that *The Origins of Totalitarianism* provoked much criticism.

General Criticism

The most important general criticism came from three scientists: Robert Burrowes, a political scientist at the University of New York; Raymond Aron, Hannah Arendt's friend from Paris and Eric Voegelin, like Arendt a refugee from Germany. Their criticism can be summarized in five points.

One: the unitotalitarian concept of the book is confusing, because there are fundamental differences between Nazism and Stalinism. Moreover, this approach does some harm to the systematics of the book. Two: the onion structure does not properly represent the structure of Nazi-totalitarianism. Because of the onion structure, Arendt's description of Nazism is based on feelings rather than on reality; it appears to be a fantasy and it tends towards a demonic concept. Three: her style tends to be judging and moralizing. Data are ordered untidily and are sometimes incorrect. However, it is surprising that none of the critics gives convincing examples of incorrect historical data. Four: objections have been raised against Arendt's alledged "logicality" of the totalitarian system. This means that on the one hand Arendt was accused of emotionality and on the other hand of too much rationality. Five: the title of the book is not in line with the contents.

In a reaction to Eric Voegelin's criticism Arendt enters into a number of the above-mentioned points. She agrees that the title of the book is somewhat ill chosen, because it is about the elements that crystallized into totalitarianism and not about the origins. Because of the fact that she has tried to describe the various elements, some readers may find that the book lacks unity, but she is aware of this. She comments on her style and says that it was impossible for her to write objectively about totalitarianism and that the analysis of the elements could not be free of value judgments. Arendt says that she started her book "sine ira et studio", but that sorrow and anger influenced her style in the end. However, she considered this as an aspect that goes with the subject.

> When I used the image of Hell, I did not mean this allegorically but literally. . .
> In this sense I think that a description of the camps as Hell on earth is more "objective", that is, more adequate to their essence than statements of a purely sociological or psychological nature. (EU, 404)

Her book did not have the intention to be value free and the onion structure is nothing more than a metaphor to get a better understanding of the totalitarian system, even though the actual organization may have been different. It has been said that the onion structure was no more than a fiction, but this fiction explains more of the essence of Nazism than a real organizational scheme would do. The facts about the destruction camps and the police battalions that were revealed after 1945 showed that the ideology, which definitely had a demonic character, was enforced in a logical way, to an extent that was beyond common sense. Arendt did, however, later admit that she probably overestimated the influence of the ideology on the individual person.

I agree with one point of criticism. Mixing Nazism and Stalinism in one book is indeed sometimes confusing. The contents of the book are mainly based on Nazi-totalitarianism and one sometimes gets the impression that Stalin-totalitarianism was woven through it. This is sometimes disturbing, because in spite of the similarities between the two systems, there were also important differences, such as a difference in ideology and the absence of the Shoah in Russia.

I consider all other points of criticism to a large extent irrelevant. It seems to me that it is criticism of people who have listened to the pianist to count the mistakes, but who lost track of the overall performance. In this respect Arnold's vision is a relief. Arnold does indeed observe a number of mistakes and inaccuracies, but he does not lose sight of the totality.

> There is a sweeping synthesis, which confidently takes the whole of modern history for its province; the shotgun marriage of philosophy and empirical sociology; the relentless search for all-embracing explanations; the cataract of learned footnotes and allusions, and the ingenuity, which discovers a latent significance in relatively ordinary happenings. The wonder is that with all these glaring faults her book is not merely readable, but fascinating and at times moving. It is an essay in the grand manner, with great passionate gusts of argument blowing and

swirling through its pages, and the wealth of information it displays is staggering, though much of it is badly organized, redundant, or irrelevant to the main theme. That theme is the catastrophe of European society before and during the Hitler years, and on this infernal subject Mrs. Arendt, for all her vagaries and her numberless faults of style, throws more light than an entire regiment of ordinary historians. (Arnold, 30–31)

Criticism on the Unicity of Totalitarianism

First of all I should like to differentiate between the unicity of totalitarianism and the unicity of the Shoah. In the case of totalitarianism a new type of political structure is involved; in the case of the Shoah we speak about an event within this structure. I will first focus on the unicity of Nazi-totalitarianism and then on the unicity of the Shoah.

What exactly is the meaning of the word unicity? By unicity I mean the historical incomparability of the totalitarian Nazi system with existing political systems. The question is whether Nazism is a unique system and not a variety of an earlier one.

I have said that totalitarianism in Arendt's book mainly relates to Nazi-totalitarianism and in the second place to Stalinism. Although I restrict myself to an analysis of Nazism, this doesn't alter the fact that Stalinism was also a unique totalitarian system, comparable to, but not identical to Nazism.

When reading the criticism on *The Origins of Totalitarianism,* one cannot escape the impression that originality provokes a kind of scientific jealousy. The result of this jealousy is that many critics have done their utmost to demonstrate that Arendt's vision of totalitarianism was absolutely not original or unique, but rather a modern variant of an already existing structure, or even pure fiction. The political scientist O'Sullivan goes too far in this respect. He says that Arendt's abstract style of writing puts her "on the brink of essentialism" and also that "she assumes that because we happen to have the word [totalitarianism], we must therefore be able to find a phenomenon corresponding to it." (O'Sullivan, 192) As I said before, the word totalitarianism existed before 1940, but Arendt gave it a special meaning and I cannot see what is wrong with that.

Carol E. Adams approaches the problem of unicity by pointing to the ideology of Nazism. She stresses the role of Hitler and states that, in fact, only he and his direct subordinates believed in the ideology.

Are we then not back to tyranny, but a tyranny in which the ruler has a madness in his method, seeking power because he—especially he—believes in an ideology that is all compassing . . . There is further inconsistency here. Arendt insists that it is the anti-utilitarian character of its ideology that distinguishes totalitarianism from tyranny. Yet she also defines totalitarianism as having an ultimate aim, namely absolute domination. This implies a degree of rationality and purpose and the existence of a leader seeking power—all of which are indices also of tyranny . . . But this leaves open the question whether totalitarianism is something new, or whether Nazism is simply "Tyranny with new technocratic methods." (Adams, 40–41)

Adams' conclusion is clear: totalitarianism is a variant of tyranny and not a new phenomenon.

John L. Stanley, in his article "Is Totalitarianism a New Phenomenon?" is also of the opinion that the unicity of totalitarianism is exaggerated in *The Origins of Totalitarianism*. Stanley also says that Arendt underestimates the role of Hitler. In her book the ideology seems to live a life of its own, separated from the leader, but this, according to him, is incorrect. It is especially the leader's longing for power that creates the similarity with tyranny. Stanley goes back in history to the beginning of the nineteenth century and points to the regime of the Zulu king Shaka. He is of the opinion that, on the basis of the descriptions of king Shaka's regime it is comparable to totalitarianism and that Arendt to a large extent ignores this historical figure.

Stanley asks a question more or less identical to that of Carol E. Adams: "Is totalitarianism so qualitatively different from ancient tyranny that it cannot be said to overlap with it or with any other form of government?" (Stanley, 27) Perhaps, says Stanley, there is a sliding scale from tyranny to totalitarianism with many intermediate forms. In fact Stanley's criticism on the unicity of totalitarianism crystallizes into the question whether Nazism differs so much from tyranny that it may not be called a tyranny any more, but should be placed in another category of regimes.

In her book Arendt pays attention to the regime of king Shaka, but she does not want to compare his organization to Hitler's totalitarianism. She says that king Shaka united Zulu tribes in an extraordinary, disciplined, warlike organization, but that there was no question of a nation, a state or a political body. Shaka killed more than one million members of weaker tribes, but Arendt considers this destruction as an unrecorded episode in history in an unreal, incomprehensible process.[1] (OT III, 192–193)

It is obvious that Arendt was of the opinion that this was a case of violence, instead of terror. As mentioned before, these two are not identical. Terror appears when violence has destroyed all resisting powers.[2] Stanley's article is based on a book written by the historian Walter and Walter's data are based on "eyewitnesses". However, the reliability of the reports of these eyewitnesses is questionable. It seems to me that historiography in those days and in that almost unknown part of the world was insufficient to make a scientifically sane comparison.

As far as I know, there are no further comparisons with other regimes in literature. What remains is the purely theoretical question whether totalitarianism differs from tyranny to such an extent, that it may not be called a tyranny or a variety of tyranny.

In order to answer this question we must consider the difference in meaning of the terms. It seems to me that, despite the similarities, the word tyranny has another meaning than the word totalitarianism and this difference is determined by the differences in characteristics between the two concepts.

– By far the most important difference is that the actions of totalitarian leaders are based on an ideology. In behalf of the ideology, pluralism changes into monism, which is a synonym for totalitarianism. Personal autonomy disappears and makes room for a collective autonomy that is nothing more than a façade. Tyrants have no ideology; they oppress their subjects for the sake of oppression only.

– A tyrant is not democratically elected. He comes to power in an illegal way. Hitler, however, was democratically elected.

– Tyrants come "from above", but Hitler came up from the bottom. Out of the hopeless, atomized and frustrated masses, the rise of a leader like Hitler was almost unavoidable, and therefore his ideas and opinions were supported, sympathetically observed or at least not disputed by almost the entire population. Therefore we can speak of totalitarianism: the ideas and ideology of the state convinced the totality of the society and this leads to programmatic collectivism. In contrast to the tyrant who mainly has enemies, the totalitarian leader has sympathizers, because the real opponents to the system are the first to be killed.

– The totalitarian leader identifies himself with every co-worker he has appointed and he takes responsibility for every action or crime performed by any member or functionary in his official capacity. A tyrant always keeps an absolute distance from his subordinates and subjects; he would never identify himself with them and definitely not with their actions. On the contrary, he prefers to blame and criticize them in order to save himself from the wrath of the people. (OT III, 374–375)

– Totalitarian leaders do not rule over men like despots, but they use a system in which the radical elimination of differences becomes an end, which makes part of the population superfluous. The end can be achieved by means of terror and the production of corpses. Terror is the essence of totalitarianism. Tyrants do not want to destroy their subjects because they need subjects to tyrannize.

– Tyrants only have real enemies: subjects who refuse to obey the tyrant's orders. Totalitarian leaders do not only have real enemies but also arbitrarily "designated" enemies and Arendt states that this arbitrariness negates human freedom more than would be possible in a tyranny. (OT III, 433)

– In contrast to tyrants, totalitarian leaders regard the area over which they have power only as their temporary headquarters on their way to domination of the entire world. Moreover, the totalitarian leader does not think in years but in centuries and millennia.

– In political science, says Arendt, all descriptions of governments are based on the alternative between legal and illegal regimes, between the power of arbitrariness and legal power. Legal governments and lawful power have always belonged together, just as illegal states and arbitrariness. The essence of legal governments is lawfulness; the essence of tyrannies is lawlessness. Totalitarianism shows us a new alternative. It does deny all existing laws, but it does not function without laws because it obeys the laws of Nature[3], while terror is its essence. We could even say that terror is lawful if it is in accordance with the law of Nature.

– Finally, if a totalitarian system's only characteristic were the oppression of a nation by a small group of tyrants, it would be relatively simple to bring this regime down. However, the elasticity of the system is in its capacity to involve the victims themselves in the organization of the overall terror and to make them partners in the commitment of the crimes. In this way the victims become active collaborators and accomplices. In this situation, their own position is at stake and therefore they will make sure that the very regime that tortures and oppresses them will be preserved.

I think that the above-mentioned differences between tyrannies and totalitarian systems are so significant that one may say that totalitarianism is unique and not a modern form of tyranny.

THE UNICITY OF THE SHOAH

Introduction

I have tried to demonstrate that Nazi-totalitarianism was a unique system in its totality. The Shoah was only part of it. Many people maintain their opinion that the Shoah was a genocide, which did not essentially differ from other genocides before and after the Second World War. In this chapter I want to demonstrate that the Shoah was a unique part of Nazi-totalitarianism. However, we can look at the unicity of the Shoah from two different aspects: historical unicity and moral unicity. By historical unicity I mean that from a historical point of view the Shoah is incomparable with other genocides. By moral unicity I want to indicate that also from a moral point of view the Shoah is incomparable with other actions or events. These comparisons are based on qualitative not on quantitative differences. Killing one million people is not a lesser evil than killing six million.

In the introduction I mentioned Emil Fackenheim, who considered the Shoah as a novum, but he is not the only one.

> Auschwitz is a unique descent into hell. It is an unprecedented celebration of evil. It is . . . the scandal of evil for evil's sake, an eruption of demonism without analogy; and the singling out of Jews, ultimately, is an unparalleled expression of what the rabbis call groundless hate. (Wiesel, 198)

> Auschwitz was a unique phenomenon, like the revelation at Sinai. (Rubinstein, 227)

> The concept is that there is much evil in the world and that most evil, evil as it is, is not altogether abnormal evil. Ordinary evil is evil enough: crimes of private individuals against other individuals, economic injustices of various societies, and the limits put on individual freedom. But then there appear evils, which are qualitatively different from all other evils. The paradigmatic case was the Holocaust (Wyschogrod, 68)

Arendt does not use the terms "unicity" or "uniqueness", but one may conclude from her description that she regarded the Shoah as a unique, unprecedented event. She says that death factories have no parallels and that they presented a radical evil, previously unknown to us. It is understandable that mainly Jewish thinkers and writers underline the unicity of the Shoah. To them it is an overpowering catastrophe, which must serve as a memorial for the victims and a warning for the living and for future generations. The idea that humanity would be better off by destroying part of it is an absolutely new point of view. Although most scholars agree with this, the historical unicity of the Shoah and the idea that the destruction of the Jews belongs to a unique moral category have been much critizised.

However, the fact that it took many years to find a proper word for the destruction of the Jews is already a proof that this genocide belongs to another category than other genocides. Apparently the difference with other genocides was significant enough to give it a separate and specific name with a specific meaning.

Criticism on the Unicity of the Shoah

To support their criticism, opponents of the idea of the unicity of the Shoah point at the massacre of 1.5 million civilian Christian Armenians by the Turks in 1915. This was not military violence but genocide. It was made possible by the final collapse of the Ottoman Empire, which had protected the rights of non-Muslim minorities. The new nationalistic government rejected the idea of a multi-ethnic society. In 1914 Turkey entered the war on the

German/Austrian side and the Armenians were identified as internal enemies. In 1915 the Turkish government decided to deport all Armenians to the Syrian Desert, but most of the men were shot before their deportation. (Von der Dunk, 17 and Dwork & van Pelt, 35–41) Without diminishing the atrociousness of the crime or considering it a lesser evil by comparing numbers of victims, I think that it is characteristically different from the Shoah. Nowadays we would consider this genocide as an ethnic purification on the basis of nationalistic and religious feelings, wheras the Shoah was the consequence of an ideology. However, more objections, based on historical comparisons with other genocides, have been raised against Arendt's ideas of the historical unicity of the Shoah.

In a personal discussion, Paul Gellings, emeritus professor of the University of Twente, drew my attention to the book of Esther in the Old Testament. This is Esther's story: The Persian king Ahasveros wanted a new wife and therefore he was searching his kingdom for beautiful young women. One of the chosen girls was Esther, an orphan, who had been educated by her uncle, the Jew Mordechai. Esther went to live in the royal palace and later Ahasveros made her queen. Everybody in the palace had to bow for Haman, an evil person, who had been given a lot of power by king Ahasveros. Mordechai refused to bow for Haman and out of revenge, Haman ordered all the Jews in the kingdom to be killed, because of their different laws. When Esther heard of Haman's plans, she begged king Ahasveros to save the Jews. Haman was hanged on the gallows intended for Mordechai. The Jews took revenge on their enemies and killed many of them. To day the Jews celebrate this event during the so-called Purim feast, on the 14th of Adar.

I should like to make a few comments on this interesting story. First of all, I wonder whether the story is historically correct, since the events took place in the 6th century B.C. Secondly, there were no killings, there was only an intention to kill and this intention was not based on an ideology but on revenge and on the fact that the Jews had different laws, based on a different religion. Therefore it seems to me that the plan for the massacre of the Jews was an example of ethnic purification, similar to what happened to the Armenians in Turkey and much later in Yugoslavia.

In his article "Human Status and Politics", Shiraz Dossa points out the similarity to other historical events and particularly to the massacre of 25 million Africans between 1890 and 1911, mentioned by Arendt in her book. (OT III, 185) According to Dossa, Arendt was apparently not very much impressed by this historical event and he wonders why she was shocked by the Shoah. Dossa's own answer is, that Arendt considers the Shoah exclusively in the context of a cultural and civilized society. The victims of the Shoah were civilized people, exterminated by civilized killers. This moral and cultural context influenced her concept of unicity and therefore Dossa accuses Arendt of ethnocentrism.

Dossa's criticism of Arendt, when he says that she is not emotionally shocked by the massacre of 25 million blacks, seems unfair. In her book she says that this event in the Congo, together with other genocides in Africa, is one of the most terrible massacres in recent history. She was aware of the horror of this genocide. However, the essential question is whether this genocide is comparable with the Shoah in a historical respect. Arendt situates this massacre within the framework of expansion and colonialism and therefore comparison with the Shoah, which took place in a civilized and enlightened Europe, is scientifically incorrect. She does consider race thinking and concomitant genocides in Africa as a precursor of the later events in Europe, but she refuses to compare two historical events, which, in her opinion, are incomparable in both a political and a methodological respect. Therefore, I think it is unfair to accuse Arendt of ethnocentrism.

I have also wondered what exactly Dossa meant by "ethnocentrism". I found three definitions. "Having race as a central interest", "characterized by or based on the attitude that one's own group is superior" (Webster, 393) and "the individual disposition characterized by feelings of loyalty towards the familiar, with or without negative feelings towards the unfamiliar". (van Dale, 740) If Dossa's understanding of ethnocentrism relates to the first part of the last definition, I could agree with it, making certain reservations. I reject the other two definitions, because Arendt did not think in races and did not consider her own group as superior. My opinion is based on a fragment from her letter to Gershom Scholem. In this letter Arendt wrote that she was not moved by any love of the Jewish people for two reasons. She never loved any collective but only her friends and the only kind of love she believed in was the love for persons. (JP, 246)

With regard to emotional involvedness, I would like to say that to her the massacre in the Congo was a historical event that took place on another continent and mainly before she was born. However, the Shoah was part of her own life and took place in her native country. Her friends and her family were involved. When I discuss the Shoah with my own children, they don't show emotion and this is understandable, because it is not part of their personal experience and they have never known any of the people who were killed.

This concludes the historical comparisons. I shall now discuss a moral comparison.

Douglas Lackey has philosophical objections against the positioning of the Shoah in a unique moral setting. Moreover, says Lackey, by doing this it becomes impossible to learn from it or draw lessons from it. Lackey does not explain this statement, but he probably means that it becomes impossible to understand it. Lackey tries to explain the Shoah by applying ordinary moral norms. His problem is phrased in the title of his article: "Extraordinary Evil or Common Malevolence? Evaluating the Jewish Holocaust." Lackey reviews all the arguments for placing the Shoah in a special moral category.

– It was racial murder. Lackey says that it is no more reprehensible to kill a Jew than to kill someone with blue eyes.

– It concerned the destruction of beings that were regarded as belonging to an inferior race. This, says Lackey, is morally no worse than killing blacks, which were also regarded as inferior beings.

– The Jews were said to be a destructive presence in society, but according to Lackey we need a moral argument to demonstrate that a murder on the basis of this atttitude is worse than a murder based on less dangerous arguments.

– The character of the murder was impersonal and nobody derived any benefit from the killings. The end was the establishment of a better world in the future. Lackey wonders whether murder on the basis of an impersonal goal (the ideology) is worse than murder for a personal, egoistic reason.

Lackey arrives at the following conclusion:

> The Holocaust was not qualitatively or quantitatively distinct because the intentions and vices of the mass murderer are qualitatively indistinguishable from the intentions and vices of the common murderer. The Holocaust was not quantitatively distinct either because the sum of evils in the Holocaust is quantitatively indistinguishable from six million randomly selected individual murders or because the notion of a 'sum' of moral evils is conceptually incoherent. (Lackey, 167)

As I said in the introduction of this chapter, I shall not discuss quantitative comparisons. Lackey analyzes all qualitative features of the Shoah. He concludes that killing because of anti-Semitism, feelings of superiority, demonization or the impersonal character of the Shoah is not morally different from other types of individual murders. I doubt whether his argumentation is correct. We have to consider the Shoah as a unity, because it was the ultimate, systematically executed consequence of an ideological logicality. Killing on the basis of an ideology is not worse than killing for a personal reason, but it is different. Splitting up the Shoah in various elements and regarding them separately gives a distorted picture of the totality. As I said before, the use of the word "murder" is incorrect. An individual murder, or even a series of murders, irrespective of the motives, is different from the extermination or destruction of a race. Fackenheim said that the Shoah was more than the sum of its parts; it was more negative than the individual negativity of the elements. Lackey totally neglects this and he says: the Shoah is no more than the sum of its parts. However, the sum was this:

The operation comprised, first, *defining* Jews for the purpose of isolating them from the economic, social and higher-cultural communities into which they had been absorbed or vitally connected, and second progressively *depleting* their physical, economic, and political strength by all the measures to disconnect them from the social organism, followed by all the measures to crowd them into a few holding areas where rapidly they could be further reduced by starvation and epidemics (adequate food and medicine being simply and deliberately withheld). Third, with would-be resisters forced to comply in consideration of families and whole communities held hostage, the operation was concluded by transporting them to killing centers for killing on assembly-line basis, with last effects and body products to be utilized in the Germany economy. An operation like *that*, we do not find anywhere in the history of the West, or indeed in the history of advanced civilizations. (We do not look to the holocausts of the primitives, if any, since they lacked the technology that is the practical counterpart of such a sustained purpose.) For free malevolence, there has been nothing like it.[4] (Rosenthal, 188–189)

The deciding factor for considering the Shoah as a unique historical and moral event is in the intention of a government to destroy within the legal order, systematically and for ideological reasons, a complete race and to make it disappear as if it had never existed. Steven Katz says in his extensive study *The Holocaust in Historical Context:*

The Holocaust is phenomenologically unique by virtue of the fact that never before has a state set out, as a matter of intentional principle and actualized policy, to annihilate physically every man, woman and child belonging to a specific people. (Katz, vol. I, 28)

Finally I want to point at the 28th Huizinga lecture entitled "A Century of Destruction and Reformation", given by the Spanish author Jorge Semprun in Leyden (the Netherlands) on December 17, 1999. Jorge Semprun stresses the unicity of the Shoah in comparison with other genocides. Its unicity does not lie in the number of victims, but in the understanding of its tragic exceptionality. All other massacres are, according to Semprun, based on "Realpolitik" (a politics of reality), which means a consequence of the urge for expansion, fear for power, or the intolerance towards different cultures. There is no Realpolitik as an explanation for the destruction of the Jews. Jews were dangerous only because they were Jews. It was an expression of absolute hatred, which needed no other justification than the ideology of the pure race. "Anti-Semitic hatred is intangible for critical reason, because it is an absolute hatred: hatred of the Other because of what he has in common." Semprun points in particular at the hallmark of the systematic industrial rationality. An insanely bureaucratic strictness was maintained and the whole system was

based on the cool modern logic of an entrepreneur. "The methods of Ford for
the production of Jewish corpses; that is the frightening exceptionality of the
Shoah." (Semprun, 6)

this law applies behind the wire
those who can work
shall live
those who cannot
shall be killed
to be enforced relentlessly

therefore

selections for the gas chambers
at odd times
the phantom of selection
hovers over the roll call square each morning
the sick cannot work
reporting sick is suicide
all are sick
all want to live
always the hope for a future
away from the inconceivable present

S.S. doctors decide
who shall live
or die before nightfall
unpredictable arbitrariness decides on life and death
the sick pretend to be healthy
straighten their painful backs
mothers push their daughters towards the back rows
daughters push their mothers
fruitless efforts
today or tomorrow
the gas for all

a broken shoulder
inflamed feet
frozen limbs
excessive loss of weight
any reason
will do for the selection

S.S. doctors walk along the rows
and make their choice in passing

take down their victims' numbers
struck off the list: deceased

alice
sales girl from lyon
klara
nurse from apeldoorn
sabina
student from saloniki
rachel
factory girl from warsaw
brave girl from the warsaw ghetto
names of one list
neatly typed list
of more than four hundred names
selected in one day
gassed
before nightfall
alice, klara, sabina, rachel,
and the others. . .

(Greet van Amstel, 19–20)

EICHMANN IN JERUSALEM

Introduction

In the spring of 1963, thirteen years after publication of *The Origins of Totalitarianism,* Hannah Arendt attended the Eichmann trial in Jerusalem as a reporter for *The New Yorker.* Thirteen years after her observation of a radical evil that was previously unknown to us, she was confronted by a person who played a major role in this radical evil. Some people were shocked by her choice of the magazine. *The New Yorker* had a reputation of being humoristic, entertaining, frivolous, intellectually presumptuous and not too serious.

> An investigation into mass murder in between mr. Arno's cartoons, the advertisements for Cadillacs and Oldsmobiles, gin, holidays in Bermuda, a little bit of holocaust, a little bit of Tiffany and Saks Fifth Avenue. (Laqueur, 1983, 110)

The articles in *The New Yorker* were the basis for her book *Eichmann in Jerusalem,* which was subjected to strong criticism. This criticism concerned three aspects of her book: factual and historical data, her remarks with regard to the role of the Jewish Councils and finally her expression "the banality of

evil". Especially the last two points have led to serious controversies. In the
following chapters I shall go into these subjects more deeply.

Factual and Historical Data

The most extensive criticism on factual and historical data was given by the
lawyer dr. Jacob Robinson in his book *And the Crooked shall be made
straight.* Robinson looked at Arendt's impressionistic style through a legal
magnifying glass and he came up with hundreds of alleged mistakes and inaccuracies, probably caused, on the one hand by her casual attitude with regard to facts and on the other hand by lack of knowledge. Dr. Jacob Robinson is a typical example of a person who listens to a pianist, to count the
mistakes without hearing the sonata. Robinson considered himself an expert
in Jewish history. According to the critic Walter Laqueur there was no doubt
that Arendt had made hundreds of mistakes (between four- and five hundred),
among which incorrect statistics and quotations removed from their context.
However, says Laqueur, the relevance of Robinson's remarks is not always
clear. For instance, Robinson writes that Italy joined the convention of The
Hague, while Arendt writes that this was not the case and he dedicates four
pages—as much as to the fate of the French Jews!—to the question whether
the Hungarian royal power, seen from a constitutional point of view, coin-
cided with the power of the Roman Empire. This is a lack of balance that indicates that Robinson read the text with a legal rather than with a historical
eye. Of course, Arendt was not an expert on history, but Robinson also had a
tendency to exaggerate. When Arendt calls an S.S. Obergruppenführer (First
Lieutenant) "Hans", Robinson says that it should be "Hanns". On the other
hand, Robinson's book contains mistakes as well and Laqueur gives examples of wrong historical dates and incorrect spelling. All this is in fact unimportant. Robinson looked at details without taking in the totality. Laqueur re-
grets that Robinson's historical knowledge has resulted in a book which
comments on and criticizes another book when it might have been a, much
needed, historical standard work. (JP, 252–259)

Arendt also comments on Robinson's book in a razor-sharp article entitled
"The Formidable Dr. Robinson". She states that she didn't go to Jerusalem to
write a book on contemporary Jewish history. She also remarks that, until
1963, Robinson was not a historian but a lawyer (his book appeared in 1965)
and that this is his first book on Jewish history. According to Arendt Robinson's only goal is contradicting her and his only ambition is showing his own
erudition. However, what he writes about Hungarian history can be found in
the Encyclopaedia of World History and it is not a proof of erudition. Robin-

son asks questions that have nothing to do with the context of the book such as: how many Jews lived in Rome in 1943; when did the Hitler-regime become completely totalitarian and is there a connection between the Final Solution and the earlier euthanasia-program. According to Arendt Robinson's method would establish an amazing number of mistakes in any book. This is not all, for Robinson is also psychologically colour-blind: he sees everything in black and white. When Arendt writes that Eichmann is not stupid, but thoughtless, that he was not a cunning liar, but that he lied sometimes, Robinson says that these are contradictions and that Arendt is "hopping back and forth". Another reproach is that Arendt does not explain her statements, but in most cases the explanations can be found on the next or the preceding pages.

For her part Arendt refers to two quite serious mistakes in Robinson's book. The first concerns the Nazis' legal system; the second relates to anti-Semitism in Europe, in particular in the Netherlands. Arendt speaks of the "unfriendly attitude towards refugees from Germany". Robinson denies that this was the case, but Robinson had never heard of an official letter of the Dutch government of May 7, 1938, in which refugees are described as "unwanted strangers".

> It is formidable that the book found two respectable publishers and was reviewed in respected magazines and it is awe-inspiring that for years now, simply on his having said so, the news has echoed around the globe that my book contained "hundreds of factual errors" and that I had not written a trial report but "scrutinized the data concerned with the Nazi extermination of European Jewry". (JP, 271–272)

In this light I must conclude that dr. Robinson has never understood the essence of Arendt's book. The core of the matter is the "banality of evil", the observation that evil was not radical (in Arendt's sense of the word) but a consequence of thoughtlessness, or inability to think and hence banal, without any demonic connotation. It is regrettable that the book contains mistakes. They are the result of Arendt's impressionistic style, where details are less important; the same thing happened in *The Origins of Totalitarianism,* which contains many historical mistakes.

I think that Walter Laqueur is right when he says that dr. Robinson, with his background and education, was the wrong man to criticize Arendt's book.

> Plodding, immersed in questions of detail, he could not possibly follow her to the rarified heights of abstractions where the moral philosopher could engage in a virtuoso performance, but where poor dr. Robinson would be quite lost. (Laqueur, 1983, 112)

The Jewish Councils

Much more disturbing than Robinson's textual criticism was the indignation about Arendt's remarks on the role of the Jewish Councils. These remarks caused a great deal of controversy between Arendt and her (mainly Jewish) opponents. The Jewish Councils were installed by the Nazis in a number of occupied countries such as Hungary, Poland and the Netherlands. Adolf Eichmann in particular played an important role in the formation of these Councils. The members were Jewish intellectuals who, in one way or another, cooperated with the Nazis and this is the heart of the matter.[5] It is true that the Jewish leaders tried to rescue Jews from the Nazis' claws. However, it is also true that the same leaders helped the Nazis in the persecution of the Jews. Slyly, the Nazis had placed the Jews in a dilemma, from which there was no escape.

Let us first look at Hannah Arendt's most important remarks about the activities of the Jewish Councils. Most of her remarks are based on Raul Hilberg's book *The Destruction of the European Jews.* (EJ, 282) I will focus on the situation in the Netherlands for two reasons. The first reason is that Arendt herself uses the situation in the Netherlands as a central issue in her argumentation. The second reason is that I know the circumstances in the Netherlands better, by personal experience, than in any other country. Arendt summarizes the activities of the Jewish Councils in the following paragraph.

In Amsterdam as in Warsaw, in Berlin as in Budapest Jewish officials could be trusted to compile the lists of persons and of their property, to secure money from the deportees to defray the expense of their deportation and extermination, to keep track of vacated apartments, to supply police forces to help seize Jews and get them on trains, until, as a last gesture, they handed over the assets of the Jewish community in good order for confiscation. (EJ, 118)

This is a very negative picture of the role of the Jewish Councils and she accentuates this by saying that in fact the Jewish leaders helped in the destruction of their own people and that, for a Jew, this is the darkest chapter of the whole story. (EJ, 117)

In the Netherlands there were strikes and demonstrations against anti-Jewish measures, but there was also a strong Nazi-movement and there was an abyss between native Jews and Jewish refugees, which was probably a result of the already mentioned unfriendly attitude of the Dutch government towards German refugees. According to Arendt all this made it easier to form the Jewish Council in Amsterdam. Initially the members of this Council were under the impression that only Jewish refugees would be deported. The Nazi movement had a considerable police force, among which there were Jews and all these factors resulted in a catastrophe unparalleled in any Western country, except for Poland, but in that country the circumstances were completely different.[6] (EJ, 169)

All the remarks about the Jewish Councils and Jewish cooperation resulted in a serious controversy. In a postscript to her book, Arendt says that even before the publication of the book an organized hatred campaign was started. Her opponents accused her of saying that the Jews should have defended themselves and also that the Jews had killed themselves. She was said to have told such hideous lies out of self-hatred. All this was invented. What she did say in a letter to Gershom Scholem was that there had always been the possibility of doing nothing, the possibility of "non-participation". (JP, 248)

In fact, Arendt's statements were a reproduction of Eichmann's testimony, when he said that after the Wannsee conference the Jewish Councils were put into action with one ultimate goal: the destruction of their own people. Eichmann let the Jewish Councils know how many people he needed for a transport and the Council made out the list. Their property was registered, they were taken to the collection points and boarded the trains. Those who tried to escape were caught by a special Jewish police force. According to Eichmann, no one protested or refused to cooperate. (EJ, 115)

Arendt writes that the court in Jerusalem did ask a number of witnesses why they never resisted, but not why they cooperated in the destruction of their own people. However, from the public gallery this question came during the testimony of Philip von Freudiger, member of the Jewish Council of Budapest. Because of the consternation, the court had to interrupt the session. It makes one think that there may have been an element of truth in Arendt's statements.

So far Arendt's description of the activities of the Jewish Councils. I will come back to it later, but I should first like to pay attention to the comments and criticisms on her statements. Among all the critics, Abigail Rosenthal occupies a special place, because she neither criticizes Arendt's remarks, nor the activities of the Jewish Councils. On the contrary, Rosenthal defends the Jewish Councils and we shall see in the following pages that Abel Herzberg does the same.

Rosenthal points out a number of forms of cooperation and assistance such as: moving to the ghettos, administrative assistance by supplying lists and other information, the production of armbands with a yellow star and there was more. The worst form of cooperation and for many critics the gravest accusation, is their selection of Jews for transportation to the death camps. However, Rosenthal wonders what would be the appropriate attitude if, as the Jewish leaders were, one is situated in a genocidal environment. Did they have a choice? Suicide was an option but this is not part of the Jewish culture.

Escape was almost impossible and the destruction program was extensive and merciless and all this made survival a lucky coincidence. Rosenthal concludes that anybody who had a chance to survive had the duty to do so, even if this involved participation in the selections for transports to the annihilation camps. It was a matter of survival of the species, which justified any efforts to survive. (Rosenthal, 205–207)

The problem of Rosenthal's argumentation is that it is probably based on genocidal situations in the ghettos of Riga and Warsaw. In Riga people were shot in December 1941 and the underground press of the Warsaw ghetto published information about the extermination campaign, mass executions in the Eastern territories and the extermination center at Chelmno-on-the Ner as early as the spring of 1942.[7] (Sakovska, 15–16) In the following pages we shall see that during the first period of the Dutch Jewish Council none of the members had any idea about future deportations and destruction. The essential question is whether the members of the Councils should not have refused membership in those early stages. It is well known that this became extremely difficult at a later stage, but that is different matter.

Bruno Bettelheim partly agrees with Arendt's criticism on the activities of the Jewish Councils. His opinion is that Arendt, by focusing primarily on the disasters caused by the totalitarian system, provokes a kind of ambivalence in the evaluation of the question of guilt. A superficial reader could easily arrive at the wrong conclusions that Eichmann was a victim and the members of the Councils were guilty. What Arendt wanted to say, according to Bettelheim, is that any organization within a totalitarian system that enters into a compromise with that system immediately becomes ineffective in the fight against the system and in fact supports it. Bettelheim refers to his own experience in a concentration camp and states that concentration camps could not have functioned without the cooperation of the prisoners.[8] (Bettelheim, 268–273)

On the whole, negative criticism prevailed. Lucy Dawidovicz writes that Arendt must have a disdain for historical facts, as a result of which she did not place the question of the Jewish Councils in a historical context. She refers to the events in the ghetto of Warsaw. There was no Jewish Council in this ghetto, so that the Jews were unorganized and without leaders and this would have enabled the Nazis to deport a quarter of a million Jews with "amazing facility". (Dawidovicz, 578, 586) I think this is an example of criticism based on unfounded arguments. Not only did Warsaw have a Jewish Council (chairman Adam Czerniakow) but there were also numerous committees, a Jewish Fighting Organization, a Council for Jewish Aid, and an underground organization. It was the only ghetto were the Jews fought back. (during the Jewish uprising in 1943) (Sakovska, 16–25)

Another argument comes from Lionel Abel who says that between November 1941 and June 1942 Einsatzgruppen (special forces) killed half a million Jews in the Ukraine, despite the fact that there were no Jewish Councils in that area. According to the former S.S. general Von dem Bach, the fact that the Jews were unorganized was an advantage. (Abel, 212) On the other hand, Eichmann declared during the trial that the formation of the Jewish Councils made the actions against the Jews easier, above all because less personnel was needed. The Jewish leaders had the illusion that they could do something for their people, says Abel; this and the fact that Arendt does not explain her accusation make it very hard to digest. She suggests that it would have been better if the Jewish leaders would have refrained completely from cooperation with the Nazis, but she does not indicate how they could have done this in an environment of Nazis and anti-Semites. Arendt's judgment, says Abel, is neither political nor moral. She should have investigated the moral and political alternatives, but she did not do that and therefore her judgment is an aesthetical judgment. (Abel, 211–219)

I want to make two remarks to which I shall refer later. The first is that it is absolutely incorrect to compare the actions of the Einsatzgruppen, which took place before the announcement of the Final Solution, with the actions in the occupied countries such as the Netherlands, France and Hungary. My second remark is that one can never know how many Jews would have been killed in the Ukraine if there had been Jewish Councils. Therefore Abel's reasoning is a faulty one.

The next critic is Gertrude Ezorsky. She wonders what Ahrendt means by "cooperation". Ezorsky refuses to accept that Arendt presumes that the Jews offered voluntary cooperation. She must have been well aware that the Jewish leaders who in one way or another cooperated with the Nazis were always under pressure of Nazi terror. Let us suppose, says Ezorsky, that some Jewish leaders, not the majority, cooperated. Others did, however, not. An example is Arthur Zyglbaum, member of the Jewish Council of Warsaw, who called on the Jews to refuse to move into a ghetto and to resist if they were forced. However, Arendt does not mention the name of Arthur Zyglbaum and she only pays attention to the negative aspects of the Jewish Councils. Ezorsky refers to a passage from *The Origins of Totalitarianism,* where Arendt says that the alternative under totalitarianism is not between good and evil but between murder and murder. The Jews found themselves in an identical situation. In retrospect it is easy to say that their strategy failed, but Arendt herself says that in a totalitarian state resistance is virtually impossible and she describes the people who ask why the Jews didn't fight back as "cruel and silly".[9]

I will not go so far as to say that Arendt's attack on the *Judenrate* [Jewish Councils] is cruel and silly. But where in her book is there a consideration of these

Jewish councilmen trapped in the inferno of Nazism that is sympathetic and serious? (Ezorsky, 77)

I want to use Ezorsky's remark as a starting point for a consideration of the criticism on Arendt's remarks. According to me most of the criticism is not about what she said, but how she said it. It is less a matter of content, than of her wording and tone. Nobody can deny the cooperation of the Jewish Councils with the Nazis. The Dutch historian Presser even used the stronger word "collaboration".

Gershom Scholem goes more deeply into Arendt's tone and style. What he misses in her book is the love for the Jewish people, compassion with six million victims and also "Herzentakt" (the voice of the heart) (JP, 242) Instead of a considered balanced judgment, Scholem observes a kind of demagogic wish to exaggerate, while there was at least reason for doubt about the motives of the members of the Jewish Councils. Of course there were crooks amongst the members of the Jewish Councils, who only acted out of self-interest (Presser also mentions this), but there were also heroes and saints. Scholem states that we are not allowed to judge because we were not in their situation. (JP, 243)

As mentioned in the chapter on the unicity of the Shoah, Arendt's reply is that she never loved a collective or a people, not even her own people, but that she could only love individuals. Moreover, showing love for the Jews would make her suspicious, since she was a Jew herself. She considered the role of "the heart" in political matters not only doubtful, but she was also of the opinion that it could disguise factual truths. (JP, 247)

An explanation of her harsh judgments might be that they were political judgments, while many readers mistook them for moral judgments. She felt sorry for the Jewish people that was caught between Nazis and their anti-Semitic collaborators, but she did not have much respect for the Jewish leaders. She made this clear by citing a statement made by a former prisoner of Theresienstadt: "The Jewish people as a whole behaved magnificently. Only the leaders failed." (EJ, 284) Another reason for her "heartless" judgment was her conviction that politics is not like the nursery and that in politics obedience is the same as support. Arendt finds it incomprehensible that the Jewish leaders did not understand this. (EJ, 279)

Walter Laqueur says that Arendt's style is a consequence of her tendency to exaggerate and to want to be original at all costs. He feels that Arendt was attacked because of the way she expressed herself. Laqueuer considers Arendt a very intelligent woman, but without much feeling for nuances, which, especially for a subject like this, is of extreme importance. Moreover, it looks as if she has forgotten the situation of people who live in a totalitarian state. Humbleness is required in a book about the Shoah, but humbleness was not her strongest point, while it would have been appropriate as it concerns a judgment about people who were in a situation in which she had never been herself. (Laqueur, 1983, 116) Elisabeth Young-Bruehl comments on Laqueur's remarks.

> With formulas like these a sacred preserve has been made of Holocaust history, one who did not experience its extreme situations—and certainly those who are not Jewish—are criticized for judgments out of accord with the ethos of the preserve and the prerogatives of the survivors. (YB, 472)

I agree with Young-Bruehl. I think that Arendt, with her knowledge and intelligence, was allowed to judge. On the other hand, I also agree with Laqueur that her style could have been more subtle. She has a tendency not only to judge but also to condemn. She never gave the Jewish leaders the benefit of the doubt. I will refer to this in the following pages.

Arendt's analysis of the cooperation of the Jewish Councils would have been much better received if she had emphasized the chronological history of the Councils and if she had incorporated her answer to a reader who asked her opinion about the activities of the Jewish Councils:

> There is one important excuse for them: the cooperation was gradual and it was difficult indeed to understand when the moment had come to cross a line, which never should have been crossed. (YB, 345)

Young-Bruehl adds to this:

> On the other hand it should be said that Arendt's knowledge of conditions in the Eastern European ghettoes—and thus her ability to suggest how a line was crossed—was not always extensive enough to support her generalizations. (YB, 345)

I have said that Arendt's style was one of the reasons for the crticism her book received, but it was not the main reason. I refer to the recently published biography of prof. Dr. David Cohen, chairman of the Dutch Jewish Council. The author, Piet Schrijvers, writes that in the Tel Aviv branch of the Library of Vienna there is a report written by Cohen about Arendt's book on the Eichmann trial. The report starts:

> In this book Arendt tries to help Eichmann in his defence, accuses Ben Gurion and Gideon Hausner of having brought Eichmann before a court in Israel, accuses Jewish leaders of collaboration with the Nazis and the "Zionists" of cooperation with them, does not accuse the Allied powers of not having assisted

the Jews in their catastrophe, does not accuse the Pope of not having protested (as Hochhut asserts) against the massacres and does not accuse the Nazis of having murdered six million Jews and shows no compassion with the victims, although she herself escaped the horrors. In order to prove these theses she makes many mistakes, of which I sum up some principal ones. [follow three pages of specific "remarks"] (Schrijvers, 236)

The author of the book says that Cohen regarded Arendt's analysis as a classical example of Jewish self-hatred of a renegade. His remark is based on a statement by Cohen, who once said that the Jews have a need to blame their own people for their misery and that this system was transferred to the Jewish Councils (Schrijvers, 236)

I find it incomprehensible that an intelligent man like prof. Dr. David Cohen, with his scientific background, could have written this. Like Jacob Robinson he did not understand or did not want to understand what the book was really about, but his remarks may explain why the book was so severely criticized.

I shall now discuss another point of criticism. Until now I have defended Arendt against her critics, apart from the fact that I think she could have been a little more careful in her statements. However, with regard to the next point, I am on the critics' side. Arendt makes some statements about the situation that might have been created if the Jews had refused to cooperate and the Jewish Councils had not existed. Since this is a hypothetical question the answer can only be hypothetical, but Arendt's answer is not hypothetical at all.

> Without Jewish help in administrative and police work—the final rounding up of Jews in Berlin was, as I have mentioned, done entirely by Jewish police—there would have been either complete chaos or an impossibly severe drain on German manpower. (EJ, 117)

So far, I agree with Arendt. I don't know if there would have been chaos, but it would have hampered the Nazis' work, not only in Berlin, but also in other countries.

Philip von Freudiger, member of the Jewish Council in Budapest, said in his testimony that fifty percent of the Jews who escaped were captured and killed but, says Arendt, that is always better than the ninety-nine percent of those who did not escape. (EJ, 124) Arendt suggests that escape would have been preferable and this would have been easier without the existence of the Jewish Councils. She makes the following important statement:

> Wherever Jews lived, there were recognized Jewish leaders, and this leadership, almost without exception, cooperated in one way or another with the Nazis. The whole truth was that if the Jewish people had really been unorganized and leaderless, there would have been chaos and plenty of misery but the total number

of victims would hardly have been between four and a half and six million people. (EJ, 125)

In order to prove her statement, she refers to the situation in the Netherlands, where the Jewish Council became an instrument for the Nazis. 103.000 Jews were deported to the annihilation camps and some five thousand to Theresienstadt with the cooperation of the Jewish Council. She said that only five hundred and nineteen Jews (0,5%) returned from the death camps[10], while ten thousand of the twenty to twenty-five thousand Jews who went underground survived (forty to fifty percent, like in Budapest) She also said that most of the Jews sent to Theresienstadt returned to Holland.[11] (EJ, 125)

When discussing the situation as it might have been without the Jewish Councils Arendt speaks of "the whole truth". In this context the meaning of the word "truth" is important. I think that for Arendt "truth" is more than an opinion, but it is not the absolute, objective truth. It is a truth that is a certainty for her. Siegfried Moses, the spokesman of the Berlin Jewish Council said that it gives the impression of being a demonstrable assertion and according to Young-Bruehl, Arendt felt indeed that it was demonstrable. (YB, 347)

The discussion about the meaning of truth is as old as philosophy. There are two opinions: the first is that truth is the compatibility of knowledge and reality; the second is that truth is the systematic coherence between human judgments. However, the most suitable definition of truth in Arendt's case is: truth is a judgment, proposition or idea that is true or accepted as true. (Woolf, 1256) Arendt considered her statement to be true.

In the following pages I shall pay attention to her statement because it is one of the main points of the criticism on her book. Because she took the Netherlands as an example, it seems appropriate to make use of the writings of the Dutch historians Herzberg, de Jong and Presser and finally of Cohen's defense against the accusation of having cooperated with the Nazis. They do not only judge the actions of the Jewish Council, but they also wonder what had happened if the Jews had not cooperated and the Jewish Council had not existed.

First of all I should like to say a few words about the Dutch Jewish Council in general. It was established on February 13, 1941, after irregularities in the Jewish quarter of Amsterdam[12], followed by raids and a general strike.[13] Before that, the Nazis had taken quite a lot of measures, which were an indication for an ominous future, like a ban on visiting cinemas for all Jews, a numerus clausus for Jewish students and a special registration duty for anybody who had one or more Jewish grandparents. What follows are summaries of the comments on the Jewish Councils of Herzberg, de Jong, Presser and Cohen respectively.

Abel Herzberg says that in retrospect the history of the Jewish Council in the Netherlands is a human tragedy, resulting in the ruin of both perpetrators and victims. Opposition against the establishment of a Jewish Council was not successful in any country. In Belgium the Jews refused the formation of a Jewish Council. Afterwards the Council was established by the Nazis and did the same as the Jewish Council in Amsterdam.

According to Herzberg the situation would not have been different if the Jews had hidden behind the veil of anonymity. Any resistance would not have put off the occupier. On the contrary, he would have been irritated. According to Herzberg, the answer would have been murder and this opinion is based on the fact that the destruction of the Jews was a major issue in the totalitarian system and not an incidental circumstance. Herzberg wonders whether the objections against the Jewish Council were not primarily directed against the motives behind its policy rather than against the policy itself. The motives were related to the characters of Asscher and Cohen.[14] Both were no supporters of a policy of principle, but they believed in opportunism, compromises, delaying the inevitable and making concessions. It was these tactics, which had been applied even before the war, supported by the majority of the Jews, which the fundamentalists and the uncompromising criticized afterwards. History judges and never asks who was right at the time, but always who was right afterwards. History proved the Jewish Council to be wrong, but it is questionable whether it was wrong at the time. Herzberg points at the circumstances in those days and emphasizes that the Jewish Council was not established to save people, because in 1941 there were no rumours of deportation and destruction yet. After the deportations it was held against them that they had saved friends and relations, that they had established degrees of dispensability and indispensability, that they had played Providence and that the Council was a class institute. All these reproaches are true, says Herzberg, but the members of the Council did what people do in normal circumstances. If they had to make the choice to save a friend or someone they did not know, they chose the friend and friends were found in their own class and circle. If the Jewish Council was a class institute, one must not blame the Council but society. The Council established degrees of dispensability and indispensability, but what could they have done for the "orange-Jews", as Presser calls them.[15] Would there have been any arguments in their favour? The members of the Council had the illusion that the war would soon come to an end. Nobody could imagine that the nightmare would go on for five years. Did the members of the Council know before the fall of 1943 what would be the fate of the Jews? No, says Abel Herzberg, they did not know because it was inconceivable and in fact, it still is. The Jewish Council turned out to be a failure, but are we allowed to conclude that its establishment was a mistake?

Herzberg tends to consider the formation of the Jewish Council a positive event in a period of oppression and terror. He points at the importance of the Jewish unity, which in fact did not exist. The Jews did not even form a group, because of the many social, economical and ideological differences, but the Nazis determined the group on the basis of their birth and therefore a Jewish organization was necessary. It is true that the Nazis needed the Jewish Councils for the realization of their program, but, says Herzberg, would the Jews have been able to live their lives without an organization that supported them? According to Herzberg this would have been impossible and the Nazis knew this and played their devilish game.

> The Jewish population of the Netherlands, their natural bonds with society and fatherland cut off, and made into a disjointed collection of individuals where everyone had to fend for himself, had to find its place in Jewish history. It would have been a mistake to think this could be done without the Jewish Council. (Herzberg, 168)

It is remarkable that Herzberg suggests that this was one of the reasons for the formation of the Jewish Council. He even justifies the establishment of the Jewish Council on grounds of principle. According to him, the Jewish Council's role in the evacuations was a very positive one and the word "collaboration" is inappropriate. What would have happened if the Council had not been established? According to Herzberg there would have been another council in another form and with other leaders. The stronger the opposition against the formation of the Council would have been, the bloodier would have been the Nazis' measures. There was no escape from reality. The Nazis would not have allowed their prey to escape. If the resistance had been stronger, the Nazis would have invented other methods of intimidation and it is hard to guess how many Jews in hiding would have survived. (Herzberg, 143–197)

Summarizing, we may say that Herzberg defends the course of action of the members of the Jewish Council, although he admits that it has resulted in a catastrophe. If the Jewish Council had not cooperated, the catastrophe might have reached even greater dimensions.

According to Lou de Jong the Jewish Council's objectives were: trying to befriend the occupier, striving towards delay in the hope that tomorrow never comes and eventually sacrificing a minority in order to save a majority. The majority of the Jewish population did not feel a connection with the social group from which most of the members of the Jewish Council were recruited. This was the reason that many Jews refused to behave according to the Nazis' instructions. 25,000 went into hiding and 3,000 fled abroad. The fact that the majority did not go into hiding did not imply an acknowledgement of the

Jewish Council.[16] The Jewish Council admitted that they helped the occupier, but pointed out that they also offered resistance. Their device was prolonging, restraining and delaying, but de Jong wonders if they actually did this. In the end the moment came that the Council actively assisted in the deportations. In this decision to cooperate the struggle for self-preservation played a major role. De Jong wonders whether anything positive can be said about the Council and thinks that only the actions that were in favour of the Jews, in 1941, can be seen in a positive light. De Jong disagrees with Abel Herzberg's opinion that the role of the Jewish Council was important for the Jews as a mental and spiritual basis and with Herzberg's view of the Jewish Council as a social element that made it possible for Jewish life to continue. Herzberg disconnects the Jewish Council from its origin as an organization that assisted the occupier. It was a political instrument and although all help in itself was useful, it should not be seen out of its context, because offering assistance to people who departed, meant helping with deportations and destruction.

De Jong wonders if the Jews had other options. When answering this question, the reality of the occupation of the Netherlands must be taken into account. Armed resistance was out of the question. It might have been possible for the Jewish Council to minimize their cooperation with the enemy, at the same time helping Jews to go underground, although this was extremely difficult in Amsterdam.[17] This would have been a combination of legal and illegal actions, because a refusal to cooperate would, according to de Jong, have resulted in the execution of the members of the Jewish Council, without abandoning the "final solution". Refusing help in the first phase (providing lists with names of Jewish inhabitants) would immediately have resulted in the execution of the second phase. (raids in the streets)[18] The deportation process would have accelerated and hardened. De Jong's strongest reproach at the Jewish Council is their cooperation in the decision which Jews would be deported and which would not (or, in Presser's words, making a distinction between the "orange-Jews" and the elite). This was done because the members were afraid, short sighted and egoistic. (de Jong, part 7, I, 362–374)

The third historian, Jacob Presser, says that the problem of the Jewish Council cannot be separated from a more serious problem that arose everywhere where Jewish Councils were established. There was an identical pattern in all occupied territories. The beginning was apparently innocent, but gradually it went from bad to worse, ending in disaster. There are always the same questions: could they have acted differently, were they allowed to act differently, would it have been preferable to act differently and did they want to act differently? They tried to sabotage the execution of the Germans' orders while pretending to cooperate. The question of moral responsibility is everywhere. Presser finds it difficult to judge the members of the Jewish

Councils. He is of the opinion that judging would only be meaningful if the dead could speak as well. They cannot, but one can make an assumption of what they would have said and this assumption is that they would have accused the members of the Council of having been tools in the hands of the Nazis, acting out of self-interest to save themselves, family members and members of their social class.

Most important is the question of collaboration. Their collaboration is an undeniable historical fact. They collaborated and they had placed themselves in a position where it was impossible to choose between good and evil, but only between evil and worse, although they said later that they chose "the lesser evil".[19] The members of the Council believed that they could prolong and restrain in the hope the war would end soon.

Presser also asks the question what would have happened if the Jews had refused to cooperate. What could the Nazis have done? Deportations would have been delayed, according to Presser, and more Jews would have been in a position to escape their fate. Presser concludes his account with the Nazis' order to the Council to select 7,000 persons for deportation. They tried to save "the best" in the opinion of the chairman: intellectuals, the rich, peers or in other words, people of their own social class. "Orange-Jews were sacrificed for the benefit of the caste of the rich and the scholars". Presser finds that on the list with 7,000 names two names were missing: Cohen and Asscher. (Presser, 452–526)

At the end of 1945, David Cohen, the chairman of the Dutch Jewish Council, wrote a justification, which was recently integrally published in Schrijvers' biography of Cohen. I shall give a summary of the 27 pages.

Cohen starts by saying that he has a clean conscience and that, considering the circumstances, he followed the right track. The Council has been accused on a number of points:

– The chairmen were informed about the ultimate fate of the Jews. Cohen absolutely denies this. Illegally transported letters from deported people had convinced them that the situation in the Eastern territories was bearable. Later these letters turned out to be forged.

– The Council prepared lists with names of Jews for deportation. This is not true, says Cohen; the lists were made up by the Germans or by Dutch officials. The Council had no idea where the lists came from.

– The chairmen are accused of a weak attitude towards the occupier and of cooperation. However, the Council repeatedly made strong protests against various measures.

– The chairmen were primarily seeking their own advantage. Out of the question, says Cohen. He could easily have fled, but he did not want to because he had always put his best efforts into Jewish affairs and wanted to continue doing so.[20]

– The Council should have resigned and all Jews should have gone into hiding. However, says Cohen, most Jews did not want to go into hiding or were unable to. If the members had resigned, others would have been assigned in their place and Cohen did not want to leave the Jewish people in the care of others.

– The members of the Council should have refused their appointment from the beginning, because in that case there would have been chaos and that would have been better than a well-organized system. Cohen says that in that case Germans or members of the N.S.B.[21] would have done the work and that no one would have cared for the Jews. The Council wanted to be a protective wall between the occupier and the Jews, trying to delay and to liberate arrested people.

– The most important accusation is that the Council selected 7,000 names for deportation out of a list of 15,000 and therefore played the role of the Holy Providence. The Council was accused of sacrificing the proletariat for the rich. Cohen says that this is not true, because they saved people only on the basis of their indispensability. (and these happened to be well-to-do!) Cohen is still behind this decision: "a general who is forced to sacrifice part of his army will keep the best men". (Schrijvers, 256) We could have refused, said Cohen, but the occupier would have made a selection in alphabetical order. Moreover, the occupier would have taken revenge on the members of the Jewish Council, not on the chairmen, because it was their system to punish innocent people. Cohen understands the bitterness of the deportees, but feels they have to understand that someone in a leading position should not decide for himself but for the community. Cohen acknowledges that they were naïve; they misjudged the character of the Nazis, but they were not the only ones. Nobody ever knew what the final destination of the deportees would be. The B.B.C. (British Broadcasting Cooperation) mentioned it, but the members of the Council always supposed that this was the fate of the Eastern European Jews exclusively and not that of the Jews in the occupied countries.

So far the statements of Herzberg, de Jong, Presser and Cohen. I should like to make a few remarks on Cohen's defense. There is not a single word of regret, guilt, apology or sympathy for the victims. There is no doubt about the Council's decisions. People have to understand, says Cohen, but I am afraid they do not. The essential question for many others and for me is, whether the Council knew of the existence of annihilation camps. Cohen denies this, but Schrijvers has his doubts, based on Cohen's lecture in 1961 about "The problem of truth". In this lecture Cohen defends telling white lies: one has to veil the truth if it might harm victims. Did Cohen withhold the truth from them? We don't know, but if he did he did indeed play the role of the Holy Providence in the selection of the 7,000 names, in which "the best" were saved.

Arendt remarks on this subject that there are people who regret the fact that Germany sent Einstein packing, but that it was a much greater crime to kill little Hans Cohn from around the corner.

Cohen reacts:

> As for her comparison between Einstein and little Hans Cohn, she is right from the human point of view; but she forgets that for the community of men in times of danger the rescue of men like Einstein is of more importance. (Schrijvers, 256)

I should like to draw the attention to Arendt's statement that there would have been fewer victims in Europe if the Jewish Councils had not existed. Her statement is based on Freudiger's over-simplified remark[22] and on the figures of the Dutch victims, which she uses to estimate the total number of victims in Europe. Let me summarize the ideas of Herzberg, de Jong, Presser and, although he is not objective, Cohen, about the situation in case the Jewish Councils had not existed.

> The stronger the resistance would have been, the bloodier their measures. (Herzberg, 195)

> It is certain that there would have been a crisis; we are convinced that the occupier would have taken rigorous measures to try and avert this crisis. (de Jong, part 7, I, 374)

> . . . and in any case the deportations would have been delayed, the solidarity between Jews and gentiles increased and more Jews would have seized the opportunity to escape their fate. (Presser, I, 520)

> Germans or members of the N.S.B. would have done the job and no one would have cared for the Jews. (Schrijvers 248)

Not one of them says explicitly that there would have been fewer victims, although Presser states that the Jews would have had a better chance to go into hiding. It can never be proven. In natural sciences the correctness of a statement can be proven by means of experiments. The advantage of these experiments is that one can determine the circumstances and above all that they can be repeated. Obviously such experiments are impossible in the field of history. Historical events are unique and can never be repeated under the same circumstances and with the same people. We shall therefore never know if there would have been fewer victims had there been no Jewish Councils. Comparisons with countries without Jewish Councils, such as Denmark and with the activities of the "Einsatzgruppen", fall short because the circumstances were very different.

In fact any statement about the number of victims if there had been no Jewish Councils is mere guesswork. One can guess, suppose or set up a hypothesis, like Herzberg, de Jong, Presser and Cohen do. For Arendt, however, it is the "whole truth". From a scientific point of view, this is wrong, because it cannot be verified.

However, there is more. Arendt does not believe in causality where human actions are concerned. Historical events and circumstances do not have predictable results, because human action and human freedom are involved. Human beings are free to change direction, which may result in an unexpected situation. Moreover, coincidence plays an important role. In the case of the Jewish Council she abandons her own theory. Her statement: If there had been no Jewish Councils there had been fewer victims is causality: if not . . . then. . . It presupposes that history follows a fixed pattern, but that is not correct. Virtual survivors do not carry much weight because history could have taken another direction. We may believe or think that there would have been fewer victims without Jewish Councils, but in all fairness we have to admit that we do not know and can only make an assumption.

It is possible that her conviction is based on her personal experience in 1940 in Gurs, an internment camp in France. She managed to escape from this camp and in 1962 she wrote a letter to a magazine, saying that after she had spent some time in the camp France was defeated and all communications broke down. In the resulting chaos she succeeded in obtaining liberation papers with which she could leave the camp. (YB, 155) She also speaks of chaos when she refers to a situation without Jewish Councils. However it is not right to compare these two types of chaos. The circumstances were completely different and it is questionable whether chaos in the ghettos would have resulted in fewer victims.

From the above I must draw two conclusions. The first is that Arendt should have made a clearer distinction between her political and her moral judgment. Political judgments may be harsh but her moral judgment could have been more subtle and balanced and since she did not differentiate between the two types of judgment, her readers were shocked. The second conclusion is that her statement "The whole truth is. . ."[23] is unscientific and contradictory to her own idea of history. It would have been preferable if she had not given her opinion about what would have happened without Jewish Councils or had made a carefully balanced assumption. If she had been more careful, many readers might have agreed and it would have spared her criticism and sorrow.

Anybody who is accused has a right to defend him or herself. Is it possible to defend Hannah Arendt's view? I have tried to find a witness for the defense and I found Marc Van den Bossche, who refers to Gadamer. He says that with the rise of modern science and technology we have the possibility to control and to repeat. However, this leads unavoidably to a restriction of the truth. If controllability determines if something is true, our yardstick of knowledge is no longer truth but certainty. The possibility of repetition is important to test a scientific statement. In social sciences truth can have another meaning. We can speak of a "formative" truth, which is based on motivations, prejudices and presuppositions. Scientific truth negates these. If we analyze these motivations, we end up with a question. The basis of each statement is a question, which was the motivation for the statement and the question itself is an answer. By asking a question we bring something out into the open and the openness exists in not providing an answer. (Van den Bossche, 159–163)

Let us go back to Arendt's statement. Let us accept that her statement was an opinion that cannot be verified. The basis of her statement could have been: "Wouldn't there have been fewer victims if there had been no Jewish Councils?" The question suffices. Why did she not leave it at that? The point is that, in this particular case, by giving an affirmative answer to this painful question she accused the members of the Jewish Councils of having killed a considerable number of their own people.

The Banality of Evil

We have seen that, after the Eichmann trial, Arendt changed her notion of radical evil, in the sense of beyond comprehension, in banal evil, which means evil without depth and without motives. We also noticed that the word "radical" has another meaning for Arendt than for Kant. For Arendt it has a quantitative and qualitative meaning and it cannot be explained by human motives. Kant's notion of "radical" refers to the origin of evil and it can be explained by human motives. Arendt said that she used the term "the banality of evil" willy-nilly. She had not really thought about it and there was no theory or thesis behind the term, although it went counter to the philosophical and theological tradition of evil. Nevertheless, her opponents were of the opinion that Arendt, by using the term "banality of evil", paid too little attention to the devilish maliciousness of Eichmann. The point is that she could detect no devilish maliciousness in Eichmann; in her opinion he was a common, ordinary, banal, non-thinking and non-judging bureaucrat who executed orders. An important question is how the banality of evil relates to Arendt's radical evil. Are these qualifications completely different or do they have something in common?

Richard Bernstein tries to connect the two expressions. He refers to the correspondence between Arendt and Jaspers. In a comment on Karl Jaspers' book *The Question of German Guilt* Arendt writes in 1946 that the Nazi crimes explode the limits of the law and that for these crimes no punishment is severe enough. Hanging is totally inadequate. (C, 54) Jaspers answers that he is not pleased with her view, because a guilt that goes beyond all criminal guilt inevitably takes on a streak of satanic greatness, which for him is inappropriate. He also says that one must see those things in their total banality.[24] Bernstein remarks that the essence of Jaspers' letter in 1946 is similar to Arendt's letter to Scholem in 1964.[25] Both Jaspers and Arendt deny a devilish character of the Nazi crimes, which is in accordance with Kant's negation of the possibility of devilish people.[26] This means that there is no demonic element in Arendt's radical evil, or in the banality of evil.

Bernstein sees another similarity between radical evil and the banality of evil. Arendt says that radical evil cannot be explained by human motives such as self-interest, greed, resentment, lust for power or cowardice. (OT, 459) However, fifteen years later she says the same about Eichmann, namely that he did not act on the basis of evil motives but as a result of thoughtlessness. (LM, 33–4)

On the basis of these two arguments Bernstein concludes that there is no essential difference between Arendt's radical evil and the banality of evil. In both terms there is no question of demonic elements or evil motives. Arendt did not change her mind because the two expressions can be united. Bernstein agrees that there is a shift of focus in Arendt's thoughts. The shift is in her key concepts. "Superfluousness", the key concept in radical evil, has been replaced by "thoughtlessness" in the banality of evil. (Bernstein, 1996, 137–153)

Bernstein's idea is interesting. He tries to solve the apparent contradiction between radical evil and the banality of evil. I have two objections. The first objection is based on Arendt's own statement in a letter to Mary McCarthy, that banal evil is contradictory to radical evil. (BF, 148) My second objection is that Bernstein's argumentation is based on the absence in both expressions of evil motives and satanic elements. However, the fact that neither a cat nor a canary can bark, does not indicate that the two animals have something in common.

It is my opinion that radical evil has another meaning for Arendt than the banality of evil. Radical evil is a crime against humanity. Radical evil tries to destroy the characteristic components of human existence—spontaneity, openness and plurality—and to change people into beings whose reactions are totally predictable, without surprises or differentiation. Radical evil creates another kind of evil, which Arendt calls banal evil. The perpetrators of this banal evil do not identify their actions as evil. This automatism is only possible within a totalitarian regime that has created a radical (and even legal) evil. Radical evil, which destroys humanity, brings people to the banality of evil. Banal people start to commit crimes and therefore some investigators prefer to speak of "the evil of banality", because despite their crimes most of the actors were and remained banal, ordinary people.

It is quite possible that Eichmann and many others had no evil motives, but that their actions were a result of thoughtlessness. However, it is questionable whether this is true for all Nazis. Is it also true for the people in the center of the onion such as the direct subordinates of The Leader or for the executors like concentration camp guards or members of the police battalions? I will revert to this in the chapter on thinking and judging in the Third Reich.

The next question is whether the banality of evil can be placed in Kant's theory of radical evil. Eichmann's thoughtlessness led to an extreme example of a lack of judgment. Arendt also speaks of self-deception (EJ, 51–52), referring not only to Eichmann, but to the entire German people. Although Kant explicitly refers to self-deception only in connection with the third level of evil doing, it nevertheless plays an important role in all three levels of evil doing as described in chapter two.

The first level is the level of weakness, the frailty of the human heart. Since human beings are no angels, good intentions are sometimes weaker than wrong inclinations. This means that we have the intention to do good, but we are unable to do it because adverse motives are stronger. (Rel, 34 [21–22]) Moral weakness means nothing else than to be open to the temptation to give preference to self-interest over the moral law. One is responsible for this weakness and as such it is an expression of freedom and therefore a self-imposed weakness. Self-deception transforms this temptation into a fact. By means of self-deception one can persuade oneself that self-interest prevails over compliance with the moral law.

The second level is the level of impurity i.e. mixing unmoral with moral motives. (Rel, 34 [21–22] Also at this level self-deception explains how we can take ourselves to be acting from duty alone, when, in fact, we require some extra-moral incentive in order to do what duty dictates.

The third level and highest degree of evil is the level of wickedness. It is the propensity to adopt evil maxims. At this level the moral law is made subordinate to motives of self-interest, and self-deception plays an important role. (Rel, 35 [22–24]

In fact it plays an important role at all levels of evil and for Kant it was the main mechanism people use to avoid their responsibility. Self-deception is a form of inner lying, enabling human beings to deceive themselves. How can the concept of self-deception be used to explain the attitude and actions of Eichmann?

In order to answer this question we must look at Kant's view on moral deliberation. According to Kant, this deliberation consists of subjecting one's maxim to the universalization test to determine whether it can be universalized without giving rise to contradiction. It is this test that provides the major opportunity for self-deception. Immoral maxims can pass the universalization test because they neglect or obscure certain moral aspects of a particular situation. Evil persons can misapply the categorical imperative, without denying its authority.

This can be clarified with the following theoretical example. Suppose person A does not like person B. A obtains information on B, which he knows will give B much pain if he hears of it. A has the intention to hurt B and decides to give him the information. He justifies doing so by saying that B has the right to know. Thus, instead of it being an evil act to make B suffer, A pretends it is a commendable act of telling the truth. A might even convince himself that it is his duty to tell B the truth. It is obvious that this justification procedure is based on self-deception and obscures the real intention. (Allison, 181)

Arendt states that Eichmann was not a fanatical anti-Semite. This implies that he had to hide his true feelings during the organization of the deportations. Arendt describes his real feelings in her book, when she reports Eichmann's visits to Lublin, Chelmno, Minsk and Treblinka. What he saw made him sick, but in fact what he saw was the final result of his own preliminary work. Instead of resigning (which would have been possible without serious consequences) he soothed his conscience by means of self-deception based on deliberate thoughtlessness. He tried to overcome his horror of the results of his own work by simply not thinking about it and not visiting the places where he could see the destruction of the Jews with his own eyes. (EJ, 87–93) The result was that he acted on the basis of faulty maxims and on the idea that duty comes first and that orders had to be executed regardless of their contents. According to Allison, Eichmann can be seen as a "virtual limiting case of Kantian wickedness" because his thoughtlessness and self-deception are examples of the neglect of morally salient features. (Allison, 182) However, Eichmann said that he complied with Kant's moral concepts by respecting the laws of the country, but Arendt says rightly that blind obedience is not in accordance with Kant's ethical concepts, because it denies the possibility of an autonomous judgment. Man must follow his own individual judgment and act accordingly.

My question was whether Eichmann's banality of evil can be placed in Kant's levels of evil. I think we all agree that it has little or nothing to do with the first level of moral weakness. As I have said before, men are no angels and we all suffer from moral weakness from time to time. What about level three, the level of the wicked character? Eichmann had no purely wicked character; he did not act out of self-interest, greed, covetousness, resentment, lust for power or cowardice. If he does not fit in level three, only level two, the level of impurity remains. It is true that Eichmann mixed pure maxims with impure maxims, but I think that the majority of men are from time to time guilty of this. Moreover, Eichmann is still regarded as one of the worst criminals of the last century and criminals usually do not fit in level two. So, it seems that Eichmann's banality of evil does not fit in Kant's theory. How is this possible? The answer is that there is an enormous discrepancy between Eichmann's character and intentions on the one hand and the result of his actions on the other hand and the explanation is that he was a cog in the wheel of the totalitarian system. Totalitarian systems did not exist in Kant's time. Of course there was murder and theft in those days, but "desk murderers" were unknown. Kant's theory is insufficient to explain the evil in totalitarian systems, also because particular crimes, which would be punishable in a normal society, would be considered legal in a totalitarian system. "Thou shalt not kill" was reversed into "Thou shalt kill" and this is the main reason why Arendt states that the crimes were incomprehensible, unforgivable and unpunishable.

The Death Penalty

Despite the fact that Arendt said that certain crimes committed in a totalitarian system are unpunishable, the last words of her book were that Eichmann must be hanged, because of not wanting to share the earth with the Jews and a number of other groups of people. Was this an adequate punishment? Let us first see what Arendt thinks about it herself.

Usually punishment is justified on one of the following grounds: protection of society, improvement of the criminal, frightening effect on other criminals and finally revenge. These motives are inadequate in the case of war criminals, because they are no ordinary criminals: it is unlikely that they will commit more crimes; protection of society is not necessary; there is little chance that they will better their lives and the frightening effect is very limited because of the extraordinary circumstances during which the crimes were committed or would be committed in the future. Even the notion of revenge is not applicable in the light of the magnitude of the crimes. Despite all these arguments it would be ridiculous not to punish them. Here is the dilemma: we punish out of a sense of justice, while the same sense of justice tells us that all our ideas about punishment and justification are totally inadequate. (VO, 57–58)

Tvetan Todorov says that if we punish somebody for crimes committed twenty years earlier, we assume that he is still the same person, but that is contradictory to human biology and psychology. Most people are capable of improvement but by enforcing the death penalty we deny them this possibility. Therefore the death penalty is a form of barbarism. Todorov says that we should not make an exception for war criminals, because if we do, we separate their actions from other forms of human behaviour and make them even more incomprehensible, which does not mean that we must give up the idea of crimes against humanity. (Todorov, 302–304)

Jacques De Visscher wonders whether Arendt's conclusion is unavoidable. Was not Eichmann a prospectless victim in Jerusalem? Of course he was guilty, but it is questionable whether he had to be killed legally. The death penalty was a solution for the sake of convenience and it was the most obvious. Would forgiveness have been impossible? Would Eichmann ever have repented his crimes? Although it seemed unlikely, the court did not give him the opportunity. De Visscher wonders if the death penalty was only based on revenge and resentment. (De Visscher, 90)

I agree with Todorov and De Visscher. From a humane point of view it would have been better not to hang him. I think there were two reasons why he was hanged. In the first place it was an Israeli court; the Jews were the main victims of Eichmann's actions and revenge can be found in the Jewish tradition.[27] It is questionable whether an international court would have decided on the same punishment. Possibly the most important reason for the verdict was the fact that Eichmann was regarded as the personification of the totalitarian system. Hanging Eichmann was symbolic for the death of Nazi-totalitarianism and it is my opinion that the death penalty had been decided upon before the beginning of the trial.

THINKING, JUDGING AND ACTING IN THE THIRD REICH

In the totalitarian Nazi-system we can distinguish the following groups: The Leader and his direct subordinates, who determined the strategy, the executors, the party members and finally the bystanders. Apart from some remarks, Arendt never paid attention to the first group. The Eichmann trial gave her an insight in the thinking, judging and acting of the executors. It is possible that this group was even more important than the first group judging by the following statement:

> The foundation of the greatest of political evils is not to be found in the few who deliberately choose to inflict evil on the world but in the heteronymous evil of those who elect to defer to evil, practices or policies. For this destroys not only the personal judgments on which a meaningful political life must be based but also permits the domination of communal life by evil policies, persons and practices. (Clark, 439)

Three conditions must be fulfilled before someone may be accused of heteronymous evil: his behaviour must have evil consequences, his behaviour must be based on heteronymous maxims and he must submit to an evil-minded person. Eichmann met these conditions and his trial gave Arendt the idea of the banality of evil, evil executed by a banal, ordinary citizen. Eichmann was an executor of the Nazi ideology. The trial has given us a better insight in Eichmann's way of thinking, judging and acting, but Eichmann was only one of many who did not determine the strategies and policies, but only decided how these could be executed. This group gave shape to the ideology. Moreover, this group can be divided into two types of co-operators. The first type were office clerks, people like Eichmann. The second type were people who worked in the field: camp guards, members of the Gestapo, police battalions or Einsatzgruppen. What kind of people where these executors? Were they criminals, people with a satanic or demonic character? On the contrary, they were common people; people who apparently were not very different from the average citizen. For the first time in history we saw the phenomenon of ordinary people who, under certain circumstances, could commit the most horrible crimes.

> The simple and rather frightening truth is that under circumstances of legal and social permissiveness people will engage in the most outrageous criminal behaviour who under normal circumstances perhaps dreamed of such crimes but never actually committing them (CR, 70)

Arendt points at Bernt Naumann's report of the Auschwitz trial in 1963, where 23 people stood trial. These 23 people were "intolerable cases" selected from around two thousand members of the S.S. who worked in Auschwitz between 1940 and 1945.

> Auschwitz was the camp of systematic extermination, but the atrocities almost all the accused had committed had nothing to do with the order for the "final solution"; their crimes were punishable under Nazi law, and in rare cases such perpetrators were actually punished by the Nazi government. These defendants had not been specially selected for duty at an extermination camp; they had come to Auschwitz for no other reason than that they were unfit for military service. Hardly any of them had a criminal record of any sort, and none of them a record of sadism or murder. Before they had come to Auschwitz and during the eighteen years they had lived in post-war Germany, they had been respectable and respected citizens, undistinguishable from their neighbors. (CR, 71)

All had been respectable citizens until they found themselves in a situation that was completely different from their normal situation, which appears from their various professions: office clerk, teacher, farmer, butcher, book-keeper, gynaecologist, piano constructor, pharmacist and dentist. The trial had two more interesting aspects. Witness expert dr. Buchheim testified that there was no "Befehlsnotstand" in the camps. This means that the execution of an order was avoidable if it provoked an inner moral conflict in the executor. According to dr. Buchheim it was even possible to refuse to execute orders without giving a reason; this was acknowledged by a number of other witnesses and also stressed by Christopher Browning in a recent study.

> I think that the new evidence clearly confirms my latter conclusion about the presence of a minority exceeding 10 percent (indeed in Mir and Marcinkance even exceeding 20 percent!) that evaded taking part in the killing itself but with very rare exceptions did not hinder or protest against the killing process. Evasion was easily tolerated, but protest and obstruction most empathically were not (Browning 2000, 175)

The second interesting aspect is that neither in Neumann's report nor in the Dutch report by Jacobs and Stoop, reference is made to a mental disturbance or diminished responsibility of the suspects and none of the eighteen defending counsels put it forward in their defence of the suspects. I must conclude from this that the suspects were normal persons. Recent investigations by Daniel Goldhagen and Christopher Browning confirm that the perpetrators were generally normal persons and, thanks to Arendt, the best-known normal person in the group of office clerks is Adolph Eichmann. In order to understand the thinking, judging and acting of all perpetrators, I make the assumption that Eichmann was a prototype of this group. My final conclusions about Eichmann will, to a large extent, apply to all the other office clerks.

Arendt said that Eichmann was "thoughtless"; he was unable to think or unable to think properly. In the film "The Specialist" we can hear the public prosecutor ask Eichmann whether he had never thought about his position and actions. His answer is: "Ja, natürlich, mitgedacht hab ich wohl". (Yes, of course, I have thought along) He had "thought along", but with whom? Definitely not with the victims, but most probably with his superiors, about the way the deportations could be organized. Eichmann's acts were to a large extent determined by thinking along with his superiors. "Thinking along" is, contrary to thinking, not an autonomous process. What is the significance of Eichmann's "thinking along", but not thinking?

In the chapter on "Thinking" we have learned that thinking itself does not lead to a final result, but that it has a liberating effect on our ability to judge. Thinking is a necessary condition for judging; it is a conversation with our conscience. During the process of thinking all preconceptions, ideas and opinions are considered and reconsidered until one is "empty" and this is the moment that one is able to judge and to say, "this is right" or "this is wrong". This judgment is not necessarily final. It may be considered as temporary and it can at any time be replaced by a new judgment, but only after thinking about new facts or new events. Arendt situates judging not only between thinking and acting, but also at the same level.

If we depart from the idea that thinking is a necessary condition for judging, it seems obvious that persons who are unable to think cannot have an inner discussion with their conscience and hence are unable to judge. Arendt said that Eichmann was unable to speak (except in officialese) and that this incapability was closely related to his incapability to think, especially from the standpoint of somebody else. (EJ, 49) However, this, as Kant calls it "Erweiterte Denkungsart" (enlarged thought), is the basis of judging. There can only be one conclusion: Eichmann was unable to think in a way that is a condition for judging. His "thoughtlessness" made him "judgementless". Eichmann and probably many others in the same layer were unable to judge their situation and they silenced the voice of their conscience. Eichmann did this after his visit to the extermination camps in Chelmno and Treblinka. Arendt describes Eichmann's horror of the things he had seen and his attempt to resist this horror by avoiding having to witness similar situations and scenes. He did not want to put himself in the place of the other man; he only wanted to arm himself against his own horror of the crime. (EJ, 87–93)

Eichmann's answer to the question whether there had never been an inner conflict between his conscience and his duty was, that he had been aware of his split personality, caused by the situation, but that he had finally forced himself to do his duty as a nationalist. The most important factor in the soothing of his conscience was that there was nobody around him who was against the Final Solution. (EJ, 116) This is exactly what Bettelheim meant when he said that living in a totalitarian society is so desperate, because there is nobody to turn to for guidance and there are no voices from the outside, because the totalitarian leaders had silenced these voices long before.[28]

If we conclude that Eichmann was unable to judge, what were the consequences? We have seen that Kant distinguishes determinant and reflective judgments. Determinant judgments subsume particulars under given universals, which are rules, principles or laws and these judgments play an important role in practical reason. Individual actions are subsumed under and determined by the categorical imperative. Reflective judgments are different. Here the particular is given and it has to be decided to which universal it belongs. We have seen how Eichmann misused the categorical imperative because he considered it his duty to comply with the Nazi laws and this was a result of his "judgmentlessness". We also learned that reflective judgments of the spectators are especially important because spectators are impartial, while the actor is partial by definition. Eichmann and his colleagues were no spectators but actors. However, an actor does not act continuously. Every now and then he looks at his actions from a distance and judges the results. In doing so he becomes a spectator and impartial to a certain extent. Eichmann was a spectator during his visits to the concentration camps. Here he saw the results of his actions. Instead of giving his reflective judgment "this is wrong", he suppressed his horror and from that moment he was a cog in the wheel. The people who organized and executed the Shoah were all in the same level of the organisation and of the same kind. They must have been aware of the effect of their actions; only very few people, if any, lack a conscience. These people's conscience was silenced by their inability or unwillingness to think and judge.

What made ordinary citizens become a cog in the Nazi wheel? The answer to this question can to a large extent be found in Arendt's description of Himmler's method for the formation of his S.S.- and Gestapo organization. Himmler was not a perverse fanatic, no adventurer, no sex maniac, but a real bourgeois, a good family man and he built his entire organization on his conviction that people, first of all, must be good employees and family members. When the economic circumstances in Germany became chaotic, their position became unsteady.[29] Already in the early days of the Nazi period, it became clear that these respectable citizens were prepared to sacrifice their human dignity for the sake of their pension, life insurance and the security of their families. Himmler made use of this knowledge. He employed citizens as workers in the destruction machine and took away all their responsibilities, because only on this condition were the citizens willing to execute their tasks. It was the fact that they had no responsibility that made them into "cogs in a wheel". (EU, 128–129)

As I mentioned earlier, there was a second group of executors besides the desk people. These were the people who worked "in the field". It is not certain whether thoughtlessness and judgmentlessness played an equally important role as in the first group. Arendt did not pay specific attention to this group, but it fits in the framework of this essay to say a few words about it. I should like to mention two investigators who studied the fieldworkers: Daniel Goldhagen and Christopher Browning. I shall pay some more attention to Christopher Browning because Goldhagen's vision is quite simple, wheras Browning's view shows more nuance. Both investigators made a study of the same police battalion: Reserve Police Battalion 101, a group of ordinary middle class and middle aged citizens, not specially selected for murder, who committed atrocious crimes in Poland.

Daniel Goldhagen thinks that the actions of this group were based on the one and only motivation: "elimination anti-Semitism" that had existed for many centuries. His conclusion is completely different from Browning's vision, which is more nuanced and seems more logical. First of all Browning remarks that this group was not in the "luxury" position of the so-called desk murderers. Between the members of the last group and their victims was a functional and physical distance. Eichmann and his co-workers never saw their victims and this depersonalizing aspect, which could explain their behaviour, was not applicable to Reserve Police Battalion 101. According to Browning there are three other major factors that could explain the behaviour of the members of this group: the influence of the specific circumstances and situation, obedience to authority and ideological education.

With regard to the situation and circumstances in which the members of Reserve Police Battalion 101 found themselves, Browning refers to the famous study of Philip Zimbardo at Stanford University. Zimbardo demonstrated that during an experiment students showed sadistic behaviour, even though they had no sadistic personality. Zimbardo randomly divided a group of students into "guards" and "prisoners" and placed them in a simulated prison. This situation caused unusual, antisocial behaviour of the "guards". One third of the "guards" were "cruel and tough"; a middle group was "tough but fair" and only two (less than 20%) were "good" guards. These two did not punish the "prisoners" and sometimes they rendered small services. This spectrum shows a remarkable similarity with the behaviour of the members of Reserve Police Battalion 101: a core of enthusiastic killers; a larger group of people who only took part in the executions and raids if they were ordered to, but who did not look for opportunities to kill and sometimes even refrained from killing, when nobody was monitoring their actions and finally a small group (less than 20 %) of refusers.

The second factor is obedience to authority. Stanley Milgram investigated whether persons are able to resist authority not backed by threat, but by "scientific" arguments. He asked a group of volunteers to inflict an escalating series of fake electric shocks upon a victim, who responded with programmed complaints, calls for help and cries of pain. The experiment showed that two thirds of the volunteers were obedient to the point of inflicting extreme pain. Milgram saw similarities between the human behaviour in his experiments and the behaviour of some people under the Nazi regime: "Men are led to kill with little difficulty". (Browning, 1998, 173) Nevertheless, Milgram was aware of the differences between the two situations: the volunteers knew that they did not cause permanent physical damage to their victims; there was no coercion or threat and no ideological indoctrination. These differences, says Browning, create too many variables to draw scientific conclusions, but many of Milgram's observations are confirmed by the behaviour and the testimonies of the members of Reserve Police Battalion 101.

The last factor is the influence of the ideology. To what extent was the behaviour of the members of Reserve Police Battalion 101 a result of ideological indoctrination? Browning wonders whether the members of the group were brainwashed. We have seen that Hannah Arendt asked the same question. Initially she thought that the ideology was of major importance for the individual behaviour, but later she had her doubts about it. Browning's study shows clearly that the members of the police battalion were indoctrinated with regard to race, the Jewish Question and the purity of German blood. This indoctrination was done by means of lessons given by one of the officers. Apart from these lessons, there was a weekly pamphlet with articles written by Joseph Goebbels and Alfred Rosenberg. Careful study of two hundred of these pamphlets demonstrates that there was indeed instruction about racial theories, but not specifically on anti-Semitism. Only one pamphlet was an exception. In this pamphlet the question of a "Europe without Jews" was brought up. Furthermore, there was a second series of pamphlets appearing two to four times a year. One of these pamphlets, distributed in 1942, was specifically devoted to the question of "S.S. members and the problem of blood relationship". A number of points have to be taken into consideration.

– The most detailed article appeared in 1943, but at that moment the Lublin district, in which Reserve Police Battalion 101 was operating was already "Judenfrei" (free of Jews). Therefore this article cannot have played a significant role in the indoctrination for the commitment of mass murders.

– The pamphlet on blood relationship was specifically meant to influence young people in their choice of partners and was in fact irrelevant for the members of the police battalion, since most of them were married and had children.

– Many Nazis were young men. They had been raised and educated with Nazi values and Nazi norms. They probably did not know better and killing Jews was not in conflict with the value system of their education and hence indoctrination was easier. However, things were different for the members of Reserve Police Battalion 101, because the majority consisted of middle-aged men. Their moral education took place long before 1933.

– The pamphlet about "a Europe without Jews", tried to explain why this should be achieved, but it did not urge people to kill innocent Jewish men, women and children in order to reach this goal.

Browning's conclusion is therefore that the influence of ideological indoctrination on the individual members of the police battalion was limited.

> Influenced and conditioned in a general way, imbued in particular with a sense of their own superiority and otherness, many of them undoubtedly were; explicitly prepared for the task of killing Jews they most certainly were not. (Browning, 1992, 184)

The example of the story of the members of Reserve Police Battalion 101 is given to see to what extent thoughtlessness and the inability to judge played a role in the activities of the "fieldworkers". We have seen that Reserve

Police Battalion 101 consisted of three different kinds of people: a few fanatic murderers, members who only took part in the killing if they received an order and finally some refusers and evaders. In another study, Browning said of the first group that these were "eager killers", ideologically educated people, who were willing to kill any Jew or real enemy of the Third Reich. In this group the ideology obviously played an important role. Browning put them on a par with Hitler or Heydrig, but on a local level. (Browning, 2000, 175) I do not think that their actions were a result of thoughtlessness or the inability to judge; they were based on evil maxims or pure maliciousness. The refusers and evaders, on the other hand, have probably formed the proper reflective judgment, that taking part in the killing would be wrong. I think that thoughtlessness and an inability to judge only played a role in the middle group: people who only participated after having received an order.

Browning concludes by saying that the story of the members of Reserve Police Battalion 101 is worrisome, although their story is not everybody's story. People who committed the crimes cannot be cleared by saying that anybody would have acted in the same way had he or she been in the same circumstances, because among them were people who protested and others who refused. This is in accordance with Arendt's remark in 1962:

> Politically speaking, it is that under condition of terror most people will comply, but *some will not* (EJ, 233)

The fundamental problem is why ordinary people in specific circumstances are willing and able to commit horrible crimes. With regard to these special circumstances, Browning points at the danger of the complexity of modern society, in which, as a result of specialisation and bureaucracy, people who execute the official strategy lose the sense of personal responsibility.

> Within virtually every social collective, the peer group exerts tremendous pressures on behaviour and sets moral norms. If the men of Reserve Police Battalion 101 could become killers under such circumstances, what group of men cannot? (Browning, 1992, 189)

I will come back to Browning's question in the epilogue, but one of the possible answers to Browning's rhetorical question was given by Jan Gross in his book *Neighbours. The extermination of the Jews in Jedwabne.* He describes how on the 10th of July 1941 in the Polish village of Jedwabne the non-Jewish inhabitants killed practically all 1600 Jewish inhabitants. This happened under the leadership of a small group among which the major of the village and with the knowledge, but not the cooperation of the German Army, which had occupied the village one month earlier.

Forty years earlier Hannah Arendt made a remark similar to Browning's, when she said that under certain circumstances people are obviously prepared to do anything. Under these extreme conditions, characterized by Arendt as "when the stakes are on the table" or "when the chips are down", the ability to think and judge plays an important role and it also shows what kind of person one is.

We have seen in Germany that at the moment when, because of unemployment, his life, future and self respect were at stake, the respectable family man was willing to do anything, even to become a mass murderer in a destruction machine. This story of a Jew who was released from the concentration camp Buchenwald is characteristic. Leaving the camp he saw a former school-friend among the S.S. guards. The man looked at him and said: "You must understand, I have five years of unemployment behind me. They can do anything they want with me". (EU, 129)

Finally I want to emphasize that these stories are in accordance with Kant's theory. In principle the inclination towards evil is present in everybody, but it depends on the person's character and his situation whether he will partially or completely yield to the inclination or not.

The question of the influence of the bystanders' judgment in the Third Reich is important. In the chapter about judgment I spoke about the importance of the judgment of "impartial bystanders", people who witnessed certain events, but who were not involved personally. In fact there were two kinds of bystanders in the Third Reich: the bystanders in Germany during the rise of Hitler and the bystanders in the entire Third Reich after 1940.

The rise of Hitler and the Nazis was partly made possible by the attitude of the bystanders. Part of these bystanders helped him up; another part was silent.[30] The reasons for this behaviour were given in the chapter on totalitarianism. In my opinion, protest would only have been effective in the early days of the movement. There was some protest at the time, but it failed, because too many people supported the Nazi movement. Passive behaviour will not do, because passivity means in fact obedience and obedience means support and even the most powerful king and the cruellest tyrant are powerless if no one supports them by obedience. (OR, 228)

A lack of protest may give the Leader the impression that the population supports his actions. Lack of protest in Germany and abroad undoubtedly supported Hitler in the execution of his plans.

What can be said about the bystanders in the occupied territories? Were they real bystanders? I think they were, especially in situations in which they were not personally involved.

One of the best examples is the attitude of the Danish population and the Danish royal family during the German occupation. It should be mentioned that in Denmark there were hardly any Nazis or collaborators and there was no Nazi organisation. The German army occupied Denmark and despite the occupation Denmark remained a neutral state until the fall of 1943. When the Nazis tried to force the Danish Jews to wear the yellow star, they were told that if the Jews were forced to wear it the king would be the first to do so and that anti-Jewish measures would lead to the resignation of government officials. By doing so, the Danish government not only protected the 6400 Danish Jews, but also the 1400 German Jews who had become stateless after their escape from Germany. The attitude of the Danes was unique in Europe and the result was that all measures against the Jews were postponed until the fall of 1943. In August of that year there was a strike of Danish dockworkers, who refused to repair a German ship. Headquarters in Berlin demanded measures, but it did not take into account that the soldiers of the German occupation army were no longer the same obedient people and more or less refused to execute the orders, or even sabotaged them.

On the 1st October Berlin decided on raids to be executed by the German police, but they did not dare to enter the houses for fear of intervention of the Danish police. Only people who voluntarily opened the door were arrested, but there were only 477 out of 7.800 who did that.

The story goes that the German plan was given away by one of the occupiers to a Danish government official, who in his turn informed the Jewish leaders. These leaders warned the Jews during the celebration of the Jewish New Year in the synagogues. The majority of the Jews went into hiding and that was not difficult because everybody wanted to help them. Fortunately, neutral Sweden was close and with the help of Danish fishermen almost 6.000 Jews escaped to Sweden. Rich Danes paid the expenses of the crossing (about a hundred dollars) for those who could not afford it. The German operation against the Jews was a complete failure. The most interesting part of the whole story is that the German occupiers probably changed their attitude because they met with resistance. (EJ, 171–175) This shows that protests from bystanders could be effective, not only in the beginning but also in a later stage.

I mentioned the lack of protest of the German population against the rise of Hitler and the Nazis. Too many people were enthusiastic and supportive. We all know the pictures of hysterical crowds with their right arm lifted in the Hitler salute and this brings me to the matter of guilt and responsibility of the German people and the question whether we are right in speaking about a collective guilt or not.

NOTES

1. In 1999 I visited "Zululand", an artificial Zulu village for tourists in South Africa. Some episodes of a Hollywood film on Shaka were shown. In a discussion with our guide he told me that Shaka is still regarded as a hero, like Napoleon, who tried to unite all Zulu tribes. He was mainly depicted as a soldier who invented new weapons, such as a short spear that was much easier to handle than the long one.

2. See also chapter 1.

3. See also chapter 1.

4. The fact that Rosenthal does not look at the Holocausts of the primitives indicates that he disagrees with John Stanley's comparison of the Shoah with King Shaka's regime.

5. For the question of cooperation in a totalitarian system, see also chapter 4.

6. The estimated pre-Final Solution Jewish population in the Netherlands is 140.000. The estimated number of annihilated Dutch Jews is 105.000, which is 75%. This is by far the highest percentage in the Western European countries. (Dawidowicz, 544)

7. Chelmno-on-the-Ner was the first extermination camp in Poland, situated about 100 km West of Warsaw.

8. see also chapter 4.

9. It is not correct to say that the Jews did not fight back. Apart from the ghetto uprising in Warsaw (April/May 1943), there were uprisings in the extermination camps of Treblinka (August 1943) and Sobibor (October 1943).

10. This figure differs considerably from the data in Lucy Dawidowicz' book. She writes that in the Netherlands there were about five thousand survivors from the annihilation camps. (Dawidowicz, 498)

11. According to Presser this figure is wrong. He says that only 1273 of the 4897 persons that were deported to Theresienstadt survived. About 75% of the deportees died, mainly because they were sooner or later transported from Theresienstadt to Auschwitz.

12. Eighty percent of the Dutch Jews lived in Amsterdam.

13. The strike is known as the "February strike" and every year there is a memorial ceremony in the former Jewish quarter of Amsterdam.

14. Vice chairman and chairman of the Dutch Jewish Council.

15. "Orange Jews" is a nickname for the poorest Jews, who tried to make a living by selling oranges from a barrow in the street or at the market.

16. One of the major reasons was that the Western part of the Netherlands, including Amsterdam, is an extremely difficult area for people who want to go into hiding. It is an open, flat area without major woods or other hiding places and a town is the worst place for hiding. Moreover, the population was reluctant to hide people, because detection meant reprisals.

17. The majority of hidden Jews were in the country.

18. In 1943 I was in a raid (in Amsterdam we used the word "razzia") myself during a visit to my uncle and his Jewish wife. The whole area was cut off and all Jewish residents were summoned by means of loudspeakers to leave their houses. My

aunt came back thanks to a special permission because of her mixed marriage. Jews without permission had to pack for deportation.

19. Hannah Arendt says that the weakness of this argument is that it is very often forgotten that they did choose for evil. (VO, 66)

20. Hannah Arendt's comment on a statement like this would have been that apparently no distinction was made between helping the Jews to emigrate (before the war) and helping the Nazis to deport them. (EJ, 284)

21. N.S.B. = Nationaal Socialistische Beweging (National Socialist Movement)

22. see also chapter 6: The Jewish Councils

23. see also chapter 6: The Jewish Councils

24. It is remarkable that Jaspers uses the word "banality" in a letter to Arendt in 1946. This might have been the reason for Arendt to use this expression in 1962.

25. see also chapter 4.

26. see also chapter 3.

27. see also chapter 6: the revenge of the Jews in the story of Esther.

28. see also chapter 4.

29. In January 1933 there were six million unemployed. This was twenty-five percent of the German workforce. For many Germans this meant that democracy had failed. (Dwork and van Pelt, 63)

30. In Germany, the difference between executioners and bystanders was not very significant. In fact, it was supposed to be inexistent. Göring's proposal in 1938 to build Jewish ghettoes in all German cities was rejected by Heydrich, who preferred control of the Jews by the German population. (Hilberg, 2004, 171)

Chapter Seven

Guilt and Responsibility

The public prosecutor asked Eichmann whether he felt responsible for and guilty of the destruction of the Jews. He answered that he did not feel responsible, since he only executed his superiors' orders. He did not invent the Final Solution, but he felt bound by his oath to obey orders and to organize the transports. Therefore, from a legal point of view, he did not feel guilty, but morally he did. Eichmann used various terms in his answer, like responsibility, moral guilt and legal guilt. How should we look at responsibility and guilt in the Third Reich? In fact an entire society was involved in giving shape to and executing an insane ideology, but does this allow us to speak of a collective responsibility?

As early as 1946, Karl Jaspers tried to answer these questions in *Die Schuldfrage*, which, with the help of Hannah Arendt, was published in the United States as *The Question of German Guilt*. Jaspers distinguishes four types of guilt and although they are different there is a certain relationship between them.

– Criminal guilt. This type of guilt can predominantly be found in the inner layers of the onion. It concerns violations of the law. Examples are: crimes against peace, war crimes and crimes against humanity. Jaspers says that the consequence of these crimes is punishment, but Arendt put this in doubt. According to her, the crimes of the Nazis go beyond the limits of all legal systems and therefore no punishment is severe enough. Hanging is completely inadequate. We are not equipped to deal, on a human political level, with a guilt that is beyond crime. (C. 54) Jaspers defends himself by saying that guilt that goes beyond criminal guilt takes on a streak of "satanic greatness", which is inappropriate for the Nazis. We must consider their actions in their total banality and their prosaic triviality. (C, 62)

I do not agree with Jaspers that guilt that goes beyond criminal guilt takes on a streak of "satanic greatness". Arendt said that Eichmann's criminal actions were also beyond the existing laws; that, considered from a purely legal point of view, we did not have an adequate punishment for him, but she never said that his actions were characterized by any form of "greatness".

– Political guilt. A nation is collectively responsible for the state. For crimes committed in the name of the German Empire all citizens are responsible. The counter-argument that there are "apolitical" people like monks, hermits, scientists and scholars is not a valid argument, because they can lead their particular lives thanks to the organization of the state. There are no exceptions: everybody is politically responsible and a wrong political action, like allowing and even supporting the rise of Hitler and the Nazis, leads to political guilt. Political guilt results in "Wiedergutmachung": compensation, financial or otherwise, of damage or harm inflicted by the state.

– Moral guilt. Any individual who in one way or another has cooperated with the system or made its existence possible is morally guilty. Jaspers gives a number of examples of moral guilt.

Sanctimoniousness and hypocrisy because one wanted to survive, such as false declarations of loyalty or standing at the Nazi salute, in short, doing things to make people believe that one belonged to it.

Closing one's eyes for everything that was going on.

Partial approval of National Socialism, half-heartedness and inner adaptation to the situation.

Self-deception: everything will be different tomorrow, but today one must participate to change the system from within.

Passiveness: not making use of every opportunity to commit sabotage and to resist injustice.

Sympathizing with the Nazis. Jaspers uses the German word "Mitläufertum" (joining a group of followers), to refer to people who became a member of the party out of self-interest.

According to Jaspers, admission of moral guilt starts an inner process of penance and renewal.

– Metaphysical guilt is guilt caused by a lack of absolute solidarity with human beings as human beings. It is a kind of inner guilt of the survivors vis à vis the victims: it is my fault that I am still alive. Metaphysical guilt provokes a change of human self-awareness in its relation to God. Men's pride is broken. This may lead to a new life, which nevertheless is linked to an eradicable consciousness of guilt that expresses itself in a humble attitude towards God.

Arendt objected to this passage. She felt that Jaspers wanted to "redeem" the German nation, with his pre-war nationalism and his protestant piety.

Heinrich Blücher's judgment was even harsher. In a letter to Hannah he wrote that in the first place there should be a discussion about the outrages and that these only could be wiped out with blood and not with feelings of guilt and sin. (YB, 215)

One of the most important questions with regard to guilt is whether we may speak of a collective guilt. I agree with both Jaspers and Arendt, who deny the existence of a collective guilt. However, Jaspers did say that although there is no question of a collective criminal, moral or metaphysical guilt, there is a collective political guilt in the sense of collective political responsibility for the rise of the Nazi regime and for the crimes committed by this regime.

As early as 1945, Hannah Arendt brings up the subject of collective guilt. According to her, the idea of a collective guilt is a result of the structure of the totalitarian system, because it made the existence of all Germans depend either upon committing crimes or on complicity in crimes. (EU, 124) This idea is the result of the fact that Hitler divided the Germans into two categories: those who supported him and the bystanders. The third group, those who actively resisted the system, was eliminated. As I explained in chapter four, not only the supporters but, in a way, also the bystanders cooperated with the system and this introduced the idea of a collective guilt.

Almost twenty years later she comes back to the subject in the postscript of *Eichmann in Jerusalem*. She rejects all theories about a collective guilt of all Germans, although she agrees with Jaspers that there is a collective political responsibility. In an article written in 1964 entitled "Personal Responsibility Under Dictatorship" she says that the whole idea of collective guilt is a misconception, since it practically ends up in glossing over actions of the real offenders, because if everybody is guilty, nobody is guilty. There is no such thing as collective guilt or innocence; the notions of guilt or innocence only have a meaning if they are applied to individuals. (RJ, 21, 29).

I agree with Jaspers and Arendt that we cannot speak of a collective guilt. As far as a collective political responsibility is concerned, Arendt makes the following remarks:

Two conditions have to be present for the collective responsibility: I must be held responsible for something I have not done, and the reason for my responsibility must be my membership in a group (a collective) which no voluntary act of mine can dissolve, that is a membership which is utterly unlike a business partnership which I can dissolve at will. (RJ, 149)

and moreover:

This vicarious responsibility for things we have not done, this taking upon ourselves the consequences for things we are entirely innocent of, is the price we pay for the fact that we live our lives not by ourselves but among our fellow men, and that the faculty of action, which, after all, is the political faculty par excellence, can be actualised only in one of the many and manifold forms of human community. (RJ, 157/158)

If we take this into consideration our conclusion must be that all Germans who were adults in 1933 had a collective political responsibility for the rise and actions of the Nazi movement. Despite all objections against the notion of a collective guilt, the idea still exists judging by Daniel Goldhagen's book: *Hitlers Willing Executioners.* Goldhagen describes the behaviour of ordinary Germans who took part in the mass destructions. In his opinion the only reason for their behaviour was: "elimination anti-Semitism", a kind of culturally determined tendency to destroy all Jews. Goldhagen makes a classical mistake by drawing conclusions for the total population on the basis of the findings in his small-scale biased sample survey. In fact he reverses "the murderers were ordinary Germans" to "ordinary Germans were murderers", a point of departure that he tried to prove. By doing this Goldhagen suggests the existence of a collective guilt, although he denies it.

Although, according to Jaspers, we cannot speak of a collective moral guilt, since guilt is an individual feeling, there is a moral aspect in the way of life and the capacity to feel and to sympathize of a total population, which must influence its individual members. Jaspers' remark might be the reason why some authors (Goldhagen among others) are of the opinion that Nazi-totalitarianism could only develop in Germany.

Today, 58 years after the publication of *'The Question of German Guilt'*, there are still discussions about guilt and penance. I agree with Arendt's view that the Nazi crimes, in particular the Shoah, go beyond the limits of existing laws. Jaspers approached guilt and punishment from a pre-war point of view, which becomes obvious in the following remark:

We must purify ourselves from the guilt, as we feel it, as far as possible, by compensation, penance, inner renewal and transformation. (Jaspers, 1946, 78)

Like Arendt and Blücher, I feel somewhat uncomfortable with this statement. If these outrages are ever to be forgiven, purification and compensation seem to be totally inadequate reasons.

Summary and Conclusions

SUMMARY

Although the word "totalitarianism" existed, Hannah Arendt gives it a specific and special meaning. For her, totalitarianism is the most radical denial of freedom. Nazism is, together with Stalinism, the most important representative of totalitarian regimes. Arendt describes a number of elements, which crystallized into Nazi-totalitarianism. These elements are not to be considered as origins of Nazism and hence Nazism is not a product of these elements. Arendt rejects causality and determinism, because she strongly believes in human freedom. These same elements could have crystallized in a different way and in any case coincidence plays an important role.

The most fundamental element of totalitarianism is expansion. Expansion is an effect of Western imperialism, which in fact means colonialism. Colonialism originally had an economical purpose, but later became a political goal in itself and resulted in the exercise of power and "totalitarian" imperialism.

Race thinking and racism are the next elements. Race thinking originated in the 19th century, mainly in Germany, France and the colonies. Race thinking is the precursor of racism. Racism is race thinking in combination with discrimination. Race thinking also played an important role in Pan-Germanism, a sort of tribal nationalism with an element of chosenness and affinity with race thinking and racial theories. Pan-Germanism was the origin of a new type of anti-Semitism that was not based on personal experience but on jealousy. The Jews formed a perfect model, being in a position where they had no homeland, had a common origin and considered themselves as chosen.

The alliance between the capital and the mob is a third element. The mob is a group of people consisting of those of the unemployed who have become active, a sort of residue of the bourgeois society with identical egoistic tendencies and partly criminal. This was the beginning of a dangerous alliance between gangsters and the established order.

The decline of the German nation-state, a fourth element, started after the beginning of World War I in 1914. Internal cause for the decline was an increase in the number of refugees, mostly stateless Jews and minorities. External causes were Pan-Germanism and imperialism.

The last element is anti-Semitism. Many consider this the most important element. Existing anti-Semitism was intensified with the aid of propaganda. Arendt rejects the "scapegoat" theory as an explanation of anti-Semitism. Jews are partly responsible for the existence of anti-Semitism, because they neglected their responsibility to defend their own rights. This is the main reason why they became a political plaything of history. So far the elements.

On analysis of Nazi-totalitarianism, we initially discover the masses. Masses consist of isolated, atomized, lonely and often desperate individuals. Masses are, among other things, formed as a result of unemployment and frustration and are characterized by the loss of plurality. An important reason for the formation of masses was the return of the soldiers from the battlefields in France and Belgium after the Treaty of Versailles. Members of masses will go to great lengths to belong to a new "home". As a result, many members answered the call of the totalitarian leaders and became responsive to the ideologies and promises of a better future. However, other things were concealed behind the improved situation as became clear during the Kristallnacht in 1938, when more than a thousand synagogues were destroyed.

To illustrate the structure of Nazi-totalitarianism, Arendt uses the pyramid and the onion as metaphors. The pyramid represents authoritarian regimes, such as tyrannies. Power is at the top and authority descends to the base. Totalitarian regimes are structured like an onion. The leader is situated in the middle and in the various layers are the staff members, the executors, the party members and finally the bystanders. This structure has the advantage of being "shockproof" and obscure to the outside world. The organization is not a party but a movement, because Nazism is always moving towards a new goal and is therefore amorphous. It is a misconception to think that the leader, Hitler, is the origin of the totalitarian system. The origin of Nazism is in the masses and it was almost unavoidable that the masses finally produced someone like Hitler. Finally, the movement had two kinds of enemies: real, mainly political enemies and fictitious, designated enemies, the Jews.

The most important characteristics of the movement were ideology and terror. Ideology is literally what its name indicates: it is the logic of an idea. Nazi ideology sees world history as a war between the races in which the final victory is won by the superior race, the Aryans. It gave new hope to the desperate masses, but in reality it was a fiction. In order to get the support of the masses, totalitarian leaders made use of pseudo-scientific statements and anti-Semitic propaganda, especially of the fiction of the Jewish world conspiracy. Propaganda was used to contaminate the masses and Karl Jaspers rightfully compares it with an infectious disease.

Terror, the second characteristic, is not identical to violence. Terror manifests itself when the real enemies have been destroyed by violence. Terror never ends and is directed towards innocent people. Their living space is reduced and in most cases eliminated, because terror accelerates the movement of nature. Within this framework everything was possible, because terror and genocide became purposes in themselves.

This resulted in an experiment of total domination in which the concentration camps became the laboratories. The institutionalized terror and the death camps are, according to Arendt, unique and without precedent. In concentration camps people were transformed into superfluous, useless individuals; the death camps served only one purpose: the production of corpses. This is why Arendt speaks of the appearance of a "radical evil", unknown until then, that made the impossible possible.

The most important criticism of this concept relates to the uniqueness of the totalitarian system and the Shoah. The word Shoah relates to the systematic disintegration and destruction of the Jews. Some authors regard totalitarianism as a modern form of tyranny. However, the two regimes differ to such an extent, that they must be regarded as two different systems. With regard to the Shoah, criticism relates to the historical and the moral uniqueness. Comparisons are made with genocides in the Bible, the Congo and Armenia and with six million randomized individual murders. The decisive argument in considering the Shoah as unique is in the intention to destroy systematically a complete race for ideological reasons.

Kant originally uses the term "radical evil". Radical in the Kantian meaning refers to the origin of evil. Human beings have a capacity for doing good, but also a tendency towards doing evil. Evil deeds are the result of weakness, impurity or maliciousness. Evil is radical because it affects the basis of all maxims and because the natural tendency to do evil cannot be destroyed.

Good or evil actions are a result of establishing priorities and this is a function of the free will. Thus Kant situates evil in the free will and this means that human beings are responsible for it.

Arendt's use of the term "radical evil" indicates that she gives it a meaning, which differs from Kant's definition. In fact, she is rather vague about it and declares that she herself does not know exactly what radical evil is.

Human motivation cannot be used to explain Arendt's radical evil because there is also a link with making people "superfluous". Sometimes she also uses the word "absolute" instead of "radical". It could therefore be said that Arendt's meaning of "radical" concerns the quality and quantity of evil rather than its origin, as is the case in Kant's explanation.

After Eichmann's trial, Arendt's description changed from "radical" to "banal". She did not consider Eichmann a satanic monster, but rather a dull, ordinary, superficial or, in other words, banal person. This was why she spoke about "the banality of evil". As in the case of radical evil, there was no theory behind this expression, but there was a connection with Eichmann's observed "thoughtlessness". His evil deeds were a result of his inability to think. It is therefore understandable that after the trial Arendt made a study of a number of mental processes: thinking, willing and judging. Purpose of this study was to find out whether these processes could play a role in evil and the prevention thereof.

According to Plato, thinking is a kind of inner dialogue. Thinking becomes "visible" by means of language. The function of thinking is to understand the meaning of all the things that we see around us. Thinking does not provide a conclusion in the form of concepts, theories or guidelines, because others constantly replace them. Thinking, however, is the condition for judging and according to Arendt this is the most political human mental process.

Willing has a minor role in the prevention of evil, because the will does not determine what should be done and is not involved in the process of decision-making, but rather in the possibility of acting.

Arendt's opinions about judging are expressed in her lectures on Kant's political philosophy. These lectures are based on Kant's *Kritik der Urteilskraft (Critique of Judgment)*. In Arendt's opinion, our judgment on good and evil, right and wrong is formed in the same way as our esthetical judgment about beauty and ugliness. In order to have a good judgment, a person must be able to think from someone else's standpoint. The final judgment must transcend one's own judgment. The judgment of neutral bystanders is extremely important, because the actor is always dependent on the opinion of bystanders. Judgment is the only mental process that may prevent evil, but only provided that the judgment of bystanders is expressed in public.

The report of Eichmann's trial provoked three controversies. The least important concerned the factual contents of the report. It was said that the text contained a few hundred mistakes. However, these errors took nothing away from the value of the book.

The second controversy was more important and was related to the role of the Jewish Councils. Arendt accused these councils of co-operation with the Nazis and consequently of co-operating in the destruction of their own people. There are not many arguments against the accusation itself; it was Arendt's style that created bad blood. There was probably also a more profound cause for all the negative reactions. Some people regarded Arendt as a renegade who, out of self-hatred, claimed that the Jews had murdered their own people. My own objection to Arendt's text relates to her statement that the number of victims would have been considerably smaller, if the Jewish Councils had not existed. This is a rather unguarded remark. Investigators like Herzberg, de Jong and Presser are more careful when giving their opinions. Moreover, Arendt's statement can never be proven and it also contradicts her denial of causality.

The third controversy relates to "the banality of evil". Many considered Eichmann as the personification of demonic evil, but Arendt called him a "stinknormale", banal civil servant. This created the impression that Arendt on the one hand defended Eichmann whilst on the other hand she accused the Jews. (especially the Jewish Councils)

Some investigators have tried to combine Arendt's radical and banal evil. However, it must be concluded that the meanings of the two expressions differ and that Arendt changed her mind during the Eichmann trial. Furthermore, the characteristic of Arendt's radical evil is "superfluity", while "thoughtlessness" was the feature of banal evil. Banal evil cannot be placed in Kant's steps of evil, because "evil cogs in a totalitarian wheel" were unknown in Kant's time.

If we consider thinking as a prerequisite for judging, the most obvious conclusion is that Eichmann was incapable of placing himself in someone else's position and was therefore incapable of judging. Eichmann's place was in the layer of the onion where the ideological strategy was executed. This was done by two different groups of people: those who put the plans on paper (like Eichmann) and those who carried them out (such as members of the police battalions). Both groups consisted of "ordinary" people. Research indicates that also in the second group, at least to a certain degree, thoughtlessness and hence an incapability to judge, played a role.

Kant pointed out the importance of the judgment of bystanders. This is demonstrated by the attitude of the Danish population with regard to the persecution of the Jews in their country. Of even greater importance was the attitude of the German population during the rise of the Third Reich. The majority of the population did not think about the meaning of the events and hence misjudged the situation. This does not mean that we may speak of a collective guilt, but rather of a collective political responsibility.

CONCLUSIONS

In the introduction I presented five questions.

– Which were the elements and factors that led to the development of Nazism and to the Shoah?

The most important elements that crystallized into Nazism and the Shoah were: expansion and imperialism, the alliance between the capital and "the mob", the decline of the nation-state and anti-Semitism. The structural form of Nazi-totalitarianism was that of an onion and the most important characteristics were ideology and terror. All these phenomena made Nazism and the Shoah unique historical and moral events.

– What is the relationship between Arendt's "radical evil", Kant's "radical evil" and Arendt's "banal evil" and is it possible to incorporate banal evil in Kant's theory?

Originally Arendt spoke of "radical evil" and this is related to making people "superfluous". Arendt and Kant give different meanings to the term "radical evil". During the Eichmann trial, Arendt switched from "radical evil" to "the banality of evil" with "thoughtlessness" as the keyword. Arendt's radical evil and banal evil are not identical. Finally, banal evil cannot be incorporated in Kant's theory of radical evil.

– Are Nazi-totalitarianism and the Shoah new and unique events in history and if so, why?

In my opinion both phenomena are unique in history. Nazi-totalitarianism differs from other dictatorial systems mainly because of the ideology, while the Shoah differs from other genocides, because never before millions of people had been systematically annihilated for ideological reasons only.

– Is it possible to prevent a similar catastrophe and which mental capacities could play a role in this prevention?

The most important mental process in politics is judging. The judgment of bystanders is of the utmost importance, on condition that this judgment is openly expressed. It has the greatest effect during the rise of a "wrong" political movement. During the rise of the Third Reich people did not judge, or judged wrongly, guided by false hope or self-interest.

– Are we allowed to speak of a collective guilt?

We are not allowed to speak of a collective guilt, since this practically ends up in glossing over the actions of the real offenders, because if everybody is guilty, nobody is guilty. However, we may speak of a collective responsibility, since the German people democratically elected Hitler and his party. It is the price one pays for being a member of a specific nation.

Epilogue

In the prologue I said that I wanted to try and understand the mechanisms behind Nazi totalitarianism and the Shoah and the essence of the catastrophe. For that, I have made use of Hannah Arendt's writings and related literature. Moreover, I wanted to see the final destination of the trains with my own eyes and therefore I visited the death camps of Auschwitz-Birkenau, Belzec, Majdanek, Sobibor and Treblinka.

"Ich will verstehen" (I want to understand) was one of Arendt's most famous expressions and I had a similar wish, but what exactly is meant by "understanding"? Politics and history deal with human behaviour and can be understood, neither by explaining origins and causes, nor by knowledge of facts, but only by fathoming the motives that lie behind them. For Arendt understanding is reconciliation with reality and it takes a continuous effort to achieve this.

I have tried to understand the motives that lie behind totalitarianism and the Shoah and also to project myself in the position of the perpetrators and the victims. I think that, up to a certain point, I understand the mechanisms and motives that led to the rise of Nazi-totalitarianism. However, this is much more difficult where the Shoah is concerned.

Prof. Procee of the University of Twente said that there are two possibilities: either one considers the Shoah as an event comparable with other historical genocides (and he thinks it is), or as a unique event. In the former case one must try to understand it, in the latter case one should not even try. Primo Levi said that perhaps we should not try to understand it, since understanding almost implies a justification. Nevertheless it did not prevent Levi to understand and to draw lessons from his experiences in concentration camps and he said that for a non-religious person like him it is of the utmost importance

to understand and to make others understand. Christopher Browning agrees
with him:

> What I do not accept, however, are the old clichés that to explain is to excuse,
> to understand is to forgive. Explaining is not excusing; understanding is not for-
> giving. Not trying to understand the perpetrators in human terms would make
> impossible not only this study, but any history of Holocaust perpetrators that
> sought to go beyond one-dimensional caricature. (Browning, 1992, XX/preface)

Tzvetan Todorov also says that understanding evil does not imply justification, but it provides us with the means to prevent repetition. (Todorov, 179)
    Generally speaking, I think that trying to understand mechanisms that
cause deprivation, terror and violence does not need justification, because it
is an ingrained mission of our species, one of the properties that situates us
on a higher level than the animals.
    As I said before, understanding the Shoah is difficult and may be impossi-
ble, but nevertheless we must try. Firstly it is incomprehensible that one can
invent a Final Solution: systematically killing six million people for ideological reasons; secondly it seems completely illogical that the Nazis sacrificed
so much money, material and manpower to the Shoah since this undoubtedly
went at the expense of the expansion war; thirdly it is even more difficult to
understand the perpetrators and the victims, because it is not humanly possible to put oneself in their place.

> Hitler's crime machine took in Treblinka ca. 800,000 victims. Their ashes lie
> everywhere around here. Slaughter was prepared with great accuracy. People
> were coming from the railway booking office straight to the railway station,
> which was situated next to the booking office. There were a lot of doors inside,
> but only one way out—'Way of Death'. Today only the stones are silent wit-
> nesses of this inhuman crime. Selection started in the beginning. Women were
> separated from men. Children were staying with their mothers. People were unc-
> tiously informed about the bath, which was allegedly waiting for them, were
> taking off their clothes and and putting away valuables to the 'deposit'. Then
> people were driven to the gas chambers. They were having their hands up so that
> more people could get inside. Children were thrown at the top of crowded mass.
> Gassing with fumes lasted 15 minutes. Human organisms have various resist-
> ances. Perhaps few of these people were still alive. . . Bodies were placed on the
> special grates and poured with inflammable liquid. Only grey smoke and smell
> of burning corpses was hovering in the surroundings.
> (Original text on the platform of Treblinka station)

Let us first consider the victims. We must not forget that all we know about
the fate of the Jews is based on the stories of the survivors. We do not know

and cannot understand how the victims themselves have experienced it, because they are dead. What about the perpetrators? Can we understand them? Can we understand their motives? No, we cannot, because they had not motives. Apparently part of mankind is capable, in certain circumstances, of committing atrocious crimes, because it gives them mental satisfaction. They do evil for the sake of evil. There is nothing new under the sun. Listen to Augustine in his confessions:

> Unfathomable seducer of the mind greed to do harm for fun and sport, desire for another's injury, arising not for desire for my own gain or for vengeance, but merely when someone says, "Let's go! Let's do it!" and it is shameful not to be shameless! (Augustine, 75)

The only thing we can do is to prevent circumstances in which people can say: "Let's go. Let's do it"!

Bibliography

Abel, Lionel. "The Aesthetics of Evil: Hannah Arendt on Eichmann and the Jews." *Partisan Review* 30 (1963): 211–230.

Achterberg, Gerrit. *Verzamelde gedichten (Collected Poems).* Amsterdam, the Netherlands: Querido, 1999.

Achterhuis, Hans. *Politiek van goede bedoelingen (Politics of good intentions).* Amsterdam, the Netherlands: Boom, 1999.

Adams, Carole. "Hannah Arendt and the Historian: Nazism and the New Order." Pp 31–41 in *Hannah Arendt: Thinking, Judging, Freedom,* edited by Gisela T. Kaplan and Clive Kessler. Sydney: Unwin Hyman, 1989.

Adorno, Theodor W. *Negative Dialektik (Negative Dialectics).* 8th ed. Frankfurt am Main, Germany: Suhrkamp Verlag, 1994.

Alford, C. Fred. "The Organisation of Evil." *Political Psychology* 11 (1990): 5–27.

Allen, Wayne. "Hannah Arendt and the Ideological Structure of Totalitarianism." *Man World* 26 (1993): 115–129.

—— "Hannah Arendt and the Politics of Evil." *Ideal Studies* 2 (1991): 97–105.

Allison, Henry A. "Reflections on the banality of (radical) evil: a Kantian analysis." Pp. 169–212 in *Idealism and Freedom: Essays on Kant's theoretical and practical philosophy.* New York: Cambridge University Press, 1996.

Amstel, Greet van. "Er viel geen duisternis over de aarde." (No darkness descended on the earth) Pp. 19–20 in *Antwoord aan het kwaad (Response to Evil).* Amsterdam, the Netherlands, 1961.

Antelme, Robert. *De menselijke soort (The Human Race).* Nijmegen, the Netherlands: SUN, 2001.

Arendt, Hannah. *Between Past and Future.* New York: Viking Press, 1993.

—— *Crises of the Republic.* New York: Harcourt Brace & Company, 1972.

—— *Eichmann in Jerusalem.* New York: Viking Press, 1994.

—— *Essays in Understanding 1930–1954.* Ed. Jerome Kohn. New York: Harcourt Brace & ompany, 1994.

—— *Lectures on Kant's Political Philosophy.* Ed. Ronald Beiner. Chicago: The University of Chicago Press, 1989.

—— *Men in Dark Times.* New York: Harcourt Brace & Company, 1995.

—— *On revolution.* New York: Viking Press, 1990.

—— *Rahel Varnhagen. The Life of a Jewess.* Ed. Lilian Weissberg. Trans. Richard and Clara Winston. Baltimore: The John Hopkins University Press, 1997.

—— *Responsability and Judgment.* New York: Schocken Books, 2003.

—— "The Concentrationcamps." *Partisan Review,* 15, no 7 (July 1948): 743–769.

—— *The Human Condition.* Chicago: The University of Chicago Press, 1989.

—— *The Jew as Pariah.* Ed. Ron H. Feldman. New York: Grove Press, 1978.

—— *The Life of the Mind.* New York: Harcourt Brace & Company, 1978.

—— *The Origins of Totalitarianism.* 1st ed. New York: Harcourt Brace & Company, 1951; 2d ed. New York: Meridian Books, 1958; 3rd ed. New York: Harcourt Brace & Company, 978.

—— "Thinking and Moral Considerations." *Social Research* 38, no 3 (Fall 1971): 417–446.

—— *Was ist Politik? (What is Politics?).* Munich, Germany: Piper Verlag, 2003.

Arendt, Hannah and Karl Jaspers. *Correspondence 1926–1969.* Ed. Lotte Kohler and Hans Saner. Trans. Robert and Rita Kimber. New York: Harcourt Brace & Company, 1992.

Arendt, Hannah and Mary McCarthy. *Between Friends. The Correspondence of Hannah Arendt and Mary McCarthy 1949–1975.* Ed. Carol Brightman. New York: Harcourt Brace & Company, 1995.

Aristotle. *The Nicomachean Ethics.* New York: Oxford University Press, 1990.

Arnold, G. L. "Three Critics of Totalitarianism." *Twentieth Century* 150 (July 1951): 23–34.

Aron, Raymond. "The Essence of Totalitarianism According to Hannah Arendt." *Partisan Review* 60 (1993): 366–367.

Augustine. *Confessions.* New York: Doubleday, 1960

Barnouw, Dagmar. "The Secularity of Evil: Hannah Arendt and the Eichmann Controversy." *Modern Judaism* 3 (1983): 75–94.

Beatty, Joseph. "Thinking and Moral Considerations: Socrates and Arendt's Eichmann." Pp.57–74 in *Hannah Arendt:Critical Essays,* edited by Lewis P. Hinchman and Sandra K. Hinchman. Albany: State University of New York Press, 1994.

Beiner, Ronald. "Hannah Arendt on Judging." Pp. 89–156 in *Hannah Arendt: Lectures on Kant's Political Philosophy,* edited by Ronald Beiner. Chicago: The University of Chicago Press, 1989.

Ben-Itto Hadassa. *Anatomie van een vervalsing (Anatomy of a Forgery)* Soesterberg, the Netherlands: Aspect, 2000.

Benjamin, Walter. *Sprache und Geschichte (Language and History).* Stuttgart, Germany: Universal Bibliothek no. 8775, 1992.

Bernstein, Richard J. "Evil, Thinking and Judging." Pp. 154–178 in *Hannah Arendt and the Jewish Question.* Cambridge, UK: Polity Press, 1996.

—— "From Radical Evil to the Banality of Evil: From Superfluousness to Thoughtlessness." Pp. 137–153 in *Hannah Arendt and the Jewish Question.* Cambrige, UK: Polity Press, 1996.

——— "Judging: The Actor and the Spectator." Pp. 235–254 in *The Realm of Humanitas: Responses to the Writings of Hannah Arendt,* edited by Reuben Garner. New York: Peter Lang, 1990.

Bettelheim, Bruno. "Eichmann: The System, the Victims." Pp. 258–273 in *Surviving and other Essays.* New York: Alfred A. Knopf, 1979.

Binner, Rolf, Otto van der Haar and Jan-Willem Bos, ed. *Wiens schuld? De impact van Daniel Jonah Goldhagen op het Holocaustdebat (Whose guilt? The impact of Daniel Jonah Goldhagen on the Holocaust discussion).* Antwerp, Belgium: van Reemst, 1997.

Bittman, Michael. "Totalitarianism: The Career of a Concept." Pp 56–68 in *Hannah Arendt, Thinking, Judging, Freedom,* edited by Gisela T. Kaplan and Clive Kessler. Sydney: Unwin Hyman, 1989.

Bosley Woolf, Henry, ed. *Webster's New Collegiate Dictionary.* Springfield, Mass.: G. & C. Merriam Company, 1975.

Brauman, Rony and Eyal Sivan, directors of the film *The Specialist*, based on Hannah Arendt's "Eichmann in Jerusalem."

Browning, Christopher R. *Nazi Policy, Jewish Workers, German Killers.* Cambridge, UK: Cambridge University Press, 2000.

——— *Ordinary Men, Reserve Police Battalion 101 and the Final Solution in Poland.* New York: Harper Perennial, 1998.

Bullock, Allen, *Hitler.* Utrecht, the Netherlands: Bruna & Zoon, 1958.

Burrowes, Robert. "Totalitarianism: The Revised Standard Version." *World Politics* 21, (1969): 272–294.

Camus, Albert. *L'homme révolté* (The Rebel). Paris, France: Editions Gallimard, 1951.

Canetti, Elias. *Massa & Macht (Mass & Power).* Amsterdam, the Netherlands: Polak & van Gennip, 1976.

Canovan, Margareth. *Hannah Arendt: A Reinterpretation of her Political Thought.* New York: Cambridge University Press, 1992.

——— "Hannah Arendt on Ideology in Totalitarianism." Pp. 151–173 in *The Structure of Modern Ideology,* edited by Noël O'Sullivan. Aldershot, UK: Edward Elgar, 1989.

Clark, Barry. "Beyond the Banality of Evil." *British Journal of Political Science* 10, (1980): 417–439.

Dawidowicz, Lucy S. *The War against the Jews.* New York: Bantam Books, 1976.

De Visscher, Jacques. *Een te voltooien leven (A life to be completed).* Kapellen, Belgium: Uitgeverij Pelckmans, 1996.

Dijkhuis, Hans. *Kains kinderen (Kain's Children)* Amsterdam, the Netherlands: Boom, 1999.

Dossa, Shiraz. "Human Status and Politics: Hannah Arendt on the Holocaust." *Canadian Journal of Political Science.* 13, (1980): 309–323.

Dunk, H. W. von der. *Voorbij de verboden drempel (Beyond the forbidden threshold).* Amsterdam, the Netherlands: Prometheus, 1991.

Dwork, Debórah and Robert Jan van Pelt. *Holocaust. A History.* New York: W.W. Norton & Company, 2002.

Ezorsky, Gertrude. "Hannah Arendt's View of Totalitarianism and the Holocaust." *The Philisophical Forum* 16, (1984–1985): 53–73.

Fackenheim, Emil L. "The Holocaust and Philosophy." *The Journal of Philosophy* Vol. LXXXII, no 10 (1985): 505–514.

—— *To Mend the World*. Indianapolis: Indiana University Press, 1994.

Frank, Hans. *Die Technik des Staates (The Technique of the State)*. Munich, Germany, 1942.

Garner, Reuben. "Adolf Eichmann: The Making of a Totalitarian Bureaucrat." Pp. 67–100 in *The Realm of Humanitas: Responses to the Writings of Hannah Arendt*. New York: Peter Lang, 1990.

Geerts, G. and H. Heestermans, ed. *van Dale's Groot Woordenboek der Nederlandse Taal (van Dale's Dictionary of the Dutch Language)*. 11th ed. Utrecht, the Netherlands: van Dale, 1984

Goldhagen, Daniel. *Hitler's Willing Executioners*. New York: Alfred A. Knopf, 1996.

Gross, Jan T. *Buren. De vernietiging van de joden in Jedwabne (Neighbours. The Destruction of the Jewish Community in Jedwabne)* Trans. Albert Witteveen and Jorien Hakvoort. Amsterdam, the Netherlands: De Bezige Bij, 2002.

Haarlems Dagblad (Haarlem Daily). Haarlem, the Netherlands, February 9, 2004.

Harris, William H. and Judith S. Levey, ed. *New Illustrated Columbia Encyclopedia*. New York: Columbia University Press, 1978.

Heydekker J.J. and J. Leeb. *Opmars naar de Galg. Het proces van Neurenberg (The Neurenberg Trial)*. Amsterdam, the Netherlands: Amsterdam Boek B.V., 1974.

Herzberg Abel J. *Amor Fati*. Amsterdam, the Netherlands: De Arbeiderspers, 1960.

—— "Kroniek der Jodenvervolging." (Chronicle of the Persecution of the Jews) Part 3 of *Onderdrukking en Verzet, Nederland in oorlogstijd (Oppression and Resistance, The Netherlands during the War)*. Amsterdam, the Netherlands: Meulenhof, 1949–1954.

Hilberg, Raul. *The Destruction of the European Jews*. Chicago: Quadrangle Books, 1961.

—— *Daders, slachtoffers, omstanders. De joodse catastrophe 1933–1945. (Perpetrators, Victims, Bystanders. The Jewish Catastrophe 1933–1945)*. Haarlem, the Netherlands: Becht, 2004.

Houtepen, Anton. *God, een open vraag (God, an open question)*. Zoetermeer, the Netherlands: Meinema, 1997.

Isarin, Jet. *Het kwaad en de gedachteloosheid (Evil and Thoughtlessness)*. Baarn, the Netherlands: Ambo, 1994.

Jackson, Michael. "The Responsibility of Judgment and the Judgment of Responsibility." Pp. 42–55 in *Hannah Arendt: Thinking, Judging, Freedom,* edited by Gisela T. Kaplan and Clive Kessler. Sydney: Unwin Hyman, 1989.

Jacobs, Hans and Bert Stoop. *Het Auschwitz Proces (The Auschwitz Trial)*. Amsterdam, the Netherlands: De Arbeiderspers, 1965.

Jaspers, Karl. *Die Schuldfrage (The Question of German Guilt)*. Heidelberg, Germany: Schneider, 1946.

—— "Das radikal Böse bei Kant" (Radical Evil with Kant). Pp. 107–137 in *Rechenschaft und Ausblick (Account and Prospect)*. Munich, Germany: Piper & Co Verlag, 1958.

—— *The Great Philosophers.* Vol. 1, ed. Hannah Arendt. New York: Harcourt, Brace and World, 1962.

Jong, L. de. "Jodenvervolging en Jodendeportaties." Pp. 270–462 in Part 7 of *Het Koninkrijk der Nederlanden in de Tweede Wereldoorlog (The Kingdom of the Netherlands during the Second World War).* The Hague, the Netherlands: Staatsuitgeverij, 1976.

Kambanellis, Iakovos. *Mauthausen.* Athens, Greece: Kedros, 1995.

Kant, Immanuel. *Anthropologie in pragmatischer Hinsicht (Anthropology from a Pragmatic Point of View).* Stuttgart, Germany: Universal Bibliothek no. 7541, 1998.

—— *Die Metaphysik der Sitten (Metaphysics of Morals).* Stuttgart, Germany: Universal Bibliothek no. 4508, 1997.

—— *Die Religion innerhalb der Grenzen der bloszen Vernunft (Religion within the Limits of Pure Reason)* Stuttgart, Germany: Universal Bibliothek no 1231, 1996.

—— *Kritik der Praktischen Vernunft (Critique of Practical Reason).* Cologne, Germany: Könemann Verlagsgesellschaft, 1995.

—— *Kritik der Reinen Vernunft (Critique of Pure Reason).* Cologne, Germany: Könemann Verlagsgesellschaft, 1995.

—— *Kritik der Urteilskraft (Critique of Judgment).* Stuttgart, Germany: Universal Bibliothek no. 1026, 2001.

Kateb, George. *Hannah Arendt: Politics, Conscience, Evil.* Totowa, NJ: Rowman and Allanheld, 1984.

Katz, Steven T. *The Holocaust in Historical Context, vol. I.* New York: Oxford University Press, 1994.

Kertész, Imre. *Dagboek van een galeislaaf (Diary of a galley slave).* Amsterdam, the Netherlands: van Gennep, 2003.

—— *Onbepaald door het lot (Fateless).* Amsterdam, the Netherlands: van Gennep, 1994.

Kluckhuhn,C. "Ethical Relativity: Sic et Non." *Journal of Philosophy* 52 (1955): 663–677.

Kofman, Sarah. *Paroles suffoquées (Smothered Words).* Paris, France: Edition Galilée, 1987.

Kohn, Jerome. "Thinking/ Acting." *Social Research* 57 (1990): 105–134.

Lackey, Douglas P. "Extraordinary Evil or Common Malevolence." *Journal of Applied Philosophy*, Vol. 3, no. 2 (1986): 167–181.

Lang, Berel. "Hannah Arendt and the Politics of Evil." Pp. 41–55 in *Hannah Arendt: Critical Essays,* edited by Lewis P. Hinchman and Sandra K. Hinchman. Albany, N.Y.: State University of New York Press, 1984.

Langer, Walter C. *Een psychologisch portret van Adolf Hitler (A psychological Portrait of Adolf Hitler)* Utrecht, the Netherlands: Bruna & Zoon, 1973.

Laqueur, Walter. "Hannah Arendt in Jerusalem: The Controversy Revisited." Pp. 107–129 in *Western Society after the Holocaust,* edited by Lyman H. Letgers. Boulder, Co.: Westview Press, 1983.

—— *The Holocaust Encyclopedia.* New Haven and London: Yale University Press, 2001.

Márai, Sándor. *Land, land!...,* Amsterdam, the Netherlands: Wereldbibliotheek, 2002.

Melville, Herman. *Billy Budd, Foretopman.* New York: Bantam Books, 1965.

—— *Moby-Dick.* New York: Penguin Books, 1992.

Minnich, Elisabeth K. "To Judge in Freedom. Hannah Arendt on the Relation of Thinking and Morality." Pp. 133–143 in *Hannah Arendt: Thinking, Judging, Freedom,* edited by Gisela T. Kaplan and Clive Kessler. Sydney: Unwin Hyman, 1989.

Moehle, Natalia. "Hannah Arendt." Pp. 171–195 in *The Dimension of Evil and of Transcendence: A Sociological Perspective.* Washington DC: University Press of America, 1978.

Morgenthau, Hans. "Hannah Arendt on Totalitarianism and Democracy." *Social Research* 44 (1977): 127–131.

Nauman, Bernd. *Auschwitz.* Hamburg, Germany: Fischer Bücherei, 1978.

O'Sullivan, Noël. "Politics, Totalitarianism and Freedom. The Political Thought of Hannah Arendt." *Political Studies* 21, (June, 1973): 183–198.

Plato. *Theaetetus.* London, UK: Penguin Books, 1987.

Presser, J. *De Ondergang (Going Under).* The Hague, the Netherlands: Staatsuitgeverij, 1965.

Prins, Bart. *Op de bres voor vrijheid en pluraliteit (Into the Breach for Freedom and Plurality)* Amsterdam, the Netherlands: VU Uitgeverij, 1990.

Rees, Laurence. *De Nazi's: Een waarschuwing uit het verleden (The Nazis: A Warning from the Past)* Amsterdam, the Netherlands: Jan Metz Uitgeverij, 1997.

Ricoeur, Paul. *Die lebendige Metapher (The living Metaphor).* Munich, Germany: Wilhelm Fink Verlag, 1986.

Roseman, Mark. *De villa, het meer, de conferentie (The Villa, the Lake, the Meeting-Wannsee and the Final Solution.* Amsterdam, the Netherlands: Balans, 2002.

Rosenthal, Abigail. *A Good Look at Evil.* Philadelphia: Temple University Press, 1987.

Rotenstreich, Nathan. "Can Evil Be Banal?" *Philosophical Forum* 16 (1984): 50–62.

Rousset, David. *Les Jours de notre mort (The Days of our Death).* Paris, France: Editions Hachette, 1993

—— *L'univers concentrationnaire (The Concentrationcamp Universum)* Paris, France: Hachette *Littératures,* 1998.

Rubinstein, Richard L. *After Auschwitz.* 1st ed. New York: Bobbs-Marrill, 1966.

—— *After Auschwitz.* 2d ed. Baltimore, Md.: John Hopkins University Press, 1984.

—— "Totalitarianism and Population Superfluity." Pp. 102–119 in *The Realm of Humanitas: Response to the Writings of Hannah Arendt,* edited by Reuben Garner. New York: Peter Lang, 1990.

Safranski, Rüdiger. *Het Kwaad (Evil).* Amsterdam, the Netherlands: Atlas, 1998.

Sakovska, Ruta. *The Warsaw Ghetto 1940–1945.* Warsaw, Poland: Drukpol, 2000.

Schrijvers, Piet. *Rome, Athene, Jeruzalem. Leven en werk van prof. David Cohen (Rome, Athens, Jerusalem. Life and works of prof. David Cohen).* Leyden, the Netherlands: Historische Uitgeverij, 2000.

Semprun, Jorge. *Een eeuw van vernietiging en hervorming (A Century of Destruction and reformation).* 28th Huizinga Lecture. Paper presented at the University of Leyden: N.R.C. (newspaper), december 18, 1999.

Shakespeare, William. *The Complete Works of William Shakespeare.* London, UK: Abbey Library, 1946.

Stanley, John L. "Is Totalitarianism a New Phenomenon? Reflections on Hannah Arendt's Origins of Totalitarianism." Pp. 7–40 in *Hannah Arendt: Critical Essays,* edited by Lewis P. Hinchman and Sandra K. Hinchman. Albany, N.Y.: State University of New York Press, 1989.

Staub, Erwin. *Roots of Evil: The Origins of Genocide and Other Group Violence.* New York: Cambridge University Press, 1989.

Steinbeck, John. *East of Eden.* London, UK: WDL Books, 1960.

Todorov, Tzvetan. *Herinnering aan het kwaad, bekoring van het goede (Memory of Evil, Attractiveness of the Good).* Amsterdam, the Netherlands: Atlas, 2002.

Van den Bossche, Marc. "Het oor wil ook wat" (Appearences also count). Pp. 149–164 in *Meesterstukken (Masterpieces),* edited by Marc Van den Bossche. Rotterdam, the Netherlands: Lemniscaat, 2001.

Villa, Dana R. "Thinking and Judging." Pp. 9–28 in *The Judge and the Spectator,* edited by Joke J. Hermsen and Dana R. Villa. Leuven, Belgium: Peeters, 1999.

Voegelin, Eric. "The Origins of Totalitarianism." *Review of Politics* 15, (1953): 68–76.

Wiesel, Elie. *A Jew Today.* New York: Random House, 1978.

Whitfield, Stephen J. *Into the Dark: Hannah Arendt and Totalitarianism.* Philadelphia: Temple University Press.

Woolf, Henry B., ed. *Webster's New Collegiate Dictionary,* Springfield, Mass: G & C Merriam Co, 1975.

Wyschogrod, Michael. 'Some theological reflections on the Holocaust." *Response: a contemporary Jewish review.* (1975): 68.

Young-Bruehl, Elisabeth. *Hannah Arendt. For Love of the World.* New Haven: Yale University Press, 1982.

—— "Reflections on Hannah Arendt's The Life of the Mind." Pp. 335–364 in *Hannah Arendt: Critical Essays,* edited by Lewis P. Hinchman and Sandra K. Hinchman. Albany: State University Press of New York, 1994.

Index